I0901970

"A Looking-Glass For Ladies"

"A Looking-Glass for Ladies"

American Protestant Women and the Orient in the Nineteenth Century

by

Lisa Joy Pruitt

Mercer University Press Macon, Georgia

25th Anniversary

ISBN 0-86554-888-9
MUP/P313

1400 Coleman Avenue
Macon, Georgia 31207

First Edition.

∞The paper used in this publication meets the minimum requirements of American National Standard for Information Sciences—Permanence of Paper for Printed Library Materials, ANSI Z39.48-1992.

Library of Congress Cataloging-in-Publication Data

Pruitt, Lisa Joy, 1964-
A looking-glass for ladies : American Protestant women and the Orient in the nineteenth century / by Lisa Joy Pruitt.-- 1st ed.
p. cm.
Includes bibliographical references and index.
ISBN 0-86554-888-9 (pbk. : alk. paper)
1. Women missionaries—United States. 2. Missions--Orient. I. Title.
BV2610.P78 2005
266'.0092'273—dc22
2005002526

Contents

Soli Deo Gloria

Acknowledgments

Many people provided the intellectual, emotional, and spiritual encouragement that I needed in order to see this book to completion. The project began as my dissertation at Vanderbilt University. First and foremost, I would like to thank my dissertation director, Professor Paul K. Conkin, for his encouragement and his insightful and provocative criticism. Professors Lewis Perry, Elizabeth Rose, John Fitzmier, and Dale Johnson graciously served on my committee and offered valuable feedback. Professor James Epstein offered a detailed critique of four chapters. Several of my graduate school colleagues also provided helpful suggestions. I would like to thank Brett Armstrong, Talisman Ford, Craig Kaplowitz, Katy McDaniel, Sean Smith, and Amy Sturgis for shaping a collegial environment that allowed for constructive criticism while fostering lasting friendships.

The library faculty at Vanderbilt University provided invaluable support, as did archivists and librarians at Mt. Holyoke College, the Houghton Library of Harvard University, Drew University, the American Baptist Historical Society, the Southern Baptist Historical Library and Archives, Regents Park College (Oxford), Birmingham University, and the School of Oriental and African Studies, University of London. The Women's Work Group of the history department at Middle Tennessee State University (MTSU) offered encouragement during the process of transforming the dissertation into this book. Dean John McDaniel of MTSU was unfailingly supportive during the two-year revision process. My colleague Betty Rowland at MTSU went above and beyond the call of duty to help carve out space in my schedule for working on this project.

I would also like to thank three Christian communities for the emotional and spiritual support without which I would have never begun this project, much less finished it. My friends in Greenville, South Carolina, especially Chip Brown, Vicky Burgess, Vance Jenkins, and Douglas and Lisa Rackley, helped launch me on this path. My involvement with the First Baptist Church of Nashville, especially the music ministry under the direction Mark Edwards and the Joshua Class under the direction of Lyn Robbins, helped keep me sane. Many friends in the Vanderbilt Graduate Christian Fellowship, especially Don Paul and Ginger Gross, encouraged me, prayed for me, and provided material assistance in times of great physical need.

Finally, I would like to thank my parents, Jay and Doris Pruitt, for their emotional support and especially for encouraging me to pursue my love of scholarship.

Engraving depicting the commissioning of the first group of missionaries sent out by the American Board of Commissioners for Foreign Missions, Park Street Church, Boston, 1812. From J. A. Graham, *Missionary Expansion since the Reformation*, 95.

Ann Judson. Courtesy of the Southern Baptist Historical Library and Archives, Nashville, Tennessee.

Emily Judson. Courtesy of the Southern Baptist Historical Library and Archives, Nashville, Tennessee.

Lucy Lyon Lord. Courtesy of Mt. Holyoke College Library, Archives and Special Collections, South Hadley, Massachusetts.

A Hindu woman about to perform *sati*. From John Scudder, *Voice from the East to the Young*, 47.

HINDOO WIDOW, CARRIED IN A PALANQUIN TO THE FUNERAL PILE. Page 47

HINDOO KING BEHEADING HIS DAUGHTER. Page 266.

A Hindu king beheading his daughter. From John Scudder, *Voice from the East to the Young*, 266.

Hindu Woman sacrificing her child. From John Scudder, *Letters to Sabbath School Children*, 19.

Henrietta Shuck. Courtesy of the Southern Baptist Historical Library and Archives, Nashville, Tennessee.

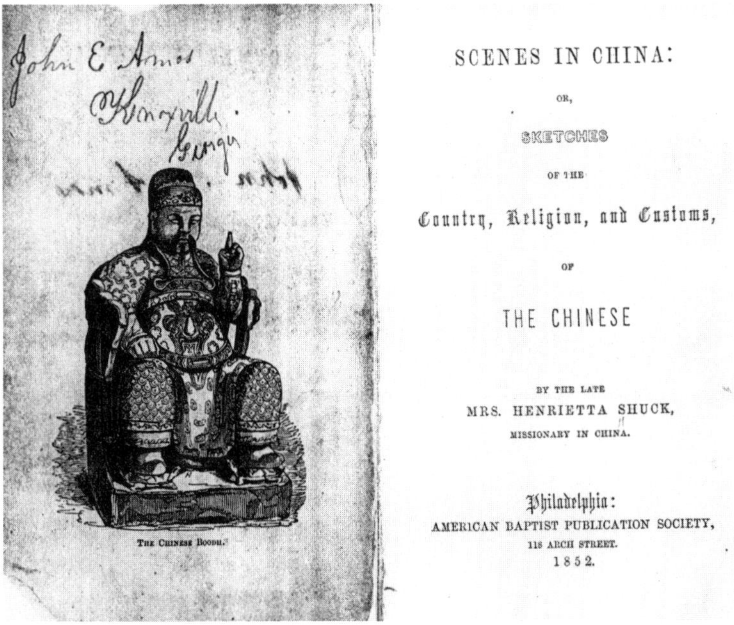

SCENES IN CHINA:

OR,

SKETCHES

OF THE

Country, Religion, and Customs,

OF

THE CHINESE

BY THE LATE

MRS. HENRIETTA SHUCK,

MISSIONARY IN CHINA.

Philadelphia:

AMERICAN BAPTIST PUBLICATION SOCIETY,

118 ARCH STREET.

1852.

Frontispiece and title page to Henrietta Shuck's book, *Scenes in China, or, Sketches of the Countys Religion, and Customs of the Chinese.*

Fidelia Fiske. Courtesy of Mt. Holyoke College Library Archives and Special Collections, South Hadley, Massachusetts.

Fiske Female Seminary, Droomiah, Persia [now Urmia, Iran]. Courtesy of the Mt. Holyoke College Library and Special Collections, South Hadley, Massachusetts.

Clara Swain. From J. A. Graham, *Missionary Expansion Since the Reformation*, 118.

Introduction

"A Looking-Glass For Ladies"

Examining the nineteenth-century mission movement by looking at the intersection of ideas about gender and ideas about the "Orient" offers insight into the reflexive influence of that movement on American evangelical culture.[1] The construction, elaboration, and reinforcement of a discourse about the female "Oriental" Other played a significant role in a movement that mobilized Protestant women on behalf of foreign missions in the half-century prior to the Civil War and culminated in the formation of denominational women's mission boards in the decades following the war. The dramatic feminization of the foreign missions movement that occurred in the late nineteenth century with the formation of women's denominational mission boards derived in large part from the cultural influence of tropes about "Oriental" women that had been circulating since early in the century. In his 1891 *Encyclopedia of Missions*, Edwin Munsell Bliss asserted that "the modern uprising of women in behalf of foreign missions had its motive in the social systems of the East.... When the degradation and suffering of Asiatic women and the darkness of their future were revealed to the western world, the conscience of Christian women was aroused."[2] Others who have written about the feminization of the American foreign missions movement have attributed that development to changes in women's roles and self-perceptions brought about by their involvement in the Civil War.[3] A close examination of popular missions literature—primarily memoirs, but also magazines, tracts, and children's books—and the official records of missionary societies and denominational boards suggests that Bliss's assessment is the more accurate.

Books and articles on the nineteenth- and early twentieth-century American Protestant mission movement proliferated rapidly in the latter half of the twentieth century. This study differs from others in the field in three important ways. First, most scholarship on the mission movement focuses on the late nineteenth and early twentieth centuries because that period represented the movement at its peak, and that peak corresponded with the emergence of the United States as an imperial power.[4] Those works, to varying degrees, identify missionaries as either willing or unwitting agents of political, economic, and cultural imperialism and necessarily focus on the people and nations that were the objects of both imperialism and evangelism. This study, in contrast, maintains the critical importance of the first half-century of the foreign missions movement and emphasizes the reflexive influence of missions.[5] In other words, it traces the influence of the mission movement on American evangelical culture rather than attempting to measure the extent to which missionaries influenced or failed to influence, for better or for worse, the cultures they were trying to transform.

Second, this study departs from earlier studies that have focused on the antebellum period but have not focused on gender. Much of the scholarship on the early nineteenth-century mission movement has an institutional or theological focus that assumes the irrelevance of gender-related issues such as the marital status of missionaries. Most of those works also simply do not discuss the roles of women in missionary work or explicitly exclude women because they generally did not hold official appointments and did not have a direct voice in denominational hierarchies.[6] This study maintains that women played significant roles in the early mission movement, as fundraisers and promoters at home and as workers abroad. Furthermore, ideas of gender had profound significance for the conceptualization of mission work from the very beginning of the movement when newly established boards debated whether a married man or a single man would make the ideal missionary. That issue held significance for early nineteenth-century evangelicals because they viewed the status of women as an indicator of the degree of civilization that a society had attained. For early nineteenth-century evangelicals, the status of women meant neither political rights nor legal privileges, but rather social and spiritual equality manifested in a woman's educational level, her position as a cherished partner in a companionate marriage, and her usefulness as a Christian, a wife, and a mother.[7] Evangelizing women in "heathen" lands meant not only proclaiming the gospel, but demonstrating it in a living parable of Christian family life. Such values in regard to family life took on added meaning when Protestant missionaries labored in the same places as Catholic priests, which they very often did.

Finally, a few excellent works of scholarship have focused on women and gender issues in the antebellum mission movement.[8] The present work differs from its predecessors by highlighting the significance of the concept of the "Orient" and of "Oriental women" in that period and by bridging the Civil War to demonstrate how ideas of the "Orient" continued to exert power over evangelicals in the decades after the war. I use the word "Orient" in the same way that nineteenth-century evangelicals did—to represent the area of the world stretching from historical Palestine to China and encompassing a wide variety of religious cultures, including Judaism, Islam, Greek and Syrian Christianity, Hinduism, Buddhism, Confucianism, and Taoism. I do not use the term in order to re-inscribe the nineteenth-century prejudices that conflated such varied cultures, for those cultures are not the subject of this study. In her path-breaking work on British women's travel literature, *Women's Orients: English Women and the Middle East, 1718–1918: Sexuality, Religion and Work*, Billie Melman wrote, "It is not as a historian of Middle Eastern Society that I approach and look at the writings—for I am not qualified to do that. It is rather as a student of the shifts and mutations in Western sensibilities, particularly the sensibilities of the Western European middle classes, that I propose to look at the materials."[9] I propose to do something similar with the writings of American evangelical women about the "Orient." I will use the terms "Orient" and "Oriental" as windows into the minds of some of the people who helped to create and shape the meanings of those terms. Nineteenth-century American Protestants somehow managed to collapse that vast region of the world into a unitary concept, the "Orient."

Evangelicals in particular were fascinated by a specific group of inhabitants of that region—its women. The idea of the "Oriental woman" carried for them a very specific set of meanings. Those meanings, and their impact on the mission movement, are the subject of this book.

Nineteenth-century American evangelicals were, in fact, motivated to action by what one might call "evangelical Orientalism." Orientalism was a powerful cultural mechanism in the late eighteenth and the nineteenth century and its influence continued, in some circles, past World War II. Orientalists, most simply put, were Westerners who developed a deep and abiding fascination with what they thought of as the "East" or the "Orient." In the late eighteenth and early nineteenth centuries, the term "Orient" comprised lands of North Africa and the eastern Mediterranean. As British imperialism extended eastward, the idea of the "Orient" grew to encompass the region then called "the Levant" (now part of the Middle East) along with the Indian subcontinent and the islands known then as the East Indies (Indonesia). By the mid-nineteenth century, the "Orient" for Americans included China and Southeast Asia and by the early twentieth century had been extended to include Japan and Korea. The nineteenth-century American evangelicals upon whom this book focuses, however, generally considered the "Orient" to encompass that region of the world extending from the ancient lands of the Bible to Burma (Myanmar), Siam (Thailand), and China.

It is important to understand, however, that the "Orient" was more of an idea—a Western idea—than it was a definable place. It was a "figment of a socially, culturally, and in the end linguistically formed imagination."[10] Likewise, "Orientals" were a Western conception—a complex idea or a fantasy or a stereotype of those who lived in the "Orient." "Orientals" lived in many places, spoke different languages, and held to a wide variety of religious beliefs and social customs. But to the nineteenth-century Westerners whom they fascinated, "Orientals" were more alike than different. They shared common characteristics that placed them in the category of "Oriental." "Orientals" were portrayed as "irrational, backward-looking, childish and feminine" in contrast to Westerners, who were depicted as "rational, progressive, adult, and masculine."[11] Effeminacy was often expressed in terms of laziness, extravagance in clothing and jewelry, and superstition. Westerners also portrayed "Oriental" societies as frozen in time—locked culturally in the distant past, bypassed by Western progress.[12]

"Orientalist" was a term first used in the nineteenth century by individuals who claimed a degree of expertise, usually acquired by extensive travel, on the "Orient" and "Orientals." Some of those individuals, including mission advocates and former missionaries, formed the American Oriental Society in 1842 to promote research into the languages, literatures, and cultures of the "East." The *Journal of the American Oriental Society* first appeared in 1843. In its first two decades, the journal regularly featured articles by current and former missionaries, particularly those of the American Board of Commissioners for Foreign Missions (ABCFM) (Congregational and Presbyterian) and the American Baptist Missionary Union (ABMU). Orientalism quickly filtered into popular culture and manifested itself in clothing styles, home furnishings, popular theater, and the circus.

The study of Orientalism as a cultural and historical phenomenon gained prominence in academic circles with the publication of Edward Said's *Orientalism* in 1977. As a result of Said's work, an entire generation of scholarship has emerged, focusing on the diverse manifestations of Orientalism in Western culture. Much of that work examines Orientalism in literature and art in Great Britain, France, and Germany in the nineteenth and early twentieth centuries. To a lesser extent, scholars have investigated the cultural influence of Orientalism in the United States. Fuad Sha'ban, for example, wrote that "Americans developed a definite Orientalist cultural attitude from its beginning and, with variations and a change in direction, has sustained it ever since."[13]

What I propose to call "evangelical Orientalism" shared much in common with and was heavily informed by those other expressions of Orientalism that have received a great deal of scholarly attention. Evangelical Orientalists, however, had a primary concern that differed substantially from those of other Orientalists. While secular Orientalists expressed fascination with and often admiration for the Eastern religions, evangelical Orientalists expressed and acted upon an ardent desire to evangelize that region of the world and witness the conversion to evangelical Protestant Christianity of millions of Jews, Muslims, "nominal" Christians (Catholics and various types of Orthodox Christians), and "pagans" (primarily Hindus, Buddhists, and Taoists). To demonstrate the urgent need of the "Orient" for the gospel, mission advocates highlighted specific aspects of "Oriental" character that they believed illustrated that need. Evangelical portrayals of the "Orient" featured effeminate men, oppressed women, and children who were either wildly undisciplined and overindulged or exploited and neglected. Evangelicals especially emphasized the character and status of women in "Oriental" societies, believing them fair indicators of the condition of those societies as a whole. In particular, they portrayed "Oriental" women as averse to anything resembling work, obsessed with clothes and jewelry but also dirty and poor housekeepers. "Oriental" women were almost universally uneducated and illiterate in American evangelical accounts. They also depicted the "Oriental" woman as a virtual slave to her husband, to the point of not being allowed to eat in his company and often being limited literally to the crumbs from his table. Most frequently, evangelicals described "Oriental" women as incarcerated in their homes—either literally behind bars, as with Persian or high-caste Hindu women or, in the case of Chinese women, immobilized by bound feet. In American evangelical literature, the penultimate degradation of the "Oriental" woman appeared in her willingness to sacrifice a male child to the gods or kill an infant daughter simply for not being male. The ultimate symbol of female "Oriental" degradation, however, appeared in accounts of Hindu women burning themselves to death on their husbands' funeral pyres in acts of misplaced (to the evangelical Christian) piety or, more commonly, because coerced to do so by family members who did not want the shameful burden of a widow on their hands.

Said depicted Orientalism as a mode of exerting Western imperial power over other nations. Many scholars have argued that American evangelical missionaries were agents of imperialism, while others have said that missionaries subverted the imperial project, or at least offered indigenous peoples the tools of resistance. I intend to leave that debate for others and instead turn my attention to the work of feminist scholars who have revised and extended Said's work by incorporating gender into their analyses of cultural contact between West and East. Melman and other feminist scholars have critiqued and revised Said's view to argue that Western European women often identified with "Oriental" women, holding up the images of those women so that their Western sisters could see themselves—equally powerless and voiceless, enmeshed in webs of masculine domination. By contrast, I will argue that American Protestant women held up images of "Oriental" women intending their American sisters to see themselves in positive contrast—educated and holding a privileged position in the home and in society at large. Protestant missionaries (both men and women) believed that evangelizing the women of the "Orient" would completely renovate those societies, releasing the women from cultural bondage while simultaneously bringing eternal salvation to all of the people.

Using constitutions and published proceedings of early nineteenth-century missionary societies, along with published sermons focused on mission work, Chapter One briefly reviews the formation of the first of those societies in the United States. It then explores in more detail the early efforts of women in behalf of missions and examines the introduction into mission literature of language about the oppressed "Oriental" woman. I conclude that, as early as 1815, women began using images of "Oriental" women to elicit sympathy for the women and financial support for missions.

Chapter Two introduces the genre of women's missionary memoirs, which emerged in 1812 with the publication of a memorial to Harriet Newell, the first American missionary woman to die abroad. Despite the fact that American missionaries spread across the globe in the nineteenth century, women's missionary memoirs focused disproportionately on those women who went to "Oriental" lands. Chapter Two outlines the form of those memoirs and places the genre in historical context. Missionary memoirs were a form of consolation literature modeled after Jonathan Edwards' *Life of David Brainerd*. The compiler of the memoir—usually a parent, spouse, or pastor—produced the memoir after the subject's (usually untimely) death by extracting passages from her diaries and letters. Two central arguments weave through this chapter. First, compilers invariably found their motivation in a desire to "sanctify" or "improve" their subjects' suffering and their own grief by holding up the life of the departed as an example for others to emulate by seeking salvation, doing good works at home, supporting the cause of foreign missions, and perhaps going abroad as a missionary. Second, the missionary women themselves were quite self-conscious of the hand of God at work in their lives. They viewed themselves as having great privileges as a result of having been born in a "Christian" nation—firm but loving parents, excellent educational opportunities, companionate marriages, and, most of all, busy and useful lives. Each woman saw in her work as a missionary a responsibility to replicate her own experiences in the lives of the women whom she was evangelizing—from the conversion of a young woman, to her education, to her preparation for a Christian marriage and motherhood, even to the point of her ability to meet suffering and death with grace. Women's missionary memoirs became quite a popular form of literature and did much to enlist women in the United States to support the cause of evangelizing the "Orient."

The remainder of the book uses the memoirs, denominational records, Sunday school literature, and other published primary sources for two purposes: first, to trace the circulation of ideas about "Oriental" women and the impact of those ideas on evangelical women, their missionary societies, and their denominations; and second, to examine the strategies that women missionaries, along with their male counterparts and their sending agencies, developed to accomplish the evangelistic goals that they shared. Chapter Three explores the role of gender in the ABCFM's formulation of policies regarding the qualifications of missionaries. I conclude first that assumptions regarding the status of women in the "Orient" played an important role in their decision that most male missionaries should marry and their wives should accompany them to the mission field as companions and helpers. Second, the chapter explains that for the first half-century of missions in Asia, the ABCFM adopted an evangelizing strategy of modeling Christian domesticity in the belief that Asian women would thus have an opportunity to see how Christianity had elevated Western women and would be drawn to the faith as a result.

Chapter Four continues the theme of Chapter Three by focusing on the modeling of motherhood as an evangelistic strategy. In this chapter, I argue that much of the motive for women missionaries and their supporters at home lay in their perception that non-Christian mothers lacked essential qualities of motherhood. That lack, according to the mission literature, made itself apparent in dirty, undisciplined children, in a refusal to educate girls, and, at worst, in infanticide. Successful evangelizing meant not only seeing "Oriental" women make professions of faith, but teaching those mothers to emulate the missionary women and nurture their children (girls as well as boys) in Christian piety, thus effecting the evangelization of Asia in a few generations. In both Chapters Three and Four, the implicit comparisons in mission literature between American evangelical wives and mothers and "heathen Oriental" wives and mothers reinforced a lesson in what made a good wife and mother. The comparison simultaneously conveyed to the female American audience a message about their own privileged position in society.

Chapter Four also points to the emergence of house schools as a strategy for evangelizing children (and subsequently reaching the mothers through the children). Missionary wives often taught dozens of children in addition to meeting their obligations to their own families. As the work of missionary wives multiplied, it quickly became apparent that, unlike the strategy of modeling domesticity and motherhood, an evangelistic strategy of reaching children (especially girls) through day and boarding schools did not require married missionaries. Chapter Five traces a shift that occurred during the 1840s and 1850s, paralleling the feminization of the teaching profession in the United States, whereby the mission girls' schools increasingly came to rely on the labor of unmarried missionary women. Girls' schools became critical sites for evangelistic activity in the "Orient" because of the pervasive belief on the part of American missionaries that opposition to girls' education (or even basic literacy) indicated the depravity of "Oriental" societies. At the same time, accounts of "Oriental" opposition to girls' education sent a message to the American audience that to be Christian meant to value the education of girls. To oppose such education was to take a "pagan" position. The ability to read, according to missionaries, opened both hearts and minds to the gospel; therefore, educational institutions for girls came to play a crucial role in the overall evangelistic strategy of American evangelical missions in the East.

Chapter Six explores another avenue of missionary vocation that opened to single women in the nineteenth century: medical missions. The arguments for women medical missionaries appeared in tandem with arguments for women's medical education generally. In both cases, proponents maintained that women made the best doctors for other women and for young children, whether in the United States or in the "Orient." Arguments in favor of training some women to serve as medical missionaries drew heavily on tropes about the seclusion of "Oriental" women. American Protestants believed that, throughout Asia, women were inaccessible to male missionaries and could only be reached through the efforts of women missionaries. As a result of their sequestration, according to mission apologists, "Oriental" women frequently had access to little or no medical care. In particular, mission literature portrayed them as being subject to the torture of "barbaric Oriental midwifery." Women physicians could potentially open doors in unprecedented ways, providing physical access into the homes of Asian women. More important, for mission strategists, securing the confidence and admiration of those women in such a perilous time as childbirth would perhaps make them more open to the Christian gospel.

Finally, Chapter Seven explores how the efforts of American women on behalf of their "Oriental sisters" led to the formation first of the ecumenical Woman's Union Missionary Society and subsequently of the women's denominational mission boards. In all cases, it was the image of the "Oriental" woman—oppressed, kept in ignorance, and accessible only to other women—that motivated women and men to inaugurate the women's boards. Twentieth-century observers and scholars have portrayed the formation of denominational women's boards as oppositional actions by women protesting their disfranchisement within the denominations. Regardless of later developments and the ultimate fate of those boards, I argue that male denominational leaders encouraged and in some cases initiated the formation of the women's boards in part because they feared the power of an ecumenical organization such as the Woman's Union Missionary Society to siphon women's support away from the denominations.

However, women *and* men formed the boards primarily because they shared a firm belief in the necessity of "woman's work for woman," especially in the "Orient." Thus, the images of oppressed "Oriental" women, circulated in popular religious literature throughout the nineteenth century, played a crucial role in decisions that significantly transformed denominational structures and feminized the foreign missions movement.

1

"The Widow's Mite"

Organizing Missionary Societies

The 1790s was a decade of religious ferment in the nascent American republic. With the Napoleonic Wars ravaging Europe, yellow fever epidemics sweeping the United States, evangelical revivals cropping up sporadically, and the turn of the century looming, pulpit and press issued forth millennial rhetoric, promising a "kingdom of God on earth" both in and flowing from the "new Israel," America.[1] The promise of the coming kingdom led both men and women to respond to their ministers' messages by participating in a united prayer movement ("concerts of prayer"), partaking of the revival spirit, and ultimately by forming separate but interdependent men's and women's missionary societies, at first to evangelize Native Americans and white settlers on the frontier and later to spread the gospel—the kingdom of God—overseas.[2]

British Baptists and Congregationalists had formed missionary societies in 1792 and 1795, respectively, with the goal of evangelizing the British colonies, especially India and the islands of the South Pacific.[3] Americans, avid consumers of British missionary publications, soon followed suit. Baptists, Congregationalists, and Presbyterians, primarily in New England, formed seven missionary societies between 1796 and

1802, hoping to evangelize both Native Americans and white frontier settlers. In order to inform the public of their own work and that of their European counterparts, some missionary societies published magazines that became popular reading for the men and women in their constituencies. The longest-lived were the *Massachusetts Missionary Magazine* (later called the *Panoplist*), the *Connecticut Evangelical Magazine*, and the *Massachusetts Baptist Missionary Magazine*. In addition to reporting on the finances and activities of the various American and British missionary societies, the magazines carried notices about concerts of prayer, described revivals, discussed the "state of religion" in particular regions, gave voice to millennial expectations, and served as a forum for mission apologetics. The missionary societies further publicized their activities by opening their annual meetings to the public and having an eminent leader deliver a relevant sermon, which the societies subsequently published and distributed.

Through missionary publications, as well as through their own personal influence, the men who organized the missionary society movement drew women into support for the cause. Women were already deeply involved with the prayer movement and revivals. Participating in the mission movement seemed to many a logical extension of those activities. As silent helpers, they gave their "widow's mites" for the support of the new missionary societies. The forceful messages of revivalist preachers ignited an enthusiasm and energy that required a new outlet in the new century, however. In the wake of the early nineteenth-century revivals, young women began to form mission societies of their own.[4] Always working in support of or as auxiliaries to the societies founded and run by ministers and laymen, the women's missionary societies nevertheless channeled the energies of a multitude of young female converts in the first decades of the nineteenth century.

One woman who proved highly influential in organizing missionary societies, Mary Webb, came into the movement after reading a sermon that Dr. Nathanael Emmons delivered before the annual meeting of the Massachusetts Missionary Society in Boston on 27 May 1800. Emmons had preached on 2 Chronicles 15:7: "Be ye strong therefore, and let not your hands be weak: for your work shall be rewarded," calling for Christians firmly to resolve "to propagate the gospel and build up the kingdom of Christ in the world."[5] Mary Webb said it was in the summer of 1800, after reading Emmons's sermon, that she "first conceived a *passion* for missions."[6] Born in Boston in 1779 and raised in a Congregationalist home, Webb had contracted a mysterious illness at age five that left her a paraplegic. When her father died in 1792, Thomas Baldwin, pastor of the nearby Second Baptist Church, befriended Webb and her mother and sister. Under Baldwin's influence, Mary Webb converted to the Baptist faith and was baptized in 1798. Baldwin, an enthusiastic supporter of missions, may well have given Webb the Emmons sermon in 1800. The sermon convinced Webb that she had neglected her duty and that physical incapacity was no excuse. She lacked not physical strength but strength of mind and faith in Christ. She acted promptly. Having devised a plan for the Boston Female Society for Missionary Purposes, she consulted with Thomas Baldwin and received his approval, along with that of the pastors of the First Baptist Church and the one Congregational church in town that, according to Webb, "stood fully upon evangelical grounds."[7] A group of fourteen women, seven Baptists and seven Congregationalists, gathered and approved a constitution on 9 October 1800. They intended to raise money through membership fees of two dollars per year for "the purchase of Bibles, Testaments, and other religious books, for distribution by missionaries in destitute places." For the first two years, those funds went to the Congregational Massachusetts Missionary Society. Thereafter, the women divided their donations between that society and the Massachusetts Baptist Missionary Society.[8]

Two years after Webb formed the Boston Female Society for Missionary Purposes, another type of women's organization had its genesis in Boston: the cent or mite society, the name and concept of which had its origin in Jesus' parable of the widow's mite in the Gospel of Luke.[9] Cent societies raised funds by requiring their members to donate one penny per week for dues. Almost without exception they followed the initial example set by the Boston Female Society by giving their receipts to male-led missionary or Bible societies for the purchase of Bibles and other Christian literature to distribute in the frontier settlements. Many cent societies, and others like Mary Webb's which required higher dues, corresponded with the male-led societies that they supported. Some of that correspondence found its way into the pages of the missionary magazines and provides a window into the motivations of the women involved, revealing that women shared the concerns of their fathers, brothers, and husbands. Women held the same millennial expectations as their male counterparts. Women often referred to themselves as "friends of Zion" and, like the organizers of the Female Association of Litchfield County, looked forward to "that happy period, when the knowledge and glory of the Lord, shall fill the earth."[10] They also shared with men a commitment to the theological tenets of the New Divinity, especially the concept of "disinterested benevolence," or doing good works for their own sake, without expectation of a return. Mary Webb wrote that being a Christian demanded "zeal and activity."[11] Another correspondent wrote that the societies gave "good women...an opportunity of knowing the Lord with their substance...believing that the approbation of their own consciences, and the tender mercies of our blessed Redeemer, will be their rich and abundant reward."[12] Women who supported the work of cent societies believed that "benevolent actions ministering to the spiritual necessities of those who are perishing...exhibit an example highly ornamental to their sex and honorable to religion."[13] Finally, the women resembled their "fathers and brethren" in their commitment to prayer as an important measure for ensuring the success of the activities that they also supported with their money. Mary Webb, for example, issued a call for concerts of prayer in a February 1812 "Address to the Female Friends of Zion," suggesting that women throughout the country meet on the first Monday afternoon of each month to pray for "general revival" and the "universal spread of the gospel."[14]

For all of their common concerns, the men's and women's societies were, nonetheless, separate. Women occasionally showed up on the membership lists of the male-led societies, but for the most part those societies excluded women from their rolls. They did not, however, exclude women from donating to support their cause. In the early years of the movement, the societies' financial reports listed every donor, and women—usually the anonymous "female friend of missions"—appeared frequently. Nevertheless, while women did not *have* to organize their own societies in order to contribute money to the cause of missions, they did. The focus of revivals and concerts of prayer on the urgency of evangelism and the duty of disinterested benevolence produced in women the same zeal that men channeled into the mission movement. Organizing to raise money for missions gave women an outlet for their religious enthusiasm, but did not represent too much of a deviation from the traditionally circumscribed roles of women—they were still "helpmeets."

Women submitted to the spiritual authority and leadership of men by turning over the money they raised to the men's societies. Sometimes they did this without qualification. The ladies of the Female Charitable Society of Whitestown, New York, for example, donated something over $130 in 1807 to the Hampshire Missionary Society "to be by them appropriated at their discretion."[15] More frequently, the women reserved the right to designate how the funds would be spent, usually requesting that the money go toward the purchase of Bibles and other Christian literature for distribution in the new settlements. The men, for their part, recognized both the right of the women to designate their giving and their own responsibility to account publicly to the women for the way they spent the funds. The Massachusetts Missionary Society, for example, established a committee each year at their annual meeting for the express purpose of spending cent society money to "the satisfaction of our female friends."[16] All of the major male-led missionary societies published annual reports in the magazines, providing details of funds received from various women's groups and the ways in which they spent the money. The women's humble relinquishment of their money and the polite gratitude of the male societies in return belied the fact that the money collected by the women became an increasingly significant portion of the societies' budgets and was often the only source of funds for religious literature. The trustees of the Massachusetts Baptist Missionary Society noted in 1811 that the "diffusive benevolence [of the women] has become one of the principal channels through which our supply is derived."[17]

The very act of publishing the letters and constitutions of women's societies and reporting on their donations represented a mark of approval on the part of male leaders of the movement. Frequently, representatives of male-led societies responded with remarks of gratitude that affirmed the women's actions and offered justifications and encouragements for their continued efforts. In the *Massachusetts Missionary Magazine's* June 1804 issue, the editor maintained that the cent societies provided an "eligible" way for women "to contribute…to the salvation of immortal souls, and the advancement of their Redeemer's kingdom."[18] Ministers also offered biblical justifications for women's involvement in missions. Thomas Baldwin, for example, replied to a letter and donation from the Warren Female Mite Society by praying that God would bless the women's "united and individual exertions, in aiding the spread of the gospel." If the women's efforts resulted in the spread of the gospel, they not only shared a common objective with laymen and clergy, but by implication, to oppose them would have the opposite effect of *inhibiting* the spread of the gospel. Baldwin's prayer for God's blessing and his subsequent statement that "*God is not unrighteous to forget your labour of love*" indicated to his audience not only that Baldwin himself supported the women's actions, but that he believed God did too.[19]

Ministers often appealed to biblical precedent as both an encouragement to women and a defense for their involvement in promoting the mission cause. Samuel Hopkins, in a trustees' report for the Hampshire Missionary Society, wrote, "If we look back to the institutions of the Old Testament, we see not only men but women and children encouraged to make vows and to bring their free-will offerings to the Lord."[20] Some writers drew on the New Testament, pointing out that a woman raised and nurtured Jesus, that women were among his most devoted followers, and that following his resurrection, Jesus appeared first to the women who had prepared his body for the grave and visited the tomb.[21] Most frequently, though, writers supported female involvement in missions by enjoining their readers to "*remember the Widow's two mites.*"[22]

Men were not the only ones who took pains to justify and defend women's participation in the mission movement. Women were acutely aware that, by organizing their own societies, they opened themselves up to accusations of misconduct. An "anonymous woman" wrote a defense of women's involvement in missions in 1804. She quoted extensively from both the Old and New Testaments, including a reference to the parable of the widow's mites. Her most interesting justification, however, compared winning souls for Christ to giving birth. "The daughters of Zion," she wrote, "are called upon to be in travail for souls," thus using the childbirth metaphor to demonstrate that efforts to save souls fell within women's sphere of concern. She called on Scripture to support her point, citing Micah 4:10 as her authority: "Be in pain, and labor to bring forth, O Daughter of Zion, like a woman in travail."[23]

Mary Webb wrote at least three lengthy defenses of women's involvement in the mission movement, two in 1812 and one in 1815. In her first address, she noted that women had the blessing of heaven because God had given them the inclination to do the work and prospered their first efforts. Even the angels, she said, "smile on our endeavours." Furthermore, "good men of different denominations" approved of their efforts, and if that was not enough, among the general public more people seemed to be for them than against them. Finally, lest anyone should bring up the Apostle Paul in opposition, she proclaimed, "And though we wish ever to preserve our place as females, we cannot view it inconsistent with that modesty and shamefacedness enjoined by the Apostle, thus openly to come out on the Lord's side."[24] Webb's second address maintained the same tone. She assured the readers that women involved in supporting missions had "no wish to go out of [their] province," nor did they have any desire to set themselves up as preachers. In a statement that was a model of deference and submission in its allusion to the Old Testament story of Ruth, she wrote, "It is our pleasure to see our brethren go before, and we are content to be permitted to 'glean after the reapers' and follow with out earnest prayers their more extensive labours."[25]

By the time of Webb's third address, in 1815, a marked shift had occurred. She maintained that it was "no longer a question whether it be proper for females to serve the church; God has too manifestly owned their labors." Citing women of the Old and New Testaments, she further declared that "since Miriam and Deborah, Priscilla and Phebe have led the way," women should not hesitate to follow in their footsteps "to facilitate the arduous work of the gospel mission." Although less apologetic than earlier defenses of women in missions, her use of the word "facilitate" indicates that women's roles in that work were still subordinate to those of men. Nonetheless, the assertion that propriety was no longer at issue indicates that an important transformation was underway.[26]

One can partially attribute that transformation to the fact that, after fifteen years, the public had grown accustomed to women's participation in the mission movement. But the advent of American participation in *foreign* missions also contributed to the transformation of women's roles. In March of 1812, the first American missionaries to India departed American shores under the auspices of the recently formed ABCFM. That same month, the editors of the *Panoplist* devoted a large proportion of the magazine to the subject of foreign missions. One letter to the editor opened by declaring that "a new and wonderful era seems to have commenced in America, the era of Foreign Missions."[27]

The British missionary societies had formed to take the gospel to the distant reaches of the British Empire. British and American evangelicals implicitly understood that the Western hemisphere remained the province of the American societies. The American societies had nevertheless followed the progress of the European societies, taking a particular interest in British Baptist missionary William Carey's work in India. In 1800, Carey and other British Baptists had settled into the Danish crown colony of Serampore just outside of Calcutta, after the East India Company had forbidden them to work in territories that they controlled. Carey had a remarkable proficiency for languages, and since locating at Serampore in 1800, he had devoted himself to translating Scripture into the various languages spoken in India. The Baptists also established a press in Serampore in order to publish and distribute the translations of Carey and other missionaries and scholars. In 1804, the British and Foreign Bible Society began to promote the work of translation around the globe. As early as 1809, the trustees of the Missionary Society of Connecticut reported "a zeal to spread the gospel, where now unknown, and to translate the holy scriptures into the various languages of the nations and to circulate Bibles and religious books, rises higher and higher."[28] Their assessment was accurate. Between 300 BCE and 1800 CE, first-time translations of all or part of the Old and New Testaments into new languages totaled seventy-four; between 1800 and 1830, that number doubled.[29]

Missionary magazines in the United States regularly published news of the Serampore mission and often suggested that their readers donate funds to support the work of translation. The *Connecticut Evangelical Magazine* noted in 1811, "The readers of this Magazine have repeatedly been addressed on the duty of giving liberally for the *Translation of the Scriptures into the Eastern Languages*." That same journal reported in 1812 that a British Baptist minister traveling through New England had "by the recommendation of the clergymen of every Christian denomination, in Boston, Salem, and Beverly,...obtained there a subscription of $4624, towards translating the Bible."[30] Numerous local societies dedicated to the support of foreign missions sprang up throughout the country, many of them specifically dedicated to supporting the work of translation.[31]

Because evangelical Protestants placed such a high value on individuals reading the Bible for themselves, they found the work of translating Scripture particularly appealing. Also, since the Bible carried the message of the gospel, translating, publishing, and distributing it would speed up the process of world evangelization and hasten the arrival of the millennium. One effect of the emphasis on translation, however, was the redirection of American interests in missions away from Native Americans and toward the "heathen" in more distant regions of the earth, specifically the "East"—India and Burma, to begin with. Translation, of course, required a written language. Despite admonitions little more than a decade earlier that missionaries did not have to civilize the "heathen" before evangelizing them, the attention drawn to translation efforts caused mission apologists to reconsider. The editor of the *Massachusetts Baptist Missionary Magazine* wrote, "Had the savage tribes which inhabit the wilds of America any written language, the friends of religion would instantly furnish them with a translation of the sacred Scriptures. There is very little to encourage missionary labours among them so long as they continue in their roving unsettledness."[32] On the other hand, "the worshippers of Juggernaut [Hindus]," he wrote, "may be fairly ranked among the grossest idolaters; yet they have the knowledge of letters, which offers the greatest facility in furnishing them with the knowledge of the sacred scriptures." The writer did not mean that he believed all Hindus were literate, but rather that Indian society had reached a level of civilization sufficient to produce a written language. While years of failed attempts to convert Native Americans proved that their lifestyle was "hostile to the introduction of Christianity among them," the missionary's eyes turned toward the East could "*behold the fields white already unto harvest.*"[33]

The transformation that Mary Webb had noted when she wrote in 1815 that propriety was no longer at issue where women's involvement in missions was concerned had serious implications for the future of women in missions. As women gained self-confidence in their mission role, they increasingly revealed a willingness to exert independence from the male-led societies by supporting causes that particularly appealed to them rather than leaving the expenditure of their funds to the discretion of their male counterparts. In her third address exhorting women to engage in the cause of missions, Webb wrote, "Particularly when we glance our thoughts to those heathenish climes never yet irradiated by the Sun of Righteousness, and see multitudes of our own sex degraded to the most abject servitude and contempt, and exposed to sufferings the most exquisite; do not our bosoms swell with mingled emotions of sympathy toward them, and indignation toward those who hold them in such a state of degradation?"[34] The rise of foreign missions and an increasing attention to the status of women in the Hindu and Muslim societies of Asia corresponded with an increasing attention on the part of women in the United States to ameliorating the conditions of their American sisters through charitable and benevolent institutions. Webb's concern for her "own sex" presaged the explicit articulation of a concept of "woman's work for woman" within the context of foreign missions.

The interest of evangelical women was aroused when the first band of five American missionaries sailed from Philadelphia for India, because three of them were accompanied by their wives. Although the ABCFM, which sponsored the mission, did not appoint the wives as missionaries, women clearly saw them as their representatives in the effort to win souls and usher in the millennium. Mary Webb captured the sentiments of many when she penned, "And do we not at times even long to cross the vast ocean and submit to all the dangers of a missionary life?"[35] Although most women could not go, they could support their sisters who did embark on the great adventure: "Will not our boldest exertions be excited by the heroic zeal and fortitude of our dear brethren and sisters, who have left their native land and are gone...to preach the precious gospel of Christ?"[36]

The missionaries were literally not yet out of the Chesapeake Bay before missionary magazines began publishing their correspondence. Letters and journals of missionaries and their wives were part of a general attention to foreign missions pervading the magazines. One particular element central to writing on foreign missions drew the attention of the female audience by arousing concern about the status of women in "heathen countries," meaning the "Orient." Articles and letters frequently pointed out that introducing Christianity would result in the "suppression of various kinds of cruelty, such as the burning of widows, and the drowning of infants."[37] In an excerpt printed from a sermon, the writer took pains to remind women of England and America that their social position derived from "the diffusion of gospel light." To illustrate his point, he went on to describe the practice in some "Oriental" countries of "destroying female infants."[38] Thus, for the first time in the literature of the mission movement, a distinct emphasis emerged on the plight of "Oriental" women and what mission advocates would later call "woman's work for woman."

With the embarkation of the first women bound for the mission field, a new genre—the woman missionary's memoir—joined missionary magazines as an important medium for stirring women's support for the cause of foreign missions. The first of the genre of women's missionary memoirs was the *Memoir of the Life of Harriet Newell*, compiled by her pastor, Leonard Woods, and initially published in 1812. Harriet Newell, a member of that first group of American missionaries to go overseas, was also the first American woman to die abroad as a missionary. She died of childbed fever at the age of nineteen on board a ship in the Indian Ocean. Despite the fact that she never reached her intended field of service (India), her memoir was something of a bestseller for early nineteenth-century America. It appeared in at least twenty-five printings in the United States and several European editions. Excerpts were still appearing in missionary magazines almost a century later. Despite the fact that Newell's memoir depicted great suffering and premature death, the book was enormously popular and seemed to inspire large numbers of women to redouble their efforts to raise financial support for foreign missions. It is certain from tributes in subsequent missionary memoirs that Harriet Newell's example persuaded others to follow in her footsteps. Leaders of the ABCFM believed that the popularity of the book was largely responsible for rescuing the missions movement, which nearly foundered in its infancy in large part because of the economic hardships that befell New England during the War of 1812.[39] Newell's memoir is significant because its popularity demonstrated the widespread interest in women's involvement in foreign missions. More important for this study, however, is the fact that the memorial of Newell's life and premature death inspired subsequent tributes to women missionaries and thus launched an entire genre of popular literature. A memorial to a woman who willingly sacrificed her life for the salvation of women of the "Orient" inspired countless men and women to give liberally to support the cause and many young women to follow in her footsteps.

2

"Sanctifying Afflictions"

Nineteenth-Century Missionary Women's Memoirs

In August 1845, Joel Hawes addressed the American Institute for Education on the subject "'A Looking-Glass for Ladies,' or the Formation and Excellence of the Female Character."[1] At a time when the "cult of true womanhood" presumably held sway over middle-class white culture, articles, lectures, and sermons on the "excellence of the female character" were no novelty.[2] The Congregational minister's text—the description of a "virtuous woman" in Proverbs 31—was hardly a more original choice than his stated purpose of depicting "all those intellectual, social, and moral qualifications, which belong to a woman of superior intellect."[3] But Hawes brought a distinct perspective to his topic. If Proverbs 31 was his text—a "looking-glass" for ladies to "dress themselves by"—the women of the "Orient" provided the subtext.[4] Hawes' lecture, like many other writings informed by the foreign missions movement, served not only as a "looking-glass" into which American Christian women could peer for an idealized standard of virtue to emulate. It also served as an "ethnological mirror," reflecting images of an antithetical, "Oriental" Other against which American women could measure their own progress and status in relation to their "degraded heathen sisters" of the "East."[5]

In 1843, the ABCFM had sent Hawes on a tour of Turkey, Syria, Persia, and Palestine to evaluate the progress of their missions and to provide his assessment of future prospects in those lands. On the trip across the Atlantic, he accompanied his daughter Mary and her new husband, Henry Van Lennep, on their way to Turkey as missionaries. Joel Hawes completed his assignment and returned safely to his Hartford, Connecticut, congregation. His daughter, however, died in Constantinople in 1844, after less than two years of service as a missionary.

In his lecture before the American Institute for Education, Joel Hawes' description of the virtuous woman served as a generic and succinct version of his daughter's life. Hawes detailed the traits of virtuous womanhood, but he also wrote the "Oriental" Other into his script. He began by exploring the opening question of his text, "Who can find a virtuous woman?"[6] Setting the biblical passage in its historical context, he pointed out that Israelite women had been superior on the whole to the women of the surrounding nations (ancestors of the Syrians, Turks, and Kurds who had become objects of missionary attention) because divine revelation had given to the chosen people the concept of the wife as a "helpmeet" deserving honor from her household. Hebrew culture, according to Hawes, nevertheless so circumscribed the roles and education of women that the writer of Proverbs felt compelled to pose the question, "Who can find a virtuous woman?" American Christian women, citizens of the new Israel, had inherited the same Old Testament precepts, but had progressed through the instrumentality of Jesus Christ to fulfill the promise inherent within those precepts. The position of women in western Asia, on the other hand—Jews, Muslims, and "nominal" Christians alike—had remained static because the light of the gospel had receded. Hawes went on to compare American women with their counterparts in western Asia, a region that he used to represent all places "where the Bible is unknown":

> In nothing is the progress of Christian civilization more remarkable, than in the elevation it has imparted to the female sex. In this view, woman's indebtedness to the Bible is greater than can be estimated. It has changed all her relations, enjoyments, duties, and prospects in life, and all her hopes for eternity. Throughout the world, where the Bible is unknown, woman is ignorant, degraded, substantially enslaved; a poor, trembling drudge, waiting on the desires of a haughty, domineering master. But wherever the Bible has diffused its light and power, there it has restored woman to her proper place in society; it has redeemed her from an Egyptian bondage of body and mind, and while it has given greater sensibility and delicacy to her affections, it has enlarged her understanding, purified her taste, adorned her manners, dignified her character, and widened, exceedingly, the circle of her influence and enjoyments; it has done all this on so extended a scale, especially in this highly favored portion of our country, that, if the question were asked, who can find a virtuous woman, we could point to thousands of mothers, daughters, sisters, who realize this character in their own persons, in all its amiable and excellent qualities.[7]

This assertion was by no means an original one. Hawes' words encapsulated a theme that had permeated mission literature since the 1790s and provided an important element for the foundation of the Anglo-American Protestant missions movement. It also supplied the framework around which the entire body of women's missionary literature was constructed.

Louisa Hawes, Joel's wife and Mary's mother, joined her husband in paying tribute to their daughter by compiling a memoir from Mary's diary and letters.[8] *The Memoir of Mrs. Mary E. Van Lennep* depicted the missionary martyr's character through explicit description of her Christian virtues and through an implicit comparison to the opposite of those virtues as embodied in the female "Oriental" Others whom Mary Van Lennep encountered in her journeys and portrayed in her communications to family and friends in the United States. The act of compiling the memoir helped Louisa Hawes to find meaning in her daughter's suffering and death, but it served a larger purpose as well. It instructed American women on the meaning of feminine virtue and reflected back to those women an image of an entire race of unvirtuous "Oriental" women in need of redemption. The memoir gave American Protestant women a vocation: working to redeem the suffering of Mary Van Lennep for the spiritual good of the "Orient" and the advancement of the kingdom of God on earth.

Protestant women's missionary memoirs, of which the memorial to Mary Van Lennep is a prime example, were among the most popular productions of the burgeoning evangelical press in the first half of the nineteenth century. When a young woman met an untimely death on the mission field, her husband, a parent, or a friend would compile the memoir as a memorial to her. Such memoirs were really spiritual autobiographies. They consisted of excerpts from the subject's diaries, private letters, and letters written for publication in missionary magazines. The excerpts generally highlighted the subject's conversion experience, her decision to enter upon a missionary career, her journeys, and her experiences on the field. The physical sufferings experienced by the woman very often provided a dominant theme of her memoir, and the descriptions of deathbed scenes, written by her husband or a colleague, could be quite lengthy. For example, Harrison Gray Otis Dwight's memorial to his wife, Elizabeth, opened with a 132-page verbatim transcript of a series of notes chronicling her death from bubonic plague. When the plague broke out in Constantinople, Elizabeth and the youngest of her three sons were stricken almost immediately. Harrison stayed with them while their missionary colleagues took the other two children to a safer location outside of the city. Several times a day, Harrison sent a note to the other missionaries offering an excruciatingly detailed account of Elizabeth's slow and painful death from the dreaded disease. Harrison thus began his memorial to his wife with a lengthy and dramatic description of her death. He then went back to the beginning of her life and constructed a rather conventional narrative of Elizabeth's birth, upbringing, conversion experience, and commitment to the life of a missionary. The account of her experiences as a missionary, covering only the last two years of her life, actually made up a relatively small proportion of the book. What clearly mattered most in Elizabeth's life was her torturous death—the death of a Christian martyr, albeit by the ravages of disease rather than by violence.[9]

Both Louisa Hawes and Harrison Dwight were engaging in the time-honored Puritan exercise of "sanctifying afflictions." [10] Hawes, Dwight, and other compilers of women's missionary memoirs sought to turn the affliction of their subjects into spiritual good for their audiences. The suffering of the missionary martyr would be "sanctified" if the testimony of that suffering caused other women to become missionaries or to support the cause of missions by participating in women's missionary societies that met to pray and raise money for the cause. Harrison Dwight, for example, noted in his introduction to the letters recounting his wife's death that he hoped the book would serve as "a very efficient instrument in exciting a still deeper interest in the cause of missions, and of hastening the triumph of our Redeemer throughout this sinful world."[11] While one might expect that repeated tales of suffering and premature death would dampen women's enthusiasm for missions, such accounts actually had the opposite effect, as the compilers and publishers clearly intended. Vivid accounts of women missionaries' suffering and early deaths inspired contemporary and succeeding generations of women to make similar sacrifices for the cause of missions.

When it came to reading the memoirs of women who died while serving as missionaries, Americans clearly preferred the stories of those who had worked and died in the "Orient." Representing Congregational, Presbyterian, and Reformed churches, the ABCFM was the largest of the nineteenth-century American Protestant mission boards. Between 1812 and 1860, it sustained a force of over 1,300 missionaries, assistant missionaries, physicians, and missionary wives. Forty-five percent of that force served in Asia, thirty-five percent worked among the North American Indians, and twenty percent went to the Hawaiian Islands.[12] The American Baptist Missionary Union (ABMU) similarly divided its mission force between Asia and North America, while the Methodist Episcopal Church (MEC) focused its efforts on Liberia. Despite the broad distribution of personnel, however, writings on Asia dominated mission literature. In an extensive bibliography appended to his *Encyclopedia of Missions*, Edwin Munsell Bliss identified seventy American missionary memoirs published before 1870. Fifty-four of them (77%) had missionaries to Asia as their subject. Twenty-six of the twenty-seven memoirs about women focused on women who served in Asia. Americans, especially American women, clearly wanted to know about the condition of women in the "Orient" and the work of missionary women to ameliorate those conditions.

Missionary women not only presented an ideal standard for American women to emulate, but they represented what the female "Oriental" Other could become if American women fulfilled their duty by extending to their sisters in Asia the same benefits that they enjoyed in Christian North America. In each memoir, the compiler devoted considerable space to tracing the subject's life from early childhood up until the point at which she departed for the mission field. The memoirs emphasized the significance of Christian family nurture, education, the conversion experience, and charitable works as preparation for the life of a missionary. Each of those stages of life also represented a benefit of living in a Christian society. The work on the mission field subsequently described in the memoirs represented each woman's attempt to reproduce those experiences in the lives of the women among whom they lived and worked. Missionary women sought to lift "Oriental" women to the same exalted spiritual and social level that they perceived themselves to hold.

Irene Quenzler Brown notes that missionary women's memoirs differed markedly from other types of female religious autobiography in the nineteenth century. While the entire genre functioned as consolation literature, missionary women's memoirs had an expressly didactic purpose more characteristic of the eighteenth-century Enlightenment than of the nineteenth-century Romanticism that informed other types of female religious autobiography.[13] Another student of the genre, Joanna Bowen Gillespie, notes that evangelical women valued "literary self expression" precisely because of "what it could do for others."[14] The compilers of missionary memoirs openly proclaimed the instructional purpose of their efforts, anticipating possible criticism for publicly exalting individual women in a culture that prized modesty as a feminine virtue. James Knowles, for example, justified compiling and publishing Ann Judson's memoir on the grounds that the Bible used biography as an instructive tool.[15] Miron Winslow said that the effort of preparing his wife Harriet's memoir would be worthwhile if it "shall kindle a spark of missionary zeal in one youthful breast—or throw the least light on the path of any follower of the Lord Jesus to a foreign land—or excite in any heart a throb of pity for a dying world."[16] Henrietta Hamlin's memorialist emphasized the utility of the genre as a whole: "From the publication of 'Harriet Newell,' the first American 'missionary sister' whose biography blessed our land, down to the last that has greeted us from the press, not one has failed of extended usefulness in the promotion of personal holiness, the increase of the spirit of missions, and the happy illustration of the grace of God."[17]

Gillespie points out that "pious memoirs...are a body of cultural artifacts demonstrating the ordinary citizen's claim to uniqueness and individuality."[18] The person who compiled a missionary woman's memoir faced a complicated task of balancing the desire to portray the woman as an exemplar of Christian faith and practice against the desire to demonstrate that she was, in fact, an ordinary person and that any ordinary person could do as she had done. In his lecture, "A Looking-Glass for Ladies," Joel Hawes pointed out that Proverbs 31 did not seek to paint a "fancy picture, or...a character so delicate and refined that few could hope to imitate or acquire it," but rather described characteristics to which all young evangelical women could aspire.[19] The memoirs of his daughter and other women demonstrated that "missionary heroines" did not possess superhuman qualities or come from especially privileged backgrounds. Rather, they came from varied stations in life and even the most sainted among them struggled with the innate depravity common to the human condition—including the condition of "Oriental" women.

Many, but not all, missionary women came from homes headed by devout, evangelical Christian parents. As a body of literature, the memoirs illustrated the importance of "parental piety."[20] Missionary women not only served as models of "parental piety" and Christian motherhood themselves; their heroic lives resulted from the early efforts of their own parents. Thus, most of the women who ended up memorialized as missionary martyrs had been "nurtured in the lap of piety," like Virginia Baptist Henrietta Shuck, or were "child[ren] of the covenant" like Fidelia Fiske or of "true Puritan stock" like Sarah

Huntington Smith.[21] A few, however, were *not* raised from infancy by evangelical parents. Harriet Lathrop Winslow's parents made public professions of faith on the same day she did, Ann Hasseltine Judson's mother did not convert until after Ann, and Elizabeth Baker Dwight's Unitarian parents opposed her conversion.[22] The memoirs of those women simply portrayed them as even more heroic and as illustrations of the sovereign power of God for having overcome the obstacle of unconverted parents. Those accounts contained the implicit message that the "call" to missions did not come only to those whose parents had raised them from infancy to embrace the teachings of evangelicalism. Of greatest importance, however, is the message that the memoirs conveyed about how a society became Christianized as a result of Christian parents creating an environment that led to their children's conversion. Faith in the role of "parental piety" lay at the heart of family-oriented mission strategy in the first half-century of mission work in Asia.

Just as most, but not all, missionary women grew up in evangelical households, most, but not all, came from similar socioeconomic backgrounds. In addition to three ministers, the fathers included two attorneys and a clerk of courts, a merchant, and a physician. One was a farmer and a cooper; the rest were probably farmers, although at least one was a "jack of all trades and master of none." None of these men possessed extraordinary wealth; three of the families included ten, thirteen, and fourteen children respectively. Sarah Lanman Huntington Smith probably enjoyed the most privileges. Her father was a prominent Connecticut attorney, and her paternal grandmother came from the Trumbull family that produced two Connecticut governors and renowned painter John Trumbull.[23] Henrietta Jackson Hamlin's father, a Congregational minister in Vermont, served as one of the first trustees of Middlebury College.[24] Even as prominent a Congregational minister as Joel Hawes, however, possessed only modest financial means. Mary Hawes had to leave school for a year at age eight in order to care for an infant brother, because her mother was ill and they could not afford to hire a nurse for him.[25] The second and third wives of Adoniram Judson probably ranked among the poorest of missionary women. Sarah Hall Boardman Judson, eldest of thirteen children, came from an impoverished family and was thus "inured to toil and care."[26] Emily

Chubbuck Judson came from a family whose poverty stemmed from the father's lack of "that practical shrewdness and energy so necessary to worldly prosperity." He failed miserably at every occupation he attempted, from farming to distributing newspapers. Hence, eleven-year-old Emily worked twelve hours a day in a woolen mill for $1.25 per week. Her memories of the experience consisted primarily of "noise and filth, bleeding hands and aching feet." She later twisted thread for a weaver and assisted a dressmaker, attending school at the same time until, at age fifteen, she began teaching.[27] Explicitly, such accounts of hardship and self-sacrifice delineated the character of a virtuous woman and exhorted young evangelical women to emulate those examples. Implicitly, the stories conveyed the message that the gospel of Jesus Christ was for people of all stations of life. Eternal salvation came to the "heathen" people of the world in the same way that it came to Americans. Likewise, salvation would bring a transformation in this life as well. "Oriental" women could achieve the same virtue as their American counterparts and could similarly replicate the salvific and transformative experience in the lives of their own children, gradually accomplishing the Christianization of Asia.

Despite the fact that most American missionary women had "pious" parents and all of their deaths were portrayed as martyrdom, the compilers of their memoirs carefully demonstrated that they had to cope with a sinful nature just like anyone else. Anyone, therefore, could imitate their examples.[28] Ann Judson, for example, suffered from high spirits and a "strong relish for social amusements" such as parties and dancing.[29] Harriet Newell, Harriet Winslow, and Emily Judson all shared that interest in dancing.[30] Harriet Newell admitted to the "wickedness" of reading novels on Sundays and the "foolishness" of reading "novels and romances" at all.[31] Judith Grant was a "wayward child," Fidelia Fiske possessed a "decidedly rebellious" spirit, and Mary Van Lennep had a "propensity to deceive."[32] Sarah Huntington Smith had revealed her depravity at a very early age. As punishment for some infraction, she was ordered to sit alone in a room and think about the fact that "God was displeased with her." In response, she "stamped her foot upon the floor and exclaimed, 'I hate God'"![33] Mary Van Lennep's mother made the point behind these portrayals of vice most clearly.

While "not exempt from the faults and imperfections incident to our fallen state," she wrote, her daughter had developed a consciousness of and repentance for her sins that provided evidence of God's grace operating in her life.[34] The same sentiment echoed through all of the missionary women's memoirs and suggested that any young woman who examined her own sinful nature and repented of it just might be an object of God's grace herself and perhaps make the same heroic sacrifice. One should read the missionary women's accounts of the depravity of the "Oriental" women whom they sought to evangelize in that same context. The sins of "Oriental" women and "Oriental" societies were not "Oriental" sins—they were simply further examples of the fallen state of the human race.

In his lecture, Joel Hawes noted that while virtuous women could come from a variety of social and religious backgrounds and all struggled with sin, they all shared certain positive characteristics, one of the most notable of which was "a cultivated and well furnished mind."[35] The memoirs of missionary women forcefully conveyed the message that educating young women played an important role in bringing about their conversion and inculcating within them Christian virtues. Education both brought about and symbolized the high status that American evangelicals perceived women to hold in the United States. Such beliefs explain the great emphasis that missionary women (and most of their male co-laborers) placed on education as an evangelization strategy for girls and women in Asia.

Missionary women, as exemplars of virtue, invariably came from families who assigned a high importance to educating their daughters. They had parents who, like Henrietta Shuck's father, "entertained enlarged and liberal views on the subject of female instruction."[36] Even Emily Judson's poverty-stricken family, though they might not have known what they would eat from one day to the next, never lacked for books. The educational experiences of missionary women whose memoirs were published between 1815 (Harriet Newell) and 1868 (Fidelia Fiske) reflected important developments in women's education.[37] Sarah Hall Boardman Judson was the exception in being almost entirely self-educated beyond the common school level. Emily Judson wrote of her, "We are accustomed to consider a self-educated man, with all his physical strength and multiplicity of resources, worthy of all praise; what, then, shall we say of the woman, who, unassisted and alone, goes beyond most of her sex, in accomplishing the same object."[38] Unlike Sarah Judson, most of these women received an academy education; many of them, though, had to work very hard to pay their own way. Harriet Winslow attended an academy for young women in New Haven, Connecticut, and Henrietta Hamlin attended several different academies at Brookfield, Haverhill, and Andover, Massachusetts. Emily Judson received a very fine education at Utica Female Seminary, attending for free in exchange for a promise to repay the school by teaching there. Sarah Lanman Smith probably attended the Female Academy at Norwich, Mary Van Lennep attended the Hartford Female Seminary, and Seraphina Haynes Everett went to Abbott Female Seminary in Andover. Lucy Lyon Lord and Fidelia Fiske both attended Mount Holyoke.

While opportunities for female education improved and expanded dramatically in the early nineteenth century, the classical curriculum at the heart of boys' education "seemed self-indulgent when found among women. Americans inherited the image of the learned woman as an unenviable anomaly."[39] Thus, while their descriptions reveal young women who sought and attained high academic achievement, the compilers of missionary women's memoirs took great care to soften their portrayals so that their subjects would not appear masculine. Most of the women were characterized as above average intellectually. The description of Ann Judson displaying an "eager thirst for knowledge" that indicated a "mind...of superior order" typified the representations of missionary women.[40] Margarette Lawrence portrayed Henrietta Hamlin as excelling in math and the natural sciences and having a particular fondness for chemistry. But to demonstrate that such aptitude was not unwomanly, she reported that "when told that she must study the kitchen as well as books," Henrietta replied, "Anyone can be a good cook who understands chemistry."[41] In the summer of 1825, Henrietta attended a school in Chester, Vermont, under the care of a Reverend Burnap. A letter from him to the compiler of her memoir recalled her as having "'a superior intellect combined with all the lovely sensibilities of her sex. There was nothing masculine in her temper or in her deportment. In all her feelings and habits she was a lady. While her recitations evinced deep thought and comprehension of the subject, they were always characterized with genuine modesty.'"[42] Judith Grant "exhibited great aptness and power" in all her studies, including classical languages and mathematics, and was "eminently qualified for the acquisition of the languages of Persia." Her great intelligence and extensive education also, however, "qualified her to adorn any circle and fill any sphere of female responsibility."[43] At Utica Seminary, Emily Judson displayed a "masculine intellect" and, as a scholar, stood in the "very first rank." Her biographer wrote, "With a woman's quickness and delicacy of feeling, she united a robust and masculine understanding."[44] While some claimed that studying the "masculine" subjects—classical languages, mathematics, rhetoric—would "unsex" young women, several of the missionary women excelled in those fields. Sarah Judson's course of self-education included rhetoric, logic, geometry, and Latin.[45] In addition to excelling in the natural sciences, Henrietta Hamlin mastered Latin and Greek at an early age under her father's tutelage, laying the foundation for her "unusual facility in acquiring languages."[46] Judith Grant "was early placed in the classical and mathematical classes in the academy, and in all her studies exhibited great aptness and power."[47] Lucy Lord excelled in math and the natural sciences, as did Emily Judson.[48]

The educational experiences of these women were just as important for their spiritual impact as for their intellectual influence. If education was a distinct and important reality of their lives, revivalism was equally so, and academic institutions were ripe settings for revivals in the early nineteenth century.[49] Most of the memorialized women reached the crisis of their conversion process during times of awakening or revival, and most of them experienced that crisis in relation to other girls experiencing the same things. The compiler of Sarah Huntington Smith's memoir noted the spiritual significance of young women's friendships when he wrote,

> The friendship of young ladies for each other is interesting and lovely, especially when it is sanctified and strengthened by religious principle. The delicacy and fervency which mark such attachments, and

> the intercourse growing out of them; the mutual confidence; the sympathy in each other's joys and sorrows; the liveliness with which they enter into each other's prospects in life; and, if Christians, the refining of these feelings which arises from their hearts being fixed upon the same Saviour, from their rejoicing in the same hope, and anticipating the same bliss, holiness, and glory in heaven;—such friendships, in this cold world, aid our conceptions respecting the love, and harmony, and purity which pervade the society of heaven. [50]

Smith's own experience of conversion is a good example of the importance of female relationships in bringing about spiritual crisis. Her memoir describes a young woman growing up in a Christian home and possessing many Christian virtues. She evidenced "dutifulness and respect," "reverence for her superiors generally," and a "readiness to receive advice or admonition." She expressed "disinterestedness and self denial for the benefit of others" as well as "enterprise, patience, and perseverance" in helping them. She displayed good self-command by being careful of the way she used both her time and money and showed "tastefulness in dress, without extravagance." Although she enjoyed socializing with her friends, she preferred to pursue those occupations that were "rational, intellectual, and useful." Even before her conversion, she turned down invitations to the theater and dances as inappropriate uses of time and effort for a young lady. But this description of her virtues built up to a crisis, for although she was moral, "she had not the religion of Christ dwelling in her heart." That is, she had the outward form of religion in her behavior, but she did not have heart religion. At twelve, she evinced a strong dislike for attending weekly prayer meetings, once even hiding to avoid going with her parents. But some of her friends at that age had already converted, and she noted the influence they had over her own heart. The death of a young woman in the community sparked an awakening among the young people. The pastor of the parish began holding meetings for young inquirers, but Sarah did not attend for fear of disappointing her friends and family. But a particular friend spoke to her "plainly, of her spiritual state" on a Tuesday evening. At her Wednesday sewing circle, "she chose the more serious part of the company," and they talked about submitting to God. At the church's regular Thursday lecture, on 19 August 1820, she prayed for "submission to the Saviour." By the end of that service, she had "[given] her heart up to God...[and] felt then, and afterwards, that it was a peculiarly rational act." Experiencing euphoric joy, she stayed up most of the night talking to her sister, but when she woke the next morning she was "under a cloud." She met with her pastor to no avail, but in an hour of solitude later in the day, she "had such views of her heart as she never had before. She felt that she was a sinner against God, and loved to sin, and she abhorred herself for it. It was an hour of intense conviction of her sinfulness. Overwhelmed with it, she went again to her Saviour, and then found permanent relief."[51]

Sarah Lanman Smith was not away at school at the time of her conversion, but clearly the young women with whom she socialized, including her own sister, had a significant influence on her spiritual development. This was true of most of the missionary women. Ann Judson and Harriet Newell both experienced conversion while students at Bradford Academy. Harriet Winslow first experienced conviction of her need for salvation while attending a women's prayer meeting.[52] Fidelia Fiske and Mary Van Lennep both converted under the influence of their female Sunday school teachers. Seraphina Haynes Everett, Lucy Lord, and Emily Judson all noted the influence of their sisters.

The importance of a nurturing Christian community for bringing about conversion experiences in the lives of young women is further evidenced by the experience of one young woman who did not have that community. Elizabeth Dwight

> labored under great difficulties on account of the religious views of most around her, they being of the Unitarian school. She rarely found the person who could direct her in her inquiries after the truth, or who took the least interest in her spiritual condition. She was obliged to go alone, and some distance, to meet with those with whom she could take sweet counsel, and have free and satisfactory spiritual intercourse. This course was not only attended with much trouble, but it brought upon her great reproach.[53]

The community of "saints" that Elizabeth found lived in a parish six miles from her home.

In addition to the influence of their peers, another common factor in the conversions of missionary women is that virtually all occurred during times of revival. When Ann Judson and Harriet Newell converted at Bradford Academy in 1807, a revival was sweeping the community and also permeated the school. The prayer meeting that Harriet Winslow was attending had been organized at the behest of a pastor who asked his congregation to meet in united prayer for a revival.[54] Judith Grant, Fidelia Fiske, Lucy Lord, and Henrietta Shuck all experienced conversion during the widespread revivals of 1830–1831. Emily Judson, who lived in the area of New York known as the "burned over district," first came under conviction during that same period, although she did not date her conversion until 1834. Her experience was almost a caricature of the revival conversion. She attended class meetings during a Methodist revival in January 1830, Baptist meetings during a revival the next month, and Presbyterian meetings the month after that. She later wrote, "I believe my solemn little face was almost ludicrously familiar to the worshipers of every denomination."[55]

Many of the women also noted the importance of their religious reading in bringing about their conversions. The most commonly noted books were *Pilgrim's Progress* and various works by Jonathan Edwards and his protégés. Ann Judson, for example, recalled reading *Pilgrim's Progress* at age fifteen, after which she "resolved to begin a religious life," which mainly consisted of trying to abstain from parties and feeling pleased with herself for having done so. This attempted reform did not last long, but after the Bradford awakening began the next year (1806), she sought guidance from Edwards' *History of the Work of Redemption*, as well as works by two of his students, Joseph Bellamy and Samuel Hopkins.[56] Henrietta Hamlin also recalled reading Edwards and Hopkins.[57] Mary Van Lennep recalled copying out fourteen of Edwards' "Resolutions" when she was ten years old and trying "to lead a consistent Christian life."[58] Seraphina Haynes Everett wrote out Edwards' "Questions for Self-Examination" as a spiritual exercise.[59] Emily Judson recalled the influence of *Pilgrim's Progress*, while Lucy Lord described her own conversion in terms drawn directly from that book: "Long had I lain bound in 'Doubting Castle,' but now the gate was thrown open, my chains were knocked off, and I was free!"[60]

Many scholars maintain that the very nature of the conversion experience underwent dramatic changes during the revivals of the 1820s and 1830s when most of these women converted. Between the spread of Methodist Arminian doctrines and the "new measures" introduced by Charles Grandison Finney—including the altar call and the anxious bench—the conversion experience was supposedly telescoped from an extended process over months or years to an emotionally charged moment at a revival or a camp meeting.[61] Most of the memorialized missionary women did experience conversion during times of revival, but their accounts of their experiences bore a remarkable resemblance to the conversion narratives of the Great Awakening of the 1740s and the earliest revivals of the Second Great Awakening between 1799 and 1802.[62] Virtually all of the women underwent months, and some even years, of conviction and searching, reading and praying, before finally making professions of faith. Even Henrietta Shuck, who converted during a Baptist camp meeting in Virginia, described a long process that began the previous year during school.

However dramatically the conversion experience changed during the first half of the nineteenth century, those changes do not appear to have had much influence on the experiences of women who became missionaries, even those who converted during the revivals of 1831, in which the use of "new measures" was widespread. One possible explanation is that most of these women came from Congregational and Presbyterian backgrounds, the denominations most resistant to new measures even in the pro-revival camps. A recent study of those denominations, however, suggests that they embraced new measures much more willingly than scholars have previously thought.[63] A more plausible explanation lies in the cultural influence of Jonathan Edwards and the fact that the American foreign missions movement was very closely connected to that branch of Edwardsean theology commonly referred to as the New Divinity. Judging by the content of their reading and the names of their pastors, most of these women seem to have come out of religious traditions strongly influenced by Edwards. Edwards' descriptions of the revivals in his Northampton parish in 1736–1737 and his *Memoir of the Life of David Brainerd* remained two of the most popular religious works of the nineteenth century.[64] Antebellum missionary women were clearly influenced by Edwards's writings, which embedded in the religious culture of those most involved in the missions movement a morphology of conversion more closely linked to eighteenth-century neo-Puritans than to nineteenth-century Methodists. Both the understanding of conversion and its influence on the practice of missions would gradually change after mid-century, when Methodists replaced Congregationalists and Presbyterians as the dominant force in the foreign missions movement.

In addition to the conversion experience, the influence of the New Divinity, and especially its most famous proponent, Samuel Hopkins, on the people who became missionaries was evident in their emphasis on benevolent activities. Missionary men and women frequently cited Samuel Hopkins and his doctrine of "disinterested benevolence"—the idea that one should devote one's life to charitable work without expecting anything in return—as an important influence in their decisions to enlist first in charitable and reform work at home and later in the cause of foreign missions.[65] If they had not already engaged their efforts even before converting, women who later became missionaries soon joined the myriad charitable and reform movements of the day. In his lecture, Joel Hawes listed "industry and economy" and "beneficence" as hallmarks of the virtuous woman. All of the missionary women exercised those virtues and participated in the reform and benevolent organizations that were ubiquitous in the early nineteenth century. Harriet Lathrop Winslow, for example, volunteered for the Society for the Relief of Poor Women and Children in 1814 because "self too much engrosses my thoughts, my time, and my labor."[66] Sarah Huntington Smith, the wealthiest of the women in this group, was "frugal and simple in her apparel" so that she would have money to give for charity and missions. She also regularly gave away the income from a "small legacy."[67] Furthermore, she and a number of her friends organized a "Charity Warehouse" through which they sold their creative productions—fancy needlework, drawings, and paintings—and gave the profits "to some of the benevolent objects of the day."[68] Relieving the poor often involved visiting in their homes; at those times the women usually distributed tracts. Some of the women, like Sarah Judson, actively participated in local tract societies. At least one of the missionary women, Mary Van Lennep, engaged in the temperance movement.[69]

The most common activities among these women, however, were teaching Sunday school and participating in or leading prayer meetings—activities they would continue when they reached Asia. Harriet Winslow, visiting friends in New York in 1816, observed a Sunday school in operation and subsequently started the first one in Norwich, Connecticut. Sarah Huntington Smith later taught in that same Sunday school.[70] Henrietta Hamlin, Judith Grant, Fidelia Fiske, Henrietta Shuck, Mary Van Lennep, and Harriet Hamlin all taught Sunday school as well.[71]

All of the women emphasized the importance of "closet duties," or daily private prayer. Seraphina Everett, for example, established a strict schedule by which she managed to cover most of the causes of her day: "Sunday, the church in our own land; Monday, the cause of education; Tuesday, the Bible cause; Wednesday, foreign missions; Thursday, home missions; Friday, seamen and temperance; Saturday, the Sabbath and Sabbath schools."[72] Most of the women also engaged in "social prayer"—prayer that took place in small groups comprised of women. Sarah Judson, for example, led a prayer meeting that included both single and married women and resulted in "all but one" making professions of faith.[73] Most of the women also participated in monthly "concerts of prayer" for revival and for missions. Harriet Winslow, on the same trip to New York that inspired her to start a Sunday school in Norwich, witnessed a revival that was preceded by united prayer and wrote home to urge her parents and sisters to try to establish a united prayer movement in Norwich.[74] Her suggestion may well have been heeded, for a few years later Sarah Huntington Smith was regularly attending a monthly concert in the same town to pray for "missions, Sabbath schools, revivals in colleges...[and] the advancement of the kingdom of Christ every where."[75]

Sarah Huntington Smith actually served as a missionary at home before going abroad. She undertook efforts in behalf of the Mohegan Indians near her home as early as 1827. In 1830, she helped raise money to build a church for them, and for eight months, in 1830–1831, she and a friend conducted a day school and a Sunday school among them. Sarah wrote to the ABCFM, the Connecticut legislature, and the U.S. Congress on their behalf, soliciting funds to support the effort to educate and evangelize the tribe. Through the help of her relative, Jabez Huntington, a representative in Congress, she eventually secured $500 for a school building and $400 to support a teacher. In her communications regarding the Mohegans, she frequently noted the "striking" resemblance of the Indians to the Jews, bringing up the subject repeatedly when writing to government officials to beg support and invoking biblical threats against nations that would rise up against Israel.[76]

Missionary women's memoirs had twin objectives: providing exemplars of feminine virtues for American women to emulate and stirring those women to exert themselves for the temporal and eternal benefit of the women of Asia. The memoirs' compilers accomplished those objectives by tracing the spiritual development of the women from birth to rebirth, and then following them to the mission field. Furthermore, juxtaposing the condition of American Christian women against that of "Oriental" women served as an extended illustration of the principle that underlay all efforts to convert women everywhere to Christianity: that "Christianity alone teaches the true rank of woman; and secures to the loveliest and best portion of our race, the respect and influence which belong to them."[77] Converting "Oriental" men and women to Christianity would not only win for them eternal life, but would liberate the women from the bondage of "heathen" social systems in this life, "elevating" them to a level of civilization in which men would recognize and value their moral and intellectual worth. The conversion of women would both provide evidence of a particular society's level of civilization and offer the means of that society's redemption. The need to convert "Oriental" women thus provided the justification for sending American women as missionary wives or as missionaries in their own right.

3

"Her Husband Shall Praise Her"

Marriage And Missions

Historians have given much attention to early nineteenth-century concepts of the innate moral and spiritual virtues of women. In the context of the nineteenth-century evangelical mission movement, concepts of the redemptive nature of women took on a special kind of power. As the primary purveyors of religious truth to young children, women had a special role in extending the kingdom of God on earth. Men, as preachers and evangelists, proclaimed good news to the present generation. Women conveyed the gospel as a sacred trust to the next. Reaching women with the gospel thus acquired urgency as American evangelicals organized missions, especially missions to Asia, where they believed women were utterly inaccessible to the public preaching of male missionaries.

When evangelical eyes turned to the "Orient," they saw an unprecedented challenge. Common assumptions placed adult "Oriental" women beyond the reach of men, incarcerated in a harem or *zenana*, confined at home by bound feet, or at best, trapped in ignorance and degradation by a culture that denied women the privilege of reading. And yet "Oriental" mothers, too, shaped the minds and hearts of future generations. Such assumptions governed the early emergence of a central role for missionary wives in the evangelization of Asia. Only women could reach their "degraded Oriental sisters" for Christ and thus secure that vast region's future place in the kingdom of God on earth. The ABCFM confronted the issue of the marriage of missionaries soon after organizing in 1810, drawing upon British testimony regarding the status of "Oriental" women and following British precedent in adopting policies reflecting their wholehearted embrace of the principle that the missionary family offered the best hope of evangelizing Asia.

The British Orientalist most widely read by American evangelicals was Claudius Buchanan (1766–1815). Buchanan, an adherent of the evangelical wing of the Church of England, initially went to India as a chaplain for the East India Company (EIC) in Bengal in 1797–1798. From 1799 to 1807, he served as vice provost of Fort William College in Calcutta, an institution established by Lord Wellesley, the governor general, to educate the sons of EIC officials stationed in Bengal. During his service in India, Buchanan traveled extensively and wrote a detailed account of his observations regarding the social and religious customs that prevailed in the various parts of the subcontinent, making particular reference to the status of Hindu women. *Christian Researches in Asia*, written in the style of a travel journal and initially published in England in 1811, and a sermon titled *The Star in the East* both enjoyed great popularity throughout the first half of the century both in England and in the United States. That Buchanan's reports on India were widely known by American evangelicals is certain. *Christian Researches in Asia* went through at least eleven American editions printed in six states by 1816. A new edition came out in London as late as 1858. *The Star in the East* enjoyed similar popularity; in America alone, twenty-one editions were published in at least nine states between 1809 and 1813. Virtually all of the American missionaries whose memoirs appeared before 1840 mentioned having read his works.[1]

In the entry for 10 November 1806, Buchanan noted that he had arrived in Chinganoor, a community of Syrian Christians in western India. "The sight of the WOMEN," he wrote, "assured me that I was once more (after a long absence from England) in a christian country. For the Hindoo women, and the Mahomedan women, and in short, all women who are not christians, are accounted by the men an inferior race; and, in general, are confined to the house for life, like irrational creatures."[2] This statement vividly illustrates the tendency of British and American evangelicals to conflate the variety of Asian religions and cultures into a single "Oriental" culture. One of the dominant features of that culture, in the view of those who constructed it, was the inaccessibility of women. It did not really matter whether an Indian woman was confined to a *zenana* or a Persian woman to a harem, or whether a Chinese woman was virtually crippled by bound feet. Nor did it matter whether a woman was rendered inaccessible by hostility to girls' education and consequent widespread illiteracy. The effect was the same in the evangelical mind: "Oriental" women were inaccessible to Western men, and only women missionaries could reach past those barriers.

Buchanan's work was not their only source of information regarding the seclusion of women in the "Orient." Hannah More opened her enormously popular *Strictures on the Modern System of Female Education* by contrasting the superior condition of English women with their unfortunate sisters of the East, who were "victims to luxury, caprice, and despotism, [and] whom the laws and the religion of the voluptuous prophet of Arabia exclude from light, liberty, and knowledge."[3] William Staughton, an English Baptist minister who immigrated to the United States, published in 1811 an account of the British Baptist mission in India, summarizing the previous fifteen years of British Baptist missionaries' writings. He noted that "women in almost every instance are unable to read" and that upper caste women were "constantly immured in their houses."[4] British and American evangelicals fully comprehended that the Muslim people to whom More referred and the Hindu people to whom Staughton referred resided in different geographical regions, spoke different languages, and practiced two very different religions. They also knew that Orthodox and Catholic Christians populated certain areas of the East (these were often called "nominal Christians," meaning Christian in name only because the Reformation had not reached them). But to evangelicals, they were all "Oriental" and thus united in the fact that they were not evangelical

Protestant Christians and their women were thus, by definition, oppressed.

Perhaps the most influential voice regarding the isolated condition of Eastern women and the consequent importance of the missionary wife was William Carey, the pioneer British Baptist missionary who arrived in India in 1793. Carey's letters (published in England as "Periodical Accounts") were widely disseminated in such publications as the British *Baptist Magazine* and *London Evangelical Magazine* and the American *Panoplist* and *Massachusetts Baptist Missionary Magazine*. Carey, motivated by his own wife Dorothy's experiences, frequently discussed the role of the missionary wife. Dorothy Carey was barely literate, had been reluctant to go with her husband to India, and suffered nothing but misery once there. Calomel, the treatment for her frequent bouts with dysentery, probably resulted in mercury poisoning and was largely responsible for her descent into madness. She died in 1807 after fourteen years in India. Dorothy was widely viewed as a great hindrance to William's ministry, thus lending power to his arguments about the critically important role that a good missionary wife could play.[5] As early as 1796, he had written the British Baptist Missionary Society about the "almost necessity of Females well qualified to communicate the Gospel of Christ in a situation where superstition secludes all the women of respectability from hearing the Word and the advantage which would arise from considerable numbers being embarked on such a cause."[6] Carey's writings greatly influenced subsequent formulations of policy by American denominations and missionary organizations regarding the marriage of missionaries.

In April 1815, the *Panoplist*, the principal organ of the ABCFM, published a notice of the board's decision to establish a mission in Ceylon and announced the appointment of James Richards Jr., Daniel Poor, and Horatio Bardwell "with their wives." In describing Ceylon, the author particularly noted its suitability as a field of labor for missionary wives:

> Whatever doubts may be entertained in regard to the expediency of females being attached to missions to be established in some parts of the heathen world; there should be no doubt that they may, very

> properly and with fair prospects of great usefulness, make a part of a mission to be established at Ceylon. The state of society and the circumstances of the people there, especially in some of the principal places, are in this regard particularly favorable.[7]

The article described the advantages of Ceylon as a field of missionary endeavor. It enjoyed a temperate climate and stable political conditions under British, but not EIC, rule. (The EIC was notoriously hostile to missionary activity.) Furthermore, the governor favored mission work.

A lengthy footnote to the *Panoplist* article offered a rationale for sending wives with their husbands to the mission field. It began with the proposition that missionaries should "live in the married state, *wherever they can obtain a settled and undisturbed residence.*" The footnote then articulated, in some detail, principles regarding the role of the missionary wives that would govern the policy of the ABCFM and other American Protestant mission organizations for decades to come.[8]

The author of this footnote offered five reasons in favor of marriage for missionaries. First, a missionary needed a wife for all the same reasons that a minister back home did, only more so. The writer did not elaborate on this point, seeming to assume its self-evident truth.[9] Second, one of the essential aspects of the spiritual development of native converts anywhere involved learning the relationships and duties of various members of a Christian family, "husband and wife, parent and child, and master and servant." A "solitary man" could not very well teach such duties, at least not so effectively as "persons who sustain these relations in a well organized family." Most important, Christian family relations could not be "*exemplified before the heathen*, unless by missionaries, who are married to well educated and pious females, who have formed all their habits and modes of thinking in a Christian country."[10] The latter phrase ruled out the suggestion made by Melville Horne, a revered Anglican chaplain in Sierra Leone, that a single male missionary struggling with sexual purity might take a wife from among his native Christian converts.[11] In other words, the author was maintaining that a Christian missionary family would teach the "heathen" Christian principles by demonstrating those principles through proper family relationships.

The third argument in favor of married missionaries involved children. Missionary husbands and wives serving together abroad had the opportunity to bear and raise children whose upbringing would uniquely qualify them to serve as missionaries in the future. The author granted that "heathen" children were "like wild asses' colts; they grow up ungoverned and ungovernable, and of consequence become idle and dissolute." But those attributes resulted from their upbringing. Christian parents should have no difficulty making their children "industrious," "studious," and "learned." The author offered as examples the sons of William Carey and his colleague Joshua Marshman, who "bid fair to be the very first [meaning first-rate] oriental scholars." Two of Marshman's sons had been trained in Chinese from early childhood and had attained fluency by the ages of eleven and thirteen. "Let it be remembered," concluded the writer, "that the Chinese is a language, which has been pronounced till lately impossible to be thoroughly learned by a European." Such a conclusion may seem cryptic to the modern reader, but one must realize that even at this early date, thirty years before the "opening" of China, mission leaders anxiously awaited the opportunity to begin evangelizing that vast empire populated by a presumably educated and intelligent people. The missions of India and southeast Asia, still in their infancy, were already viewed as staging grounds for that event. The various dialects of Chinese posed major obstacles, so raising American or English children as bilingual represented an investment that presumably would yield a huge return within a generation.[12]

The fourth justification for the marriage of missionaries hinged upon the assumption that the hallmark of a civilized society was "a just appreciation of the female character." A society (such as all of those considered part of the "Orient") might appear civilized in having a written language and an educated class and in having attained a high level of development in agriculture, manufacturing, and commerce. One could nevertheless consider that society uncivilized if its family life did not demonstrate "domestic virtue and domestic happiness." One could only find "domestic virtue and domestic happiness" in Christian societies. The author offered as proof of the uncivilized state of the "Orient" reports by the ABCFM missionaries at Bombay "of such gross, enormous, and universal violations of morality and decency, as could not be named, or even hinted at with propriety in this place." "Domestic virtue and domestic happiness," according to mission apologists, only existed in monogamous, companionate, Christian marriages, and only women who had received the advantages of education made fit companions in such marriages. American and British missionaries assumed that all "Oriental" women lived sequestered and in a state of degradation and ignorance, virtual slaves of their husbands. The social, cultural, or religious context or the particular form that oppression took did not matter. The oppressed status of women from Syria to China meant that only "females who have been educated in a Christian country" could reach those women and introduce them to Christian civilization.[13]

Finally, the author drew upon the experience and authority of those who had gone before, most notably William Carey. Carey, according to this author, viewed marriage as an "indispensable duty" on the part of a missionary. In fact, Carey "would hardly admit the possibility of a missionary being so situated as not to make it expedient that he should be married." Furthermore, British missionaries in South Africa "generally deemed it expedient," and the Moravians, "though engaged among the most savage people [i.e., Native Americans], have generally been married."[14]

Rufus Anderson, for many years secretary of the ABCFM, reiterated the same set of principles twenty years later in his essay "On the Marriage of Missionaries."[15] The essay introduced the American edition of a memoir of Mary Mercy Ellis, wife of a missionary of the London Missionary Society. Dana L. Robert has interpreted Anderson's essay as reflecting views on the role of missionary wives that were developed by women within the context of missions in the Pacific, specifically the ABCFM Hawaii mission.[16] Anderson, however, clearly addressed the roles of missionary wives in all foreign missions and explicitly placed his remarks in the context of missions to China, Japan, Ceylon, Jerusalem, and Syria (i.e., the "Orient") in addition to Hawaii. Furthermore, the views Anderson expressed reiterated and amplified those set forth in the 1815 *Panoplist* article, which predated by several years the founding of the Hawaii mission.

Anderson began by noting the circumstances under which mission boards should employ single men. For example, exploring new areas for their potential as mission fields required single men to act as "vanguards and scouting parties of an army." They should work from an established mission station with a permanent base in the home of a married couple, so that when not traveling they could "enjoy [the] advantages" of family life "without being entangled with the cares which families necessarily produce."[17] But in a paraphrase of the book of Genesis, Anderson followed up his opening remarks by writing, "Generally, it is not good for a missionary to be alone." [18]

Mirroring the priorities established by the 1815 *Panoplist* article, Anderson stated that, first and foremost, a missionary needed a wife for all of the same reasons that a minister at home did. Anderson, however, elaborated on those reasons. A major motivating factor was that "powerful law of nature, which is operative alike in all countries and climates and among all conditions and classes of people, producing the family state." In other words, being a man, the missionary needed a wife for sexual fulfillment—otherwise, he would either pine away in ill health (physical and mental) or seek solace in a native woman. Either scenario would ruin his effectiveness as a minister of the gospel. Anderson used this point as part of a running commentary on Catholicism. In virtually every mission field of the "Orient," Protestant missionaries worked in areas where Catholics also sought converts. One of the main features distinguishing Protestants from Catholics, Anderson noted, was the repudiation of a celibate priesthood. In the anti-Catholic climate of the day, it was essential for both the missionaries' target audiences abroad and their supporters at home to remember that distinction. Just being in a different climate and culture, according to Anderson, was unlikely "to reconcile [the missionary] to the monastic life." Solitude (the "cloister"), contrary to what might seem logical, would not produce closeness to God. Rather, the "perpetual cheerlessness" of a foreign field would greatly strengthen the natural desire for female companionship.[19]

Furthermore, the hardships attendant upon living far from home only magnified for the missionary the need that all ministers had for spiritual companionship. A missionary, even more than a minister at home, required a wife who would serve as "friend, counsellor, companion, the repository of her husband's thoughts and feelings, the partaker of his joys, the sharer of his cares and sorrows, and one who is to lighten his toils, and become his nurse in sickness." A woman "judiciously chosen" would prove just as capable of "endur[ing] privations and encounter[ing] dangers" as her husband. Such a woman would also fulfill the role of helper suited to the particular circumstances of the mission. Without such a "helpmeet," the missionary would devote valuable time to securing food, clothing, and shelter under difficult circumstances. A wife to oversee domestic concerns would free him from "loneliness and vexation," thus permitting him to devote his entire attention to preaching the gospel.[20]

Finally, according to Anderson, wives (and children) were even more important for the missionary than for the minister at home because they served as "symbols of peace." While some might argue that a woman should not live among "uncivilized" people, Anderson argued that missionary families offered the "best earthly protection" for mission stations. Even a "savage," he said, could fully understand and appreciate the significance of the presence of women and children as evidence of the peaceful purpose of missions.

Anderson returned to his attack on Catholicism in his conclusion: "The desire for the marriage state is a part of the original constitution of human nature and not a perversion of it." A married male missionary "will be more of a man, a better Christian, a more contented, zealous, faithful, useful missionary." One should not, he continued, compare missionaries to merchants, who often went abroad without wives. Merchants went abroad for limited periods of time to make their fortunes, fully expecting to return home. Furthermore, they were prone to "violate the laws of purity." Missionaries, on the other hand, offered themselves for life and were fully expected to adhere to accepted Christian standards of sexual purity. But that standard of sexual purity was Protestant, not Catholic: "The holy and blessed enterprise of Protestant missions must not be spoiled by introducing into it the monastic principles of the Romish church," Anderson wrote. Thus, unless a missionary's principal employment involved exploring new territory or itinerating over long distances, a Protestant understanding of the laws of human nature and the divine sanction of family order required that the missionary have a wife.[21]

In addition to the divine sanction of family life, Anderson maintained that missionary families had an evangelizing function as well. They were to serve as living parables illustrating the doctrines of Christianity for the "heathen": "The domestic constitution among them is dreadfully disordered, and yet it is as true there as every where else, that the character of society is formed in the family. To rectify it requires example as well as precept."[22] Again, Anderson elaborated principles that informed the 1815 statement in the *Panoplist*. In "pagan and Mohammedan countries" (i.e., the "Orient"), the wife was "a degraded slave having no conception of a better destiny." One simply could not expect a convert to Christianity automatically to become a "virtuous, useful, praiseworthy wife and mother" without anyone to instruct her and inculcate within her the principles of Christian womanhood. It was also patently absurd to assume that anyone other than a Christian wife and mother could effectively teach and demonstrate those principles:

> In what manner shall the images of domestic order, neatness, comfort, and whatever else sheds beauty and sweetness over domestic life, be imparted to her mind? She must have female teachers, living illustrations. She must see these things exemplified in actual life. And the Christian wife, mother, husband, father, family must all be found in all our missions to pagan and mohammedan countries.[23]

This belief in the centrality of Christian domesticity to the effective proclamation of the gospel reflected the broader conviction of the redemptive role of the wife and mother that emerged in the post-Revolutionary and antebellum periods in the United States.

That conviction of the redemptive role of the wife and mother, whether embodied in the language of republican motherhood or the "moral mother," gave rise to a demand for improved education for women, which in turn created a new and more public role for women—that of teacher. The role of teacher in antebellum America was generally justified as an extension of the domestic sphere into the community, rather than a transgression of the boundaries of that sphere.

Women who became missionary wives or missionaries in their own right in the nineteenth century were generally among the most highly educated women of their day. Missionaries selected educated women as wives in part because missionary children received much of their education from their mothers, but also because missionary wives were expected to teach. Adopting native children, gathering a small daily class in her home, instructing her servants, or teaching a Sunday school comprised the standard elements of a missionary wife's work. Anderson maintained that one of the primary reasons for requiring the marriage of missionaries rested on the fact that the wife who enjoyed good health would normally "exert a propitious influence over the whole extent of infant and female education, especially if she made herself familiar with the subject before leaving her native land." Molding the minds of young children through religious education (and training native women converts to do so as well) "would shorten the work of missions by one or two generations."[24] Anderson concluded his essay by citing a passage from a letter written by a missionary then on the field:

> It is not exegesis, it is not theology, it is not philosophy, it is not divinity, it is not law, it is not precept or command, which the people need; but it is the gospel, the pure gospel, which they want all day long. It is Christianity embodied, acted out, living, breathing. The missionary's wife, as well as himself, should be a sort of moving commentary on the Bible; everything she says or does should remind the hearer or beholder of something in the Bible; her whole life should be altogether a New Testament life. The whole spirit of the New Testament should be inhaled, and the whole spirit of the New Testament should be breathed, in every breath.[25]

Thus Anderson summarized what had in fact been the practical policy of the ABCFM for twenty-five years regarding the role of missionary wives in all foreign fields and especially in those regions designated the "Orient." The parable of domesticity as a philosophy and a policy justified a woman's vocation as a missionary and invested in the missionary wife great moral power on the field and in the minds of women at home.

Throughout the antebellum period, a belief in the efficacy and importance of modeling "Christian family relations" as an evangelistic strategy in Asia provided an important motive for missionary women. It also served as an important tool in mobilizing women at home to support the cause through money, prayer, and by raising up a new generation of missionaries and supporters of missions. Women missionaries wrote voluminously. Their correspondence was regularly published in missionary magazines and in their own memoirs. By juxtaposing their discussions of Christian domesticity with descriptions of the family life of "Oriental" women, they created contrasting images that served to heighten the already strong conviction that Christian women enjoyed an elevated social status while "heathen" women suffered degradation and oppression. Furthermore, the images of "Oriental" women that missionary wives depicted in their writings quickly hardened into tropes that, however oversimplified they may have become over time, carried great emotional power for American women and catalyzed them into action.

Early nineteenth-century missionaries regarded the husband-wife relationship as the central element of their domestic parable. The wife's relationship to her husband was one of companionship, spiritual equality, and mutual esteem. Missionary wives shared with their husbands an understanding of and commitment to the roles of companion and helper. For example, Harriet Winslow, Congregational missionary in Ceylon, wrote in 1822 that a missionary without a wife would lose much time providing for his own daily necessities—time he might otherwise devote to preaching. Even if he employed servants, their "negligence" and "dishonesty" would cause him great trouble and multiply the cost of the mission. A judicious and industrious wife, however, would liberate her husband from responsibility for such "worldly cares and from trials of temper and patience, which would hinder him in his appropriate works."[26]

Such "minute" concerns did not, however, comprise the sum total of the missionary wife's responsibilities, for if they did, her position in relation to her husband would differ little from that of the "Oriental" women whom she was trying to instruct through her example. The Christian marriage required conjugal love. Lucy Lyon, who later served with the Baptists in China, responded to her future husband's first proposal of marriage by saying that she needed more time to become acquainted with him. Proper Christian marriages, she wrote, had "mutual, rational, and abiding affection" as their foundation, and she was unwilling to marry Edward Lord until she had reasonable confidence of achieving that kind of relationship.[27] It was not enough, however, for a missionary couple to have those qualities in their marriage. Once on their field of labor, they had to make conscious efforts to demonstrate their mutual respect and affection publicly in order for those qualities to have the desired evangelistic effect. In her journal entry for 2 June 1822, Harriet Winslow reported going out with her husband when he went to preach, in hopes that her presence would bring the women out. The women did appear, and Winslow suspected from their manner that they were "wondering at the unheard of custom of a female walking arm in arm with her husband."[28]

According to Winslow, the missionary should "find all his society" in his wife.[29] That kind of companionship could only come from a woman whose mind had received the refinement of a good education. Elizabeth Dwight, Congregational missionary in Turkey, noted that the missionary wife's "education and mental endowments" should qualify her for the roles of "companion and counsellor."[30] Furthermore, her spirituality should offer a source of "encouragement" and "strength," while her advice would assist him in overcoming obstacles to his work.[31] A single man could not sustain the "cheerfulness of mind and [physical] health" necessary for effectively prosecuting the work of the mission.[32]

The introduction to the memoir of Henrietta Hamlin, wife of a Congregational missionary in Turkey in the 1830s and 1840s, echoed Harriet Winslow's views when the author noted that one of her purposes in compiling Hamlin's memoir was to demonstrate "the indispensableness of [woman's] fortitude and perseverance to the support and consolation of man in his oft-recurring seasons of exhaustion and despondency."[33] Hamlin herself predicted that she would have little to offer the Turks and Armenians of Constantinople, but anticipated that she would "enjoy all the good" that her husband would do. "If I can do anything to lighten your labors or cheer your heart," she wrote to her husband in 1838, "it will constitute both my happiness and duty."[34]

Missionary accounts portrayed "Oriental" wives, whether from Syria, India, China, or elsewhere in Asia, in stark negative contrast to their American counterparts. Nowhere was the "Oriental" woman a companion and helper to her husband. Rather, throughout the "Orient," despotic men ruled over their wives as masters ruled over their slaves. Sarah Lanman Smith, Congregational missionary in Syria, recorded in her journal on 4 November 1835 that a Muslim woman had come to her seeking a cure for opthalmia, a common eye complaint that often led to blindness. The woman told Smith that her husband had threatened to divorce her if she went blind. "Poor woman! my heart ached for her," Smith wrote. "Such is the kindly nature of the religion of Mohammed!"[35] Smith later offered an account of a Muslim wedding. She noted that the parents arranged their children's weddings and that the ceremony itself took place by proxy. The bride wore a veil for her presentation to the groom. When they met, he first lifted the veil to look at her face. If he did not like her appearance, he could reject her and have her put away. If he accepted her, the two parted to go to separate men's and women's wedding parties. Smith attended the women's party. The bride, she reported, "looked as if she were in the extreme of misery," for custom required her to sit through the twenty-four-hour-long party in a motionless position without speaking and with her eyes closed.[36]

Harriet Winslow gave an account of a marriage in Ceylon that bore a strong similarity to Smith's account, notwithstanding the fact that the one Winslow attended was a Christianized version of a Hindu wedding for two recent converts.[37] Most notably, in both instances the parents had arranged the marriage. One can account for the similarities in the missionary women's perceptions of the wedding ceremonies of two religions as diverse as Hinduism and Islam by taking note of a comment by Harriet Winslow. In a letter to a friend, written on 30 September 1830, she wrote, "Among the heathen the parties are not even consulted: every thing is settled without their consent, and perhaps without their knowledge." The elastic boundaries of the category of "heathen" contained a broad array of religious practices and customs that, in the eyes of missionaries, shared much with each other because they shared little with Protestant Christianity. The one certain conclusion that the

Protestant Christian could draw was that, in all non-Christian "Oriental" marriages, the couples "knew little of domestic happiness."[38]

Missionaries frequently pointed out the uncompanionable nature of "Oriental" marriages by suggesting that husbands would not eat with their wives or acknowledge their presence in public. Winslow noted that in Ceylon, "husband and wife must never eat together, and a man cannot even touch a woman's hand in public without disgrace."[39] Asahel Grant, husband of Judith Grant and missionary doctor in Persia, noted that in most places in "the East" a woman not only could not eat with her husband, but could only have what was left over (if anything) when he was finished. In a narrative of a journey that he made to Nineveh shortly after his wife's death in 1839, Grant remarked with surprise a difference among the people of Persia. The wife still could not eat with her husband, but she did not have to subsist from the crumbs of his table: "A portion was reserved for the females, and in all respects, they were treated with more consideration, and regarded with more compassion than in most Asiatic countries."[40] Grant's observations did not lead him to revise his views on the relationships between husbands and wives in "the East," however. His assessment is perhaps most notable in the persistence of its underlying assumption that the people he encountered on his journey in fact *deviated* from the "Oriental" norm. Through such accounts, missionaries elevated to cosmic significance the simple act of sharing a meal with one's spouse.

The missionaries saw a relationship between the lack of companionship that they observed in "Oriental" marriages and what they perceived as the universal opposition of the peoples of the East to literacy for girls and women. Missionaries uniformly condemned "Oriental" societies from Syria to China for rendering women unfit for companionate marriages by denying them education. In 1833, two missionary wives began a girls' school in Beirut (then a part of Syria). They had approached the task with "apprehension" because of the "strong prejudice" against educating girls that had persisted "from time immemorial."[41] When Sarah Lanman Smith arrived on that field a year later, she soon observed in her journal the "deplorable ignorance" of the women she met there.[42] A regular correspondent of the Young Ladies' Academy in Norwich, Connecticut, Smith wrote to her young friends that their Syrian sisters had "no books, and no means of moral or intellectual improvement. It is considered a disgrace for a female to know how to read and write, and a serious obstacle to her marriage, which is the principal object of the parent's heart. This abhorrence of learning in females, exists most strongly in the higher classes."[43] Elizabeth Dwight wrote of carrying a book with her when she went to observe a procession in the streets of Constantinople in case she had an idle moment. A shocked native woman came up to ask her if she really knew how to read.[44] Similarly, Lucy Lord in China wrote of an incident in which a woman servant observed her reading and asked if she could understand books. "Ningpo women do not understand books—men understand, but *women do not*,' she quoted her servant as saying. Lord asked one of her husband's Chinese assistants how many women in Ningpo could read, and "he replied, 'Perhaps one in ten thousand.'"[45] Likewise, a missionary in Burma wrote that, while literacy was widespread among the male population of that country, very few women knew how to read.[46] Accounts of "Oriental" opposition to girls' education reminded American women to appreciate and take full advantage of their educational opportunities. They illustrated the urgency for missionary women to infiltrate "Oriental" society by teaching girls and women.

Besides their ignorance, according to missionary observers, "Oriental" women made poor companions in marriage because of their bad character. They were, by common assent, decidedly lacking in virtue. The address given before the meeting at which American Baptists established their mission board in 1814 stated that throughout the "heathen" world, "the female character is sunk in servility and wretchedness."[47] Missionaries represented women of the various parts of Asia as habitual liars given to cunning, thievery, extortion, and, worst of all, sloth.[48] Elizabeth Dwight characterized the women of Turkey as "idle." Writing to a friend at home in 1832, Dwight said, "Where are you, dear Miss K., and what are you doing? for you are not living in idleness, like the people of this country. This disposition, I am happy to know, is not a general trait of the American character, and it ought never to manifest itself in the Christian."[49] Eli Smith wrote of his wife, Sarah, after her death that it was nothing less than a miracle that she was able to train Syrian women in "habits of industry."[50] Similarly, Ann Judson wrote that "the Burmans are surprised to see us always employed, particularly me, as the Burman women never think of doing any work if they can get their rice without."[51] Such illustrations reminded American women that, while "Oriental" women needed salvation, American women should cultivate habits of industry themselves, for idleness was a "heathen" characteristic.

Missionary women often illustrated the view that "Oriental" women lacked virtue by describing their physical appearance as dirty. Physical dirtiness, to American evangelicals, symbolized spiritual uncleanness. Sarah Lanman Smith wrote to a friend in 1835 that her husband Eli had decided that "Satan supplies filth and vermin to deter missionaries" from interacting with the Syrians. In a letter to the Young Ladies Academy at Norwich the following year, she noted that "these weak-minded Syrian females are not attentive to personal cleanliness."[52] Judith Grant remarked upon the infrequency with which Persian women bathed and washed their clothes. The fact that those women slept in the same clothes that they wore during the day and slept upon the floor meant that "*vermin* [lice and fleas] are very plenty about their persons and garments."[53] Lucy Lord wrote to the Baptist Church at Delanti in October of 1847, describing the people of Ningpo, China, as "disgustingly filthy in all their habits.... I suppose this external pollution is a fair index to their moral condition."[54] Missionary women, while reinforcing the virtue of cleanliness to their American audience, portrayed the depravity of "Oriental" women as a way to encourage women at home to support the cause financially and to inspire young women to become missionaries themselves.

Another indicator of a woman's virtue, according to American evangelicals, was the way she dressed. A virtuous woman dressed modestly and simply. Missionary women generally had one of two responses to the manner in which "Oriental" women dressed: either distress at the crudeness and scantiness of their clothing or disapproval of its lavishness. Missionaries often viewed crudeness or scantiness of clothing as an outward signifier of moral and spiritual poverty. Harriet Winslow and Henrietta Shuck shared similar reactions upon seeing

Bengalis for the first time upon their arrivals in Calcutta, Winslow in 1819 and Shuck in 1836. Winslow remarked

> The dress of the natives…is only a piece of cloth around the waist. Some, however, have a cloth thrown over their shoulders, or wear something like a tunic. Their hair is generally very black and oily.… We were, of course, a little shocked to see people so nearly naked; but in a moment the recollection of their spiritual degradation filled our minds and hearts to the exclusion of every thought of their external appearance.[55]

Later, writing from her field of work in Ceylon, she noted that women of the upper castes wore a piece of muslin draped in such a way as "mostly to cover them," while lower caste women did not cover the upper half of their bodies. Children, she said, went entirely naked until the age of five or six. "You may easily conceive," she went on, "that their minds are soon filled with all manner of impure thoughts. It is often disgusting to see them, and distressing to know their habits from their earliest years."[56] Shuck remarked in a letter to her father, "Their dress consists of a small piece of cloth wrapped around their loins. You cannot, my dear pa', tell how I feel when I see that I am surrounded by a people, who know nothing of Jesus. I feel more anxious than ever to labor for the destitute heathen."[57]

Most frequently, however, missionary women described the lavishness of dress and ornamentation in which "Oriental" women indulged. Harriet Winslow maintained that, notwithstanding the poverty of the people as reflected in their scanty clothing, even the poorest had elaborate collections of jewelry. Both men and women wore earrings and rings of "precious stones," pearls, and gold. The women also wore "a profusion of beads, bracelets, armlets, plates on their hair, clasps around their ancles, and ornaments on their toes." In another indication that missionaries saw the "Orientals" as trapped in a primitive state, Winslow noted that the ornaments possessed by Tamil women comprised the bulk of their property, "and as their fashions do not change, are handed down from generation to generation."[58] Sarah Lanman Smith described a Syrian Muslim bride elaborately dressed and ornamented, her face decorated with "rouge, "gold leaf," and "black paint." The bride "looked more like a pagan priestess than any other imaginable being," Smith wrote.[59] "Pagan priestesses," as every moderately well-read American evangelical woman "knew," were prostitutes. Elizabeth Dwight described the lavish apparel of a Turkish woman with whom she and Mrs. Goodell, another missionary wife, dined on one occasion. Their own clothing contrasted starkly with that of their hostess: "Mrs. Goodell wore a coloured muslin frock and I a white one, both made entirely plain, and neither of us could boast one valuable ornament of gold or pearl, and no doubt the lady thought we made a sorry figure, while we could only pity her." In contrast to her elaborate clothing, the woman's home contained virtually no furniture, suggesting to the American women that her depravity caused her to expend all of her income on clothing and jewels while otherwise living in apparent poverty.[60] Once, Dwight wrote to the Utica Maternal Association about the reprehensible manner in which Armenian mothers in Constantinople dressed their children. She described with consternation one boy whose mother bribed him to go to school by letting him wear a red suit with "bright buttons," a girl who looked forward to going to the Greek Orthodox church on Sundays so that she could wear "a red silk frock," and a six-year-old who wore an ornament of silver and diamonds in her hair but could not read.[61]

Missionary women spent a great deal of time condemning the lavishness of "Oriental" women's dress because their own values emphasized that women expressed their purity and Christian comportment through modesty in dress. Sarah Smith wrote the students at the Young Ladies Academy at Norwich a letter in which she contrasted their appearance to that of Syrian young women: "I see you not only comfortably, but neatly dressed, and your persons indicating that suitable attention was paid to them before leaving home." The Syrian girls in her school in Beirut, however, did not have "a neat and tasteful style of dress. Their apparel is precisely such as the Apostle [Peter] recommended that Christian females should avoid; while the ornament of a meek and quiet spirit is thrown wholly out of account." On another occasion, she wrote of Syrian women that "their energies are expended in 'outward adorning of plaiting the hair, and gold and pearls and costly array;' literally so." Smith was preaching a sermon from a biblical text that her American audience certainly knew. The Apostle

Peter had enjoined the women of the early church to adorn themselves with the holiness of a "meek and quiet spirit" while avoiding the "outward adorning of plaiting the hair, and of wearing of gold, or of putting on of apparel."[62] Smith was not, however, merely describing the "Oriental" Other to her American audience for the sake of satisfying their curiosity. She was holding up a mirror for her audience, reminding them that if *they* were absorbed in matters of dress, they were imitating the pagans rather than imitating Christ. On 12 February 1835, she wrote "An Appeal to American Christians," which was published in the *Missionary Herald* and reprinted in her memoir. She reported having heard that the mission to the Washington Islands in the Pacific Northwest had been abandoned due to a want of financial support. She decried that development and chastised the "blood-bought disciples of Christ" who spent their time "regulating the fold or fashion of an article of dress" instead of giving that money to missions and giving their time to raising additional support by participating in missionary societies.[63]

Smith's lecture recalled a similar one that Adoniram Judson, Baptist missionary in Burma, had issued a few years earlier. Judson had published an open "Letter to the Female Members of Christian Churches, in the United States of America," in which he pointed out that the "chief obstacle" to winning converts among women in Burma lay in the "principle of vanity, [the] love of dress and display." Judson maintained that Burmese and Karen women, Christians and non-Christians alike, were given to wearing bracelets, necklaces, rings, and earrings in profusion. The problem, however, was compounded by the fact that such vanity was not unique to Oriental women, but had in fact "in every age and in all countries, been a ruling passion of the fair sex, as the love of riches, power, and fame has characterized the other." Following a year's absence touring around the various mission stations in Burma, Judson had returned to his church in Maulmein to a shocking sight. During his absence, several new missionaries had arrived, and on his first Sunday in the pulpit he was confronted by the sight of their wives "dressed and adorned in that manner, which is too prevalent in our beloved native land." "The demon of vanity," he wrote, "was laying waste the female department.... I saw that I was brought into a situation that precluded all retreat—that I must fight or die."[64]

Reading in 1 Timothy 2:9 that a godly woman adorned herself with "good works" rather than "plaited hair, or gold, or pearls, or costly array," Judson determined no longer to administer the Lord's Supper or baptism to any woman who wore what he considered inappropriate attire. When a Karen woman wearing a necklace offered herself for baptism, he asked if she was willing to "give up her ornaments for Christ." She thought long and hard and then took the necklace off and replied, "I love Christ more than this."[65] Some Karen men, however, pointed out that one of the missionary wives was wearing a gold necklace, citing the apparent hypocrisy as their reason for not converting to Christianity. Thus, Judson wrote to his American audience, a Christian sister had been a stumbling block to those men's salvation. When he confronted the woman, she "willingly" gave up the necklace, but not before noting that she "dress[ed] more plain than most ministers' wives and professors of religion, in our native land." Furthermore, she said, it had been a parting gift from her mother, who asked her to wear it always as a remembrance. Having reported this conversation, Judson chastised his American audience: "O ye Christian mothers...dare you give injunctions to your daughters, directly contrary to apostolic commands?"[66] He carried his argument further by stating that as long as Christian women in America continued to follow fashion in their manner of dress, a steady flow of missionary wives wearing necklaces, earrings, and rings would continue to arrive in Burma and undo all his efforts to get the Burmese and Karen women to give up such ornamentation:

> And thus, you my dear sisters, sitting quietly by your fire sides, or repairing devoutly to your places of worship, do, by your example, spread the poison of vanity, through all the rivers, mountains and wilds of this far distant land; and while you are sincerely and fervently praying for the upbuilding of the Redeemer's kingdom, are inadvertently building up that of the devil. If on the other hand, you divest yourselves of all meretricious ornaments, your sisters and daughters who come hither, will be divested of course;—the further supplies of vanity and pride will be cut off; and the churches at home being kept pure, the churches here will be pure also.[67]

Judson went on to encourage the women of America to imitate the temperance movement and organize themselves into Plain Dress

Societies. They could then pool their efforts to divest themselves of their ornaments and use the proceeds "to feed the hungry, clothe the naked, relieve the sick, enlighten the dark minded, disseminate the Holy Scriptures, spread the glorious gospel throughout the world." "Little do the inhabitants of a free Christian country," he wrote, "know of the want and distress endured by the greater part of the inhabitants of the earth." Thus Judson attempted to harness the energy of the moral reform movement in the United States to encourage a return to the emphasis on simplicity and charity that the early church had enjoined.[68] He did so by holding up a mirror that reflected back a pagan, "Oriental" woman when the American Christian woman looked into it, using the object lesson to instruct American women regarding their duty to the women of the "Orient."

American missionary organizations routinely published accounts from the pens of missionary women, simultaneously evoking the American evangelical Christian view of marriage as divinely sanctioned, a moral duty, and a powerful evangelistic tool that empowered women. Those accounts also spelled out the ways in which non-Christian marriages oppressed women throughout the "Orient," marshalling as evidence the practice of arranged marriages, the refusal of husbands to be seen with or eat with their wives, and women's illiteracy, idleness, unclean habits, and inappropriate dress.

During the first four decades of the nineteenth century, the most commonly produced and powerful image of the "degraded Oriental woman," however, was that of *sati*, the practice whereby a Hindu widow, usually but not always of high caste, burned herself to death on her husband's funeral pyre as an act of piety.[69] The practice of *sati* was not uncommon in certain geographical regions of India, particularly Bengal. Evidence of its practice exists far back into antiquity. Westerners had long known of it; a member of the Dutch EIC had published a report of the practice as early as 1626.[70] *Sati* began to receive attention in England in the 1790s. The EIC had adopted a position of non-interference with the religious customs of the Hindus in the regions that they controlled. The practice of widow immolation, however, "aroused genuine horror among all classes of Europeans in India."[71] As early as 1789, a collector for the EIC tried to prohibit *sati* in the area around Shahabad. In 1798, the chief justice for Bengal, Sir John Anstruther, had banned the practice in Calcutta. It was in 1803, however, that William Carey and his Serampore colleague, William Ward, began to lobby for the immediate abolition of widow immolation throughout the areas under British control. They took the approach of drawing the attention of the British governor general to the practice.[72] Carey initiated a systematic study of the practice within a thirty-mile radius of Calcutta in the year 1803, recording 275 incidents that year and 109 in the first six months of 1804. He submitted his report to the governor general of India, but to no avail. Carey continued this annual survey until Lord Bentinck finally banned the practice in Bengal in 1829.[73]

Carey's reports, which included descriptions of specific incidents, received wide circulation in England and the United States when Claudius Buchanan incorporated them into his 1811 *Christian Researches in Asia*. Buchanan even extrapolated from those reports to estimate that 10,000 incidents per year occurred within British India. Although historians now consider that figure much too high, no one at the time had either the information or the inclination to contest it. As historian Kenneth Ingham has noted, the figure became entrenched in writings on the subject and "creat[ed] an impression by its vastness."[74] Ingham also suggests that the subject of *sati* received considerable notice in England when William Wilberforce addressed the subject in an 1813 speech before the House of Commons. Wilberforce advocated revising the EIC charter to require the company to permit missionary activity within the areas under its jurisdiction and used the issue of *sati* as an example of why such activity was needed.[75]

In his "Memoir on the Expediency of an Ecclesiastical Establishment for British India," Buchanan described the practice of *sati*:

> The usual mode of performing the rite of burning is the following: When the husband is dead, the widow, if she intend to burn, immediately declares her intention; and soon after goes to the river side, where the corpse of her husband is laid. The Brahmins and common people assemble. The pile being erected, the dead body is placed upon it. After a few ceremonies (differing in different districts) the widow lays herself down by the side of the corpse. Combustible materials are thrown upon the pile, which is pressed down by bamboo

> levers. The heir at law then kindles the fire. The surrounding multitude set up a shout, which is necessary to prevent her cry from being heard, if she should make any, and the life of the victim is soon ended. The following circumstances contribute to the frequency of this act: When a husband dies, the wife has the choice of burning with him, or of forsaking the comforts of life. She must put on no ornaments, must be clothed in sordid apparel, and must eat but one scanty meal in the day.
>
> If she attempt[s] to escape from the fire, any person of the very lowest caste may seize and carry her home as his own property. But in this case her relations generally bring her forcibly back to the fire, to prevent the disgrace of her being carried away.[76]

This account, originally published in 1805, appeared in the *Massachusetts Baptist Missionary Magazine* in December 1809 under the heading "Hindoo Superstition."[77] In addition to his general description of the practice in this essay, Buchanan's *Christian Researches* included his account of "The Sacrifice of the Koolin Brahmin's Three Wives, Calcutta, 30th Sept. 1807." As early as 1811, a letter to the editor in the American magazine the *Panoplist* stated that among the principal reasons for engaging in foreign missions was "the suppression of various kinds of cruelty such as the burning of widows."[78]

A number of widely popular works on missions described the practice of *sati*, including William Ward's *A View of the Idolatry of the Hindoos*, Thomas Smith's *Origin and History of Missions*, and Baron Stow's *A History of the Baptist Mission to India*.[79] The image of *sati* as representing the degradation of all "Oriental" women was so pervasive that it even received some attention in children's Sunday school literature. Writing in 1859, John Scudder, ABCFM (and later Dutch Reformed) missionary to Bombay, India, devoted three chapters, totaling sixteen pages of his book *A Voice from the East to the Young*, to the subject of widow immolation. Scudder pointed out that while the British had banned the practice in the parts of India under their control, Hindu women continued to fulfill the rite "to an awful extent in some of the native Rajah's territories." "Even while you are reading these lines," he wrote, "perhaps some poor widow is stretched on the pile with the dead body of her husband, and will be in eternity in a very few moments. I will mention a few instances of the burning of widows, that you especially, my dear little girls, may be thankful that you were not born in this dark land."[80] Scudder then proceeded to detail an incident in which a thirty-year-old woman carried out the practice in Tanjore. He described the procession in which a palanquin bore the widow, richly attired and bejeweled, to the site of the funeral pyre. An engraved illustration depicted the "multitudes of people [who] stretched out their hands towards her, to show how much they admired her conduct." The widow, he noted, maintained a "serene and even cheerful" demeanor until actually arriving at the place where the sacrifice would occur. Then she began to panic. She had to complete a ritual walk encircling the funeral pyre three times before sitting down upon it. To prevent her escape, her relatives, "armed with muskets, sabres, and other weapons," formed an outer circle. She fainted before completing the ritual walk, her relatives threw her bodily upon the pyre, and the woman "entered eternity, suffocated at once, most probably, by the flames."[81] Scudder related this story in order to demonstrate that, while *sati* encompassed a religious tradition in which the women concurred, the actual practice of the ritual involved the use of force and thus demonstrated not only the degradation of Indian women, but their virtual enslavement as well. Scudder's two succeeding chapters gave additional examples, also in gruesome detail, emphasizing the fact that the widows thus burned were sometimes as young as eight years old—probably the age of many of the children to whom he directed his book.[82]

Modern sensibilities reel at the thought of including such violence in children's Sunday school literature. The presence of those stories, however, only serves to illustrate their pervasiveness. Missionary women and other evangelical writers wanted to demonstrate to an American audience the privileged status that American Christian women held in comparison to women of that vast and mysterious region of the world that they called the "Orient." They did so by widely circulating negative descriptions of "Oriental" marriages, ranging from accounts of men refusing to eat with their wives to widow immolation. Second only in importance to the comparisons between ideal evangelical Christian marriages and less-than-ideal "Oriental" marriages were comparative accounts of motherhood.

4

"Her Children Shall Call Her Blessed"

Modeling Motherhood

Motherhood was a fact of the missionary wife's existence, as it was a fact of the lives of the women whom missionaries were trying to reach with the Christian gospel. As with marital relationships, missionaries wrote of maternal relationships and the condition of "Oriental" mothers and children in a manner designed to demonstrate to the home audience the superiority of American evangelical culture and the depravity of "Oriental" culture and to secure support for missions as a result of that contrast. Missionaries and mission apologists considered the modeling of Christian maternal relations as a second aspect of the evangelistic function of modeling Christian family order. They adopted numerous approaches to extend that influence into the lives of the people whom they tried to evangelize. Those methods included instructing native women in proper maternal relations by example and by precept. More commonly, missionary women adopted individual children, especially girls, into their homes to raise them under the "right" influences. They also operated household boarding schools to bring large numbers of children under their influence.

One way that the missionary mother demonstrated her love for her children and modeled mother-love to the "Oriental" mother was by sacrificing her time to instruct them at home, separately from and in addition to her equally arduous work among indigeneous women and children. Harrison Dwight, missionary in Constantinople and husband of Elizabeth Dwight, noted that one obstacle to the missionary wife's work outside the home came from the fact that she was the only one available to educate her own children and oversee their moral development. Missionary children lived in great danger of "falling an easy prey to temptations unknown in America." She could not give up her own children "to ignorance, stupidity, and sin" while doing the work of a missionary, nor could she "instruct them together with native children in the same school." Thus she simply had to redouble her efforts. Elizabeth Dwight wrote to the *Mother's Magazine* in 1835 to describe some of the sinful influences that her children faced:

> No sooner has the pompous procession of priests, displaying the holy cross, followed by a train of boys bearing torches, and singing through the noise their monstrous notes, passed our windows, than our children are marching about the room with their sticks raised, chanting the same uncouth sounds. Not many days since, hearing them busily engaged, we inquired what they were doing. They replied, "We have got a picture, and are playing *worship idols*."[1]

Dwight thus described the negative environmental influences on her children in a manner that would have forcefully driven home her point to her anti-Catholic audience.

Missionaries frequently expressed reluctance or even loathing at the idea of their children having contact with "Orientals" or corrupt Europeans. Lucy Lord expressed fear that her son would "grow up familiar with idolatrous scenes" in China. She reported with optimism, however, that the number of missionary children at Ningpo was multiplying. They would provide her son with companionship, for "I do not mean," she wrote, "that he shall play at all with Chinese children."[2] When her son, Lewis, was only two-and-a-half years old, Henrietta Shuck began making plans to send him back to the United States for his education when he reached the age of ten. She cited the lack of educational advantages for an American child in Ningpo and noted with consternation that her son could speak Chinese fluently and, that although he understood English perfectly well and already knew his letters, he would "*not speak a word in English*, if he [could] avoid it."[3]

The compiler of Henrietta Shuck's memoir interjected in the text at that point with a discussion of missionary children's education. Children, he noted, would befriend whoever was at hand, whether "intelligent, refined and pious" or "ignorant, vicious and degraded." It was not only the "heathen" who posed a threat, but European and American merchants, who were "generally mere adventurers, unprincipled, vicious, eager in the pursuit of money, and unscrupulous as to the means of acquiring it." Furthermore, the very climate of Eastern nations was "ennervating." The heat could sap the "physical and mental energy" of children, offering the fearful possibility that conversion could work in the wrong direction: missionary children could actually become like the "degraded Orientals" rather than the reverse.[4]

Miron Winslow in Ceylon had made a similar argument a few years earlier. "Southern Asia," he wrote, "is no place for northern people to *colonize*. They dwindle away under a tropical sun." The foreigner with an already established character could maintain it and work much good, but his children "born and educated in the country, instead of aiding to elevate the natives, would, in all probability, gradually sink to their level."[5] Sarah Boardman Judson wrote of the great trial of sending away her son, George, but concluded that "the Anglo-Saxon blood seems to degenerate under the influence of an Asiatic sun; and the child must be sent away to develop under more favourable circumstances, or arrive at manhood, crippled in mind and muscle."[6]

Since, as the missionaries believed, God had divinely ordained parents as the instructors and preservers of their children, the best thing missionaries could do was to send their children back to the morally and physically bracing environs of North America to complete their education. The advantage, according to mission apologists, was that by the age of ten those children were already accustomed to the missionary life and had acquired fluency in an Eastern tongue. Most missionary parents hoped that their children would eventually return as missionaries themselves.

The practice of sending children back to the United States for education prevailed with daughters as well as sons. Cyrus Stone, an ABCFM missionary at Bombay, sent his two young daughters back as the result of a promise made to his wife on her deathbed. He handed them over to the care of the Maternal Association of Utica, New York, with the hope that "they may be qualified by education and grace, and return to this pagan clime, in the character of missionary laborers, to aid in raising these poor, degraded, Hindoo females from their degradation and woes, to a participation of the blessedness which the gospel confers on woman."[7] The presence of missionary children in their midst also served to sustain a personal interest on the part of some women at home in the United States, while many others empathized by reading missionary women's accounts in the pages of *Mother's Magazine* and other publications.

Another way in which missionary mothers demonstrated love for their children and modeled Christian motherhood was by detailing the suffering of those children when they died and their own suffering in mourning for their children. Lucy Lord, for example, wrote a letter to her parents from Ningpo, China, on 14 November 1849, in which she reported the death of her infant son from dysentery. She and her husband were sick as well; the doctor could do nothing for the three of them but prescribe a change of air. Despite their extreme weakness, Lucy and her husband embarked on a trip by boat to Chusan. The wind, however, did not cooperate, forcing them to lie at anchor for an entire day. The baby grew progressively worse: "Through the day…our dear little one was almost constantly uttering short, sharp cries. Meanwhile the swelling increased so much that he looked quite unnatural; and other symptoms appeared more alarming." During the night, her husband awoke her to tell her that the baby, whom he was holding in his arms, was dying. Lucy was so weak that she had to crawl over to them, and could only hold the baby's hand while he expired. She insisted upon preparing his body with her own hands, then and there. Her husband had to lift her into a chair and lay the body on a chest so she could reach it. "I shed no tears," she wrote, "but calmly washed the dear flesh, closed the eyes and mouth, composed the limbs, wrapped the body in a sheet, and covered the face. Then I felt that my work was done."[8] Less than a year later, Lucy reported to her parents that, within the last few months, five of the seven mothers among the missionary families in Ningpo had lost children. Six of the seventeen mission children had died.[9]

Missionary memoirs and periodical accounts were replete with similar stories. The American Tract Society, for example, published one book-length account of a missionary child, Judith Grant Perkins, who died of cholera in Persia at age twelve. That memoir explicitly linked Judith to the angelic character of Little Eva in Harriet Beecher Stowe's recently published and spectacularly popular *Uncle Tom's Cabin.* The novel was the last book Judith read before her death, and according to the memoir, Little Eva was Judith's favorite character: "She longed to be like Eva, and to be with her. And as Providence ordered, it would almost seem, that that seraphic character was presented to her, just at that time, as a beckoning angel, to invite her to her celestial home. The congeniality of Judith's spirit and character with Eva's, was more than imaginary, and obvious to the general observer."[10] Such accounts, even in the abbreviated form that most of them took, sought to elicit sympathy both for the parents and for the cause of missions, and sometimes, as in the case of Judith, to instruct children on the virtues of godly self-sacrifice and the importance of preparing oneself for an untimely death.

"Oriental" mothers and their children, according to American missionary women, offered a stark contrast to the portrayals of Christian maternal relationships. "Oriental" mothers, too, experienced the deaths of their children, but missionary accounts usually depicted the mothers as the agents of death, rather than as mourners. The supposedly widespread practice of female infanticide in "Oriental" cultures provided one of the most common themes in antebellum missions literature and one of the most frequent justifications for sending mission families to demonstrate ideal parental relations.[11]

As with the practice of *sati*, the American audience knew of infanticide by means of popular British missions literature, geographical works, magazines, and children's literature. Claudius Buchanan reported that the practice of "destroying female infants" prevailed among the Rajpoots and in the province of Benares. Mothers starved their infant daughters to death "without alleging any other reason than the difficulty of providing for [them] in marriage." "In some places," he reported, "not one half of the females are permitted to live."[12] Malte Brun's popular *Universal Geography* noted that female infanticide was common in the Indian province of Cutch, while William Ward emphasized its prevalence in Orissa and the Punjab.[13] The *Massachusetts Baptist Missionary Magazine* estimated in 1811 that 30,000 to 50,000 female infants "perish[ed] annually in the East Indies."[14] John Scudder reported to his juvenile audience that:

> Infanticide, or the murder of children, is very common. There is a sect of people called the Jatus who make it a point to murder their female infants. In the province of Mulva this crime is common. On a visit to one of the villages in that province, a gentleman found that it contained forty-two boys; but not a single girl could he find. They had all been slaughtered almost immediately after their birth. On the Nilgherry hills, where I resided for a short time before I left India, there is a sect of people called Todurs. When discovered a few years ago, it was found that infanticide was also common among them. In the province of Bengal alone it is supposed that one hundred and twenty thousand infants are destroyed every year![15]

In another children's book, Scudder told of a Rajah in northern India whose wife bore five daughters in succession, each of whom he ordered destroyed immediately. When a sixth daughter was born, he gave the same command, but the mother managed to have her taken away secretly. Raised by relatives, she grew into a beautiful little girl. Her mother died when she was eleven, and the relatives decided to present her to the Rajah, thinking that he would own her as his daughter for the sake of her mother and because of her beauty. Instead, when the child threw herself at her father's feet, he immediately "seized her by the hair of the head, and drew his sword from its belt, and with a single blow took off her head."[16] In his *Appeal to Christian Mothers*, Scudder encouraged mothers in America to repeat such stories to their young children and to provide them with "nursery books" that would offer accounts of such "heathen" degradation. He argued that teaching small children about the sufferings of others, far from being inappropriate for them, would in fact help them to develop the habit of sympathy and would inculturate them into the cause of missions from an early age.[17]

Just as common as the image of female infanticide, discussions of ritual child sacrifice pervaded missionary literature. Buchanan reported the practice, in parts of India among the "lower classes," of hanging an infant that refused its mother's milk from a basket in a tree as an offering to the demon that was supposedly afflicting it. If after three days the infant had survived, the mother would retrieve it. Usually, however, the infant fell victim to white ants or birds of prey if it did not die of neglect.[18] William Ward also described that practice, reporting one occasion in which William Carey discovered a basket that contained the skeleton of an infant that had been "devoured by ants."[19] More commonly, authors described the practice of sacrificing children by throwing them into a river (usually the Ganges) to drown or to be devoured by crocodiles.[20] Sarah Hall, later married first to the missionary George Boardman and then to Adoniram Judson, published a poem titled "Come Over and Help Us" when she was still an adolescent in New York. One stanza of the poem read, "By the infant's piercing cry, / Drowned in Ganges' rolling wave; / By the mother's tearful eye / Friends of Jesus, come and save!"[21]

Such accounts were also a staple of children's missionary literature. With an accompanying illustration, Scudder wrote,

> This river is considered particularly holy where it meets the ocean. Hence, the celebrity of the island called Saugor. This is the spot where hundreds of mothers annually, in times past, used to throw their children into the waters, to be devoured by crocodiles; and the spot, too, where these mothers bewailed the sacrifice as lost, if these children were not devoured before their eyes by these crocodiles. Thus you see what hard-hearted creatures a false religion can make even of mothers. The British government in India will not now allow them to throw their children into the waters, at that place; but such sacrifices will never be stopped, until the gospel of Jesus Christ shall teach heathen mothers to make no more vows that they will devote their offspring to heathen gods.[22]

The lead article in *Mother's Magazine* for November 1844 bore the title "A Scene on the Ganges." It offered a dramatized description of a Hindu woman reluctantly placing her firstborn child in a basket to offer to the Ganges: "Terror…seizes the young voyager, as the waters ooze into its narrow boat, and it calls for help, in cries that a mother comprehends, though infant lips have no words in which to utter fear…. On the banks of the river near the spot where her child has sunk to rise no more, the worn and wretched mother sinks, and pours her sorrows on the balmy air." In the account, the woman's sorrow was redeemed, however, because a missionary wife happened along just at that moment and comforted the grieving mother. Telling her of the religion of Jesus, which did not require the sacrifice of children, she planted the seed that became the woman's salvation.[23] Ironically, one could argue that the religion of Jesus *did* require the sacrifice of children, since so many of the missionaries' children died of tropical diseases while living in the countries where their parents served, or their parents sent them back to the United States to receive an education, never to see them again.

One of the principal ways that missionary women sought both to fulfill their obligations as mothers and to model Christian maternal relations before "Oriental" women was by forming maternal societies. The first maternal society had been formed in 1815 by a Mrs. Payson in Portland, Maine. Initially, organizers intended the societies to serve primarily as an opportunity for women to gather for "social" (corporate) prayer for the conversion of their children. The societies soon evolved into vehicles for disseminating the latest information on child-rearing. In such organizations, mothers "whose opportunities for mental cultivation [were] extremely limited" could "find the best works on education collected and explained, and [were] greatly assisted in bringing them to bear on daily practice." Missionary wives had, soon after the inception of the concept, transplanted maternal associations to Asia. The first issue of *Mother's Magazine*, founded in 1833 to impart information about the "science" of motherhood, noted that missionary wives had established associations in the Sandwich Islands, in Ceylon, and in Bombay.[24] Harriet Winslow wrote to the Maternal Association in Portland, Maine, on 8 October 1821 to report that she and the women of the British Wesleyan and Church Missionary Societies had organized themselves to pray for the conversion of their children and their protection in the "heathen" environment of Ceylon.[25] Likewise, Sarah Boardman Judson established a maternal society in Maulmein, Burma, around 1834.[26] Judith Grant, writing to a friend from her station in Persia, noted her pleasure at hearing of the "general establishment of Maternal Associations." "I hope that mothers in America, when they come together to implore blessings on their own little ones," she wrote, "will not neglect to put up a petition for those children and those mothers who are far from them—among the Gentiles."[27] Elizabeth Dwight expressed similar pleasure and established a Maternal Association in Constantinople in 1835. She explained the difficulties of the maternal role in a land without churches, Sunday schools, and prayer meetings. The missionary women organized to provide each other with moral support and encouragement in the midst of their spiritual isolation. They devoted their meetings primarily to prayer for the conversion of each of their children.[28]

Missionary wives were not alone in approving maternal societies. Their husbands joined them in reading *Mother's Magazine* and not uncommonly corresponded with its editors. For example, the magazine published a letter from S. Wells Williams of Canton, China, in December of 1834. He described for American women the "degraded state of females in China." Despite the complete absence of educational opportunities for Chinese women, he wrote, they nevertheless had the same power to form their children's moral character and intellect as women in America. How much would that influence increase, he queried, "if they were enlightened and Christianized?"[29] Asahel Grant addressed the magazine from Persia. He described the quality of mothers in Persia by writing, "As the impress of character is made in infancy and early childhood, I have only to point you to the lying, theft, profanity, intemperance and degrading ignorance of all classes of people around us, and you have the portrait of *mothers* in this dark land." He concluded his letter by asking the mothers of America to pray for the enlightenment and uplift of the mothers of Persia.[30]

The *Mother's Magazine* offers clear evidence that the maternal society movement was closely related to and concerned with the foreign mission movement, particularly with missions to Eastern lands. The magazine's "Prospectus," printed in the first issue, indicated that mothers had in their tutelage the "future defenders of the faith." For that reason, the "welfare of Zion"—the extension of the kingdom of God on earth in anticipation of the coming millennial reign of Jesus Christ—was to a large extent in the power of Christendom's mothers. The Christian mother in the United States participated in the conversion of the world by training her children to support and pray for the missions movement and preparing them to offer themselves as missionaries. To enforce that message, the magazine regularly printed letters from missionary husbands and wives, reported on the condition of women in foreign lands, and frequently offered articles encouraging mothers to educate their children about the missions movement. Articles such as the series on "Future Defenders of the Faith" reminded mothers that their sons could be the next "Swartz, Elliot, or Martyn" or "Brainerd, Parson, or Judson" (all of them famous missionaries).[31] The second article in the "Future Defenders" series drew a portrait of a mother in her nursery, telling her children a story about the "poor, heathen children" of India:

> Do you know, my children, that in India there is a large and deep river, in which some parents drown their children?
>
> Drown them, mother! exclaims a little girl.
>
> Yes, they take them to the river Ganges, and cast them in there.
>
> But why do they drown them, mother? inquires her boy.
>
> It is a part of their cruel religion, my children. They worship idols. And they think it will please their idols to have children sacrificed to them.
>
> But don't the children cry?
>
> Indeed they do; but their ignorant and cruel parents push them off into the deep water, and see the little sufferers struggle and drown without a tear.
>
> Do parents ever drown their children in America?
>
> No; we are taught better. Here we have the Bible, and that Bible tells us of the only living and true God, and how we should worship him.
>
> But why are not parents in India told better?
>
> They have no Bible there, no Sabbaths, no ministers. Had they them, they would know that God is to be worshiped "in spirit and

> in truth," by prayer and praise, and not by drowning poor little children.

The mother in this scenario went on to tell her children that, when she died, she hoped they would visit her grave, remember what she had told them about missions, and make contributions to the missionary society.[32]

In addition to such fictional sketches, the magazine often included articles to instruct mothers on exactly how they could accomplish the task of raising their children to support the cause of missions or, better yet, to be missionaries. One such article declared that "the mother of a missionary is an honored woman" and went on to instruct mothers on how to enter those ranks: pray for her children, "portray the condition of the heathen world," and let her children know that she had consecrated them in infancy to become missionaries.[33] The March 1836 issue included an article on how to interest children in missions. Suggestions included having the children make small items or contribute one of their own books for "missionary boxes," taking the children to the monthly concert of prayer for missions, and requiring them, while at the concert, to learn the names of the missionaries and their stations, then following up by having them study geographies, maps, and the *Missionary Herald*.[34]

One series of articles specifically addressed the issue of raising daughters to become missionaries. The author offered the standard argument that maternal influence was key to extending the influence of the gospel from one generation to the next and that the conversion of the world thus required female missionaries to reach their "heathen" sisters. American mothers should train their daughters in the cause of missions so that they could either go themselves or become the means of training up the next generation of children who might go abroad and "stand upon some heathen shore, and tell the melting story of Calvary to a group of gathered Hindoos." The next article in the series suggested that mothers accomplish their goal first by telling their daughters stories about "the cruel gods the heathen serve, how many children like herself are sacrificed even by their mothers hand." Another strategy involved teaching her geography by pointing out the places of service and death of famous missionary women such as Harriet Newell and Ann Judson.

Far from being too "gloomy" a subject, young children needed early exposure to the fact that they lived in "a world of sorrow and sin." Furthermore, mothers should take their daughters to the monthly concert of prayer, preparing in advance by reading from the missionary magazines and geographies. Finally, the author suggested that girls should produce fancy needlework to sell for the cause of missions, giving the example of a three-year-old who made a quilt for the benefit of the Cherokee and Choctaw missions.[35]

In 1835, Elizabeth Dwight wrote to the *Mother's Magazine* to encourage women to educate their daughters as missionaries. Her words encapsulated the concept of marital and maternal relationships as a part of the evangelistic enterprise of missions. To prepare a daughter for life as a missionary, a mother must first educate her to engage herself in works of "benevolence" for the church. She might someday "be a solitary example of true female piety" to the heathen. In all probability, however, if she went to the mission field, she would go as someone's wife. The next step in her preparation, therefore, involved training her in all of the qualities desirable in a wife, for "she may, at some future period, be the sole companion and helpmeet of a man of God, under labours the most weighty, and trials the most severe." Finally, a mother should educate her daughter for the maternal role. "Multitudes of parents who never witnessed a pious family circle," Dwight wrote, "may look with wonder and profit at the manner she trains up her offspring, and admire the sweetness of behaviour, their purity of conduct, or they may exclaim, 'Her religion is no better than ours.'"[36]

Efforts to involve native women in the maternal societies that they initially established for their own benefit represented one of the ways that missionary women sought to take more active steps than simply modeling maternal relations before "Oriental" women. Most missionaries, however, believed that family relations in the Eastern nations were so disorderly that the only hope lay in bringing children, especially girls, into missionary homes to live. They also believed that such informal adoptions could prove an effective mode of direct evangelization. Usually such an arrangement involved an agreement that the parents would allow their child to live with the missionaries in exchange for an education, food, and clothing. In the case of girls, the missionaries often also had to pay the parents for the privilege, since little interest existed in girls' education.

Ann Judson, in Burma, established the precedent. She "adopted" two sisters, named them Mary and Abby Hasseltine (after women in Ann's own family), and kept them with her until her death, when they went to live with another missionary family. Ann received support for the girls from the "Judson Association" at Bradford Academy, her alma mater in Massachusetts.[37]

In June of 1834, Sarah Lanman Smith, who lived in Beirut, took an eight-year-old Arab girl named Raheel into her home in order to have greater influence over someone whom she could train to work among native women. Raheel's education included household chores and needlework; in fact, "so thoroughly was she initiated into habits of industry, as never to sit down with nothing to do." Two years later, Sarah's physician prescribed a sea voyage to Smyrna to restore her health; her greatest regret was giving up Raheel, whose parents would not consent to her leaving. "Parents…in Syria have an especial aversion to parting with their children for foreign countries," Sarah wrote. She turned the girl over to a single woman, Miss Williams, who had come from the United States to assist with the girls' school in Beirut.[38] It was just as well that Raheel's parents objected. The Smiths were shipwrecked on their way to Smyrna, and although they were rescued, Sarah died of consumption soon after arriving.

Lucy Lord, in China, wrote to her former pastor suggesting instructions to the missionary wife: "Gather a few little girls into your house, take the entire charge of their education for as many years as you can secure them and there in an *appropriate* and quiet way cast a healing influence into the very fountain of social life." According to Lord, taking young girls into her home was one of the most useful evangelistic activities that a missionary wife could adopt and a strategy beyond the reproach of even the most staunchly conservative mission societies.[39] Other examples of missionary wives "adopting" children included Elizabeth Dwight in Constantinople, Judith Grant in Persia, and Henrietta Shuck in China.

Besides the usual practice of bringing girls into their homes by arrangement with their parents, missionary wives on several occasions rescued young girls from slavery. Sarah Lanman Smith in Syria and Henrietta Shuck in China each reported rescuing a slave girl and taking her in to raise. A German missionary wife in China, Mrs. Gutzlaff, reported to the *Mother's Magazine* that she had purchased four blind slave girls to save them from an unspeakable fate. "They are *bought* slaves," she wrote, "and bought that they may be redeemed." She went on to implore American mothers to raise money with which she could rescue more slave girls and give them an education.[40]

The most well-publicized account of a missionary rescuing a girl from slavery came from the experience of Deborah Wade at Amherst in Burma in 1827. The father of seven-year-old Meh Shway-ee had sold her as a slave to a Burmese magistrate's interpreter, who later turned out to be her half-brother, she being the product of an illicit liaison between her father and a woman other than his wife. The *American Baptist Magazine* reported in 1829 from Deborah Wade's account that

> Meh Shway-ee's master had treated her with the utmost barbarity, in consequence of which, one of her arms was broken, and her body covered with scars. When her arm was partially cured, he satiated his cruelty by inflicting upon her a peculiar kind of torture by fire, which cannot, for reasons of delicacy, be described, but which, beside the exquisite agony of infliction, is calculated to ensure a return of torment every few hours, until death comes to the relief of the wretched sufferer.[41]

The Burmese themselves did not officially permit slavery, but apparently those who knew of Meh Shway-ee's existence had remained silent because the abuser had the power to retaliate against anyone who reported his actions. Neighbors became concerned, however, when the child disappeared from sight and her owner said that she was sick. The British governor was absent from Amherst, the Burman colonial capital at the time, but someone managed to get word to Adoniram Judson, head of the Baptist mission. Although an American, Judson's position as a white man in a region recently conquered by the British placed him in a position of power. He went to the man's home and demanded that he hand the child over, threatening to have him arrested if he refused. Under duress, the man complied. His Burmese neighbors soon took courage and reported him to the authorities; he was later sentenced to four years hard labor, but committed suicide.

Judson, a widower, took Meh Shway-ee to Jonathan and Deborah Wade, who had recently arrived in Burma to serve as Judson's colleagues. The bulk of the first published account of Meh Shway-ee consisted of extracts from Deborah's journal in which she noted the girl's physical and spiritual progress. Meh Shway-ee's physical condition was poor, and the resident European surgeon offered little hope of her long-term survival. Under Deborah's care, she did, however, regain enough strength to begin receiving religious instruction. Most of Deborah's account assumed the form of a lengthy conversion narrative. Meh Shway-ee survived for about one year, during which time Deborah tried to "improve" the child's affliction for her eternal good. In the end, Meh Shway-ee became a Christian, and her story was told and retold in anecdotes and poems for the next thirty years. Her experience became a parable used to inform American girls and women about the terrible things that could happen to their "Oriental" sisters and to inspire them to support the cause of missions with their money or their lives.

A number of missionary women went beyond taking in one or two children and instead opened their homes as boarding schools with up to thirty students. Those domestic establishments in some cases grew into full-scale educational institutions, but in the early years they were more like extended households with the "mother" (missionary wife) as primary teacher. At first, the missionaries could attract only boys, but sometimes they gradually added girls by requiring parents to bring them a daughter for every son. Harriet Winslow in Ceylon, for example, began in 1820 with nine boys, added the first girl in 1822, and by 1823 had added several girls to that number.[42] In 1839, Henrietta Shuck reported that she had nine children (besides her own) living with her and another six day students. "I should much prefer taking girls exclusively," she wrote, "but so great is the opposition of Chinese parents to have their female children educated, that I find I must take boys in order to get girls." By 1844, the Shucks had thirty-two children, four of them their own, living with them in Hong Kong.[43]

Mary Van Lennep wrote to a friend in 1844 to report that they had received a new assignment in Constantinople. Her husband, Henry, would work among the Armenians, but the board was transferring them primarily because they wanted Mary to start a "female seminary." They did not intend for it to function like a traditional American boarding school, but instead, she wrote, "What they want is the influence of a Christian family to be exerted over those who are to become the wives and mothers of the Armenian nation." The school would provide Mary the opportunity "to become acquainted with Armenian females generally, and thus to preach to them the gospel." In sum, the ABCFM sought a means that would extend "sweet Christian family influence" over the minds of young women in a more direct way than simply modeling that influence for women to observe from casual contact with the family.[44]

A sense of personal vocation, a philosophical and practical commitment to the role of "helpmeet," and a simultaneous unwillingness (on the part of both husbands and wives) to permit that role to restrict the women's evangelistic activities all characterized the experiences of antebellum missionary wives. Despite an early commitment to a mode of evangelism centered on establishing Christian family order as a living parable that would reach "Oriental" women, it gradually became apparent that the field was too large and the possibilities too great for such an indirect and limited approach. Missionary wives soon developed more direct approaches to evangelism. In addition to establishing maternal societies and adopting children into their homes for full-time religious instruction, the "family boarding school" represented another way in which the efforts of missionary wives could extend beyond their immediate families, even if those efforts did not take her outside her home. But missionary wives all brought with them a model of Christian service from their own experiences in churches and from observing and understanding the roles of pastors' wives in the United States. Neither they, their husbands, nor their sending agencies expected that they would confine themselves to their own firesides, even if those firesides had thirty children gathered around them. Establishing Sunday schools, reading the Bible and tracts to women in their homes, leading women's prayer meetings, and translating the Bible and other Christian literature into Eastern languages represent several of the ways missionary women extended their roles.

Most missionary wives established and led Sunday schools. Just as Sunday schools were becoming an increasingly important means of evangelizing children in the United States, the missionaries viewed them as essential to the task of evangelization in "Oriental" countries. Harriet Winslow had established a girls' Sunday school in Ceylon by the spring of 1823. The children received reading instruction using the gospels and a sacred history textbook written for children. They also spent a portion of each class memorizing and reciting the catechism and reviewing the previous week's sermon.[45] Ann Judson and Sarah Boardman Judson each established similar institutions in Burma, as did Sarah Lanman Smith in Syria, Judith Grant in Persia, and Mary Van Lennep in Turkey.[46]

Missionary wives also devoted a considerable amount of time to visiting women in their homes. Sarah Lanman Smith devised a systematic program of visiting the mothers of the students at her Beirut girls' school. She described this household visitation plan as akin to what "the Tract distributors in America do, for the purpose of personal religious conversation." The missionary women agreed to go out on their visits at appointed times, and then return to a central meeting room at the mission "to report to each other our success." Sarah and the other missionary women knew that the work would be painstakingly slow, however. Sarah herself anticipated that it would require consistent monthly visits over the course of at least a year with any given individual for any progress to occur.[47] The experience of a few months in this project taught her, however, that she would seldom succeed in making more than one or two visits on a given day. As it happened, the presence of a missionary in any one person's home drew a whole crowd from the neighborhood so that she would often have "quite a congregation" when she had intended a private visit with one woman.[48] Informally, it would seem, missionary women engaged in what resembled itinerant preaching.

In addition to visiting in homes, missionary wives often tried to organize formal prayer meetings akin to the prayer meetings in which they all had participated back in the United States. Ann Judson wrote in her journal in March of 1812, while en route to Burma via India, "I desire no higher enjoyment in this life, than to be instrumental of leading some poor, ignorant heathen females, to the knowledge of the Saviour. To have a female praying society, consisting of those who were once in heathen darkness, is what my heart earnestly pants after, and makes a constant subject of prayer." Within seven years, Ann had realized her goal, for she reported in a letter to her sister in 1819 that she continued to hold regular meetings with fifteen Burman women, some of whom had indicated that they might soon convert.[49] Most missionary wives led some type of indigenous women's Bible study since it provided the primary opportunity for evangelistic work among adult women.

Another evangelistic activity of missionary wives involved translating religious literature into indigenous languages. Sarah Judson prepared twenty hymns for a new *Chapel Hymn Book* and also wrote articles for the Burmese newspaper.[50] Many of the women also engaged in translating tracts, Sunday school lessons, and portions of Scripture. Sarah Lanman Smith translated the weekly Sunday school lessons into Arabic, while Harriet Winslow translated tracts into Tamil. Perhaps the most prolific of the women translators and writers, however, were Ann Judson and Sarah Boardman Judson. Ann Judson studied Thai and translated a catechism, several tracts, and the Gospel of Matthew. Sarah Judson studied the language of the Peguan minority around Maulmein, Burma. She eventually translated numerous tracts, the entire New Testament, and *Pilgrim's Progress.*[51]

Missionary wives also wrote voluminously to promote missions at home. Those writings drew attention to the "plight" of "degraded Oriental women" in images and stories designed to cause American women both to reflect on their privileged social position and to desire to use that position to impart comparable privileges to their "Eastern sisters." All of the missionaries maintained an extensive correspondence with supporters in the United States, and writing those letters usually fell to the lot of the missionary wife. The significance of that activity was great, since many such letters eventually found their way onto the pages of missionary magazines, the *Mother's Magazine*, the popular *Godey's Lady's Book*, and even into secular newspapers. Sarah Lanman Smith reported that she often received as many as fifteen or twenty letters per delivery (it is not clear how frequently the mail was delivered), all of them requiring a reply.[52] Lucy Lord wrote to Reverend and Mrs. Hawkes of South Hadley, Massachusetts, in a slightly complaining tone: "I would ask my dear Mrs. Hawks to recur to the time when her firstborn was a babe in her arms, herself the wife of a Christian minister, and when perhaps she, like myself, had some fifty correspondents, several of whom expected to hear from her quarterly, and all at least annually." [53] Smith and Lord also each reported assisting their husbands by transcribing letters, reports, and other writings, as well as keeping financial accounts.[54]

The fact that both the sending agencies and the missionaries themselves sanctioned the concept of a divine calling for married women also left open the possibility that agencies might at some point recognize a similar call in the lives of unmarried women. In fact, the very success of missionary wives in firmly establishing a role for themselves working among their "heathen Oriental sisters" opened the way for single women to enter the field. While the *tableau* of family life required marriage, the more direct approaches, as it soon became apparent, did not. Missionary wives, burdened by the sheer scope of the work and following the lead of their English counterparts, began to request assistance from single women at home. They met with only limited success during the antebellum period, largely because the ideal of the missionary family as living parable persisted with such strength throughout the period. Other reasons for limiting the roles of single women in the Asian mission fields during this period included financial constraints, apparent conflicts between single women and missionary wives in the Sandwich Islands mission, difficulties arising from the problem of housing single women in cultures and under political conditions that could prove dangerous or where the indigenous people might misinterpret a single woman living with a married couple as polygamy, and a theological perspective that regarded "civilizing" activities as secondary to, or even subversive of, the traditional preaching of a "pure" gospel and the founding and indigenization of Christian churches. The work of missionary wives and that of the few single women who went to Asia to assist them, however, established precedents and laid the philosophical and practical groundwork for the dramatic feminization of the entire foreign missions movement in the decade following the Civil War. That feminization had its roots in the establishment of formal educational institutions for girls—institutions requiring teachers—as a key component of mission work.

5

"A Cultivated And Well-Furnished Mind" Education For "Oriental" Women

The efforts of missionary wives to extend their activities beyond their homes offered an oblique commentary on the "idleness" of "Oriental" women. But perhaps more pointedly, their actions also offered a lesson to American women. The positive example of missionary women and contrasting image of "Oriental" women offered justification to American women whose evangelical activism could sometimes bring complaints that they overstepped their bounds. To be idle was to be like the heathen. At the same time, such injunctions, along with stories of missionary women apparently working themselves quite literally to death, could turn the privilege of activism into an urgent requirement. Popular missionary literature made clear that the "fields were ripe for harvest, but the laborers few." Some educated young single women began to feel restless at the limited scope that America offered for their energy. They found in their reading and their missionary society meetings that much of the work missionary wives were performing did not, in fact, require a husband. Single American women began to recognize that a woman unencumbered by her own family might be in a position to accomplish great things for God. In the 1840s, as mission boards began to develop more formal educational institutions in their "Eastern departments," single women, along with their married counterparts, found their opportunities multiplying, and a subtle transformation in the entire mission movement began.[1]

On 26 February 1836, Sarah Lanman Smith, missionary to Syria, addressed a letter to the students at her alma mater, the Young Ladies Academy at Norwich, Connecticut. "God is furnishing American females their high privileges," she wrote,

> with the intention of calling them forth into the wide fields of ignorance and error, which the world exhibits. I look over my country, and think of the hundreds and thousands of young ladies, intelligent, amiable, and capable, who are assembled in schools and academies there; and turn my eye to Jerusalem, Hebron, Nazareth, Sychar, Damascas, Tyre, Sidon, Yafa, etc. and to the numerous villages of Mount Lebanon, and think, Why the inequality of condition and privileges? Why can there not be stationed at every one of those morally desolate places, at least one missionary family and one single female teacher?[2]

Smith's delineation of biblical place names was no accident. She was reminding her youthful audience that they had the high privilege of dwelling in the new Israel (America), to which the blessings of God's chosen people had passed. Those blessings received their clearest illustration in the privileged condition of the daughters of New England, (presumably) beloved of their families, blossoming spiritually under regular preaching and Sabbath observance, and receiving an unparalleled education befitting their social position atop the pedestal of American womanhood. Those privileges, however, simultaneously conferred upon them an obligation to carry the gospel to the world. And what better place to start than the very lands from which it had sprung? Hence, Smith recited the most familiar of biblical place names to evoke the sympathy of her audience.

Smith issued her echo of the Macedonian cry on the heels of a most telling illustration intended to demonstrate the importance of education in the evangelization and moral uplift of young women. She opened her letter with a literary device common in correspondence of the day. She first imagined herself in the presence of her audience as an omniscient and invisible observer and described her mind's image of them at that moment. She saw the young ladies of Norwich gathered for the day's lessons, all of them freshly scrubbed and "neatly" attired. Each student had spread before her everything she needed for the day's tasks: books, paper, pens, and other implements of learning. The day opened with Scripture reading and prayer, to which the students offered respectful attention. Exercises designed to advance the girls in knowledge and "usefulness" filled the hours. "Kindness, gentleness, and respect," she observed, "characterize your deportment towards your teachers and companions; and intellectual cultivation as well as amiable feeling, beam in every countenance."[3] After school, loving families who desired nothing more than their daughters' intellectual and moral improvement welcomed the girls home.

"I hasten to present the contrast, which is not before my imagination only, but before my eyes," Smith continued. Having just drawn for the girls at Norwich an idealized sketch of their own happiness, she held up for their reflection an image of the "Oriental Other": their counterparts, "the young Syrian females at large, moving in one unbroken line to the land of darkness and sorrow." Despite the claim of eyewitness authority, Smith did not limit herself to "our little female school of twenty or thirty," but instead extrapolated from her observations to paint a grim picture of the "unhappy condition of the females of Syria":

> Select from among your acquaintances a young lady who is excessively weak, vain, and trifling; who has no relish for any intellectual or moral improvement; whose conversation is altogether confined to dress, parties, balls, admiration, marriage; whose tempers and faults have never been corrected by her parents, but who is following unchecked all the propensities of a fallen, corrupt nature.... Then place the thousands of girls, and the women too, of this land, once the land of patriarchs, prophets, and apostles, in her class.[4]

Smith went on to describe young women who, while obsessed with lavish, gaudy dress, took little interest in personal cleanliness; who not only had no books, but deemed it a "disgrace for a female to know how to read and write." Although "nominal" Christians in the Syrian Orthodox Church, they knew virtually nothing about the Bible. Their annual attendance at church served as a social occasion, "to which [they attached] no solemnity." While their families abounded in affection, it was expressed in indulgence and lax discipline rather than "respect" and actions designed to "elevate the character."[5]

Smith subtly designed her contrast as both a warning and a call to service. By telling her Norwich audience to "select from among their acquaintance," she in effect told them that the "heathen" Syrian women had their counterparts in America—that heathenism was not a matter of where one lived, but was manifested in the way one behaved. Hence, American women who indulged in worldly, superficial concerns were no better than their Syrian counterparts. American women, however, were also without excuse, for they lived surrounded by the means of effecting their own moral transformation. They could hear the gospel preached and observe Sunday as the Lord's Day when they chose; they could read, had access to books, and could attend excellent schools; they were enmeshed in webs of family ties and social institutions that gave them a respected and even revered position in society. If they devolved into heathenism, it was their own fault. But the warning also carried a plea. Syrian women did not have similar advantages. If American Christian women did not carry to the Syrian woman the means of hearing the gospel to effect her soul's salvation for eternity and the means of educating her mind so as to effect her moral redemption in this life, the Syrian woman was without hope.

As the illustration from Smith's experience indicates, education for girls became an important strategy in American Protestant missions to the "Orient." The importance that women missionary teachers attached to their own education and the significant role that reading played in their conversion experiences help to explain missionary women's emphasis on teaching "Oriental" women to read. Schools were a place where conversion might occur through the instrumentality of the written word in the form of Scripture, catechisms, tracts, and other Christian literature. In addition to introducing the gospel, such readings also helped to inculcate moral values such as discipline and the importance of hard work, respect, and personal cleanliness. Missionaries believed that the lack of educational opportunities for girls signified the spiritual, moral, and intellectual degradation and oppression of

"Oriental" women. At the same time, the missionaries believed that the gospel and Western education could redeem all aspects of the individual "Oriental" woman's life, while simultaneously collectively uplifting the status of women in general and thus civilizing "Oriental" societies.

Understanding developments in women's education in the early nineteenth century is crucial for understanding the significance missionary women attached to their own educational experiences and helps to explain why missionary women sought to replicate their own experiences in the lives of girls and young women in the "Orient." Prior to the American Revolution, girls of the upper classes often had access to academies or seminaries. Modeled after similar institutions in England, female academies usually taught the rudiments of reading, writing, arithmetic, geography, history, and ornamental accomplishments—French, music, drawing and painting, and fancy needlework. Following the Revolution, noted patriot Benjamin Rush called for reforming girls' education to reflect the unique conditions of an American republic. The British, he suggested, were decadent and corrupt in part because they neglected to develop the rational faculties of their women. American girls needed a different education from their British counterparts—they needed a *useful* education that included civics so that they could impart republican principles to their sons.[6] By the 1790s, prosperous and middling farmers, merchants, and artisans had joined the wealthy elite in seeking at least basic instruction outside of the home for their daughters.

Secular, politically motivated voices were not alone in calling for educational reform, however. British evangelical Hannah More, in her widely disseminated *Strictures on the Modern System of Female Education*, added pietistic moral authority to calls for reforming girls' education. Like Rush, More saw British society as corrupt. She believed that corruption resulted from a decline in public virtue, which in turn resulted from an erosion of Christian principles. Only wives and mothers could "preserve the ark of the Lord"—the Protestant British nation—by influencing their husbands at home and by inculcating in their children the principles of "pure religion": "Your private exertions may at this moment be contributing to the future happiness, your domestic neglect, to the future ruin, of your country.... [R]eligion is the only sure ground of morals; [and] private principle is the only solid basis of public virtue."[7]

More's arguments reflected what Ruth Bloch has called the "rise of the moral mother." According to Bloch, it was between 1785 and 1815 that writers and preachers in America began to idealize mothers as the "chief transmitters of religious and moral values."[8] A heightened awareness of the role of maternal influence in the moral and intellectual development of children contributed greatly to the force of arguments in favor of improving education for girls and young women. That awareness also governed the Protestant foreign mission organizations' formulation of evangelizing strategies aimed at wives and mothers.

If Rush directed his gaze to the decadent European (or British) Other, More directed hers toward the depraved "Oriental" Other. She compared the emphasis on elegance and ornamental learning by the British aristocracy to reputed Muslim practices:

> To use their boasted power over mankind to no higher purpose than the gratification of vanity or the indulgence of pleasure, is the degrading triumph of those victims to luxury, caprice, and despotism, whom the laws and religion of the voluptuous prophet of Arabia exclude from light, liberty, and knowledge: and it is humbling to reflect that in those countries in which fondness for the mere persons of women is carried to the highest excess, *they are slaves*; and that their moral and intellectual degradation increases in direct proportion to the adoration which is paid to mere external charms.[9]

When William Staughton, a Baptist minister intimately involved in the foreign mission movement, gave the Examination Day address at Mrs. Rivardi's Seminary in Philadelphia in 1807, he echoed More's sentiments by saying that one could only justify denying a woman an education if one believed "with the Arabians, that a female is without a soul."[10]

In 1819, New Yorker Emma Willard added her voice to arguments for improving girls' education. Willard maintained that women's education should address "moral, intellectual, and physical nature" and should prepare young women to be useful to themselves and others.[11] Most important, women's education should prepare them to serve God rather than men. According to Willard, women ought "to move, in the orbit of our duty, around the Holy Centre of perfection, the companions, not the satellites of men." If women orbited around men, then they would have to "accompany them in their wildest deviations." But if women were themselves "primary existencies" in orbit around a "Holy Centre," they could "shed" on their male companions "an influence that may help to keep them in their proper course."[12]

Willard identified several important characteristics of a good secondary school for young women. It should have ample classrooms; adequate equipment, ranging from musical instruments to scientific apparatus; and a well-stocked library. It should provide "suitable" instruction in religion, composition, literature, and science. It should also instruct students in housewifery, teaching them "neatness and order…as a virtue," and finish off the education with art and music. Young women should study for three years, beginning no sooner than age fourteen. They should meet minimal qualifications for admission, follow a prescribed course of study, and be subject to public examinations.[13]

Willard saw a number of benefits to improving women's education, not the least of which was preparing good teachers. She argued in favor of transforming the profession of teaching into a women's profession in order to free men to serve in other capacities.[14] Even more significantly, Willard tied the success of the republican form of government to appropriate concern for educating women, suggesting that the failure of other republics in history could be traced to the neglect of "the formation of female character." Historically, "loss of republican manners and virtues has preceded the loss of republican government."[15] Echoing the sentiments of More and Staughton, she maintained that only "barbarians" and "tyrants" degraded women. In other words, one could determine the degree to which a nation was civilized by measuring the status of its female inhabitants. Efforts to improve the condition and education of women were a sure sign of national progress, and Americans ought to "lead rather than follow in the march of human improvement."[16] Willard concluded, "Who knows how great and good a race of men may yet arise from the forming hand of mothers, enlightened by the bounty of that beloved country—to defend her liberties—to plan her future improvement—and to raise her to unparalleled glory?"[17]

A decade after Willard first published her views on the subject, Catherine Beecher offered a plan that bore a striking similarity to Willard's. Beecher, like Willard, emphasized the connection between motherhood and teaching. Mothers and teachers, according to Beecher, had the job of forming the character of succeeding generations.[18] A woman's "express business" was "to rear the body and form the mind," but the general neglect of appropriate female education meant that most women devoted almost no effort to learning how to fulfill those two crucial responsibilities.[19] Beecher went much further than Willard in her arguments in favor of feminizing the teaching profession. At her Hartford Female Seminary, she insisted that students not only study every subject, but that they learn how to teach each subject as well.[20] Beecher's philosophy of teaching—that a good teacher ought to "gain the affections" of her students and not have to depend upon the exercise of authority—provided a primary justification for women being teachers, based on the assumption that women represented affection and men authority.[21] In particular, women ought to teach girls because women were most adept at guiding and instructing by means of the "affections" and because good teaching required "familiarity of intercourse" inappropriate between male teachers and female students.[22] Finally, Beecher maintained that, for women, teaching represented "the road to honourable independence, and extensive usefulness, where she need not outstep the proscribed boundaries of feminine modesty."[23]

It was under the guidance of Mary Lyon that the ideals of female education articulated by Rush, More, Willard, and Beecher reached their highest expression in the first half of the nineteenth century. Lyon received her own education at Byfield Academy in Massachusetts, under the tutelage of Joseph and Rebecca Hasseltine Emerson.[24] In 1837, Lyon fulfilled her ideal of women's education by establishing Mount Holyoke Female Seminary in South Hadley, Massachusetts. Lyon, like Beecher, viewed teaching as an appropriate "sphere of usefulness" for women, but she also believed that education should "qualify ladies for other spheres of usefulness" as well.[25] Those "other spheres" she defined as the arena of "Christian Benevolence."[26] Christian women teachers would prepare workers to carry the "blessing of salvation to the 200,000,000, the estimated proportion of the inhabitants of this benighted world to be converted to the gospel through our instrumentality."[27] She viewed her new seminary as "rendering female education a handmaid to the gospel and an efficient auxiliary in the great work of renovating the world."[28]

Lyon further extended the "household" of young women to embrace the whole world, insisting that, while they were "pioneers in the great work of renovating the world," such women did not violate standards of female behavior.[29]

> All her duties are retired and private, and not public like those of the other sex. Whatever she does beyond her own family, should be but another application and illustration of social and domestic excellence. She may occupy the place of an important teacher; but her most vigorous labors should be modest and unobtrusive. She may go on a foreign mission; but she will there find a retired spot, where, away from the public gaze, she may wear out, or lay down a valuable life. She may promote the interests of a Sabbath School, or be an angel of mercy to the poor and afflicted—she may seek in various ways to increase the spirit of benevolence, and the zeal for the cause of missions, and she may labor for the salvation of souls. But her work is to be done by the whisper of her still and gentle voice, by the silent step of her unwearied feet, and by the power of her uniform and consistent example.[30]

Lyon's commitment to the cause of foreign missions was legendary. She urged the faculty and students at Mount Holyoke to give liberally to the cause, in part because she believed that the money supporters had given to found the seminary would otherwise have gone to foreign missions. Hence, the school had a lasting debt to pay. She declined the $800 annual salary the board offered her, accepting only $200 instead, and giving $90 of that each year to the ABCFM. She gave out of personal conviction and to set an example for her faculty and students. Lyon's commitment dated to her childhood when she remembered hearing tales of a heroic William Carey and the excitement surrounding the founding of the ABCFM.[31] From 1842 to 1849, Mount Holyoke faculty and students gave, on average, $1,000 annually to the cause of missions.[32]

American women who became missionaries benefited from those developments in education for girls and young women and exported them to the lands they called the "Orient." As noted in Chapter Two, those young women invariably came from families who valued their daughters' education, and most received a secondary education at female academies, including Emma Willard's Utica Female Seminary, Catherine Beecher's Hartford Female Seminary, and Mary Lyon's Mt. Holyoke. In fact, as early as 1849, thirty-five Mount Holyoke women were on the rolls of the ABCFM, and by 1860 sixty women from the school had served or were then serving the ABCFM and other boards as missionary teachers.[33] Because of the educational backgrounds of missionary women, educational practices for girls and young women as they evolved on the mission field paralleled American developments.

As the previous chapter noted, most missionary wives in the "Orient," like Sarah Lanman Smith, gathered "family boarding schools" by bringing indigenous children, especially girls, into their households and giving them rudimentary instruction in reading, writing, and housekeeping. The primary purpose of such arrangements was to provide religious instruction, with the Bible and a catechism providing the main, if not the only, instructional texts. Most mission stations soon adopted the practice of organizing more formal educational institutions. Such schools often developed as day pupils joined the family boarding schools. In some instances, missionaries established large boarding schools with separate facilities. Initially, missionary wives and daughters staffed the "infant" and girls' schools.

The ABCFM's schools in Ceylon provide a good example of those developments. In 1816, the ABCFM chose Ceylon as the site of its second mission in Asia. Samuel Newell, a member of the board's original band of missionaries, had taken refuge there in 1813 after the EIC barred him from Bombay and after the death of his wife, Harriet, at sea. At his urging, the board undertook the second mission. The primary reason for the initial focus on Ceylon was pragmatic, however: in 1816, when the mission commenced, a British governor friendly to missions ruled the island rather than the hostile EIC.

The board opted to focus on the predominantly Tamil-speaking and Hindu province of Jaffna as affording the most promising beachhead for eventually launching an effort in the southeastern provinces of the Indian subcontinent. Jaffna had been the object of missionary exertion since the sixteenth century, when the Portuguese ruled the island. The Portuguese had established thirty-seven Roman Catholic parishes in the province, each overseen by Franciscan or Dominican missionaries. Portuguese authorities provided the missionaries with churches and houses constructed of coral, as well as lands for their support. When the Dutch seized possession in the mid-seventeenth century, they ejected the Catholics (or tried to) and established the Reformed Church of the Netherlands in place of Catholicism. They banned Hindu ceremonies and required those who sought government offices to convert to Protestant Christianity. The Dutch appropriated and repaired the Catholic churches, establishing a district school in each. Rufus Anderson, long-time secretary and historian of the ABCFM, noted that the Dutch secured school attendance by fining the parents for their children's non-attendance. According to Anderson, the Dutch required little for church membership and provided only rudimentary instruction. As for preaching, he claimed that between 1642 and 1725, "only eight [Dutch clergymen] could preach in the native language, four in Tamil and four in Singhalese."[34] Nor had the Dutch attempted to disseminate the Bible and other Christian literature in the vernacular. They had operated almost entirely through the medium of interpreters, thus creating a barrier against the indigenization of Christian principles and church structures. According to American missionary Miron Winslow, the Dutch Reformed Church was a "soulless religion" that secured nominal conversions because the colonial government required religious conformity and that declined steadily until England acquired possession of the island around the turn of the nineteenth century.[35]

Unlike the Dutch, the British did not require religious conformity and secured few funds for education. When the British came to power, bringing with them a policy of religious toleration, 136,000 people in Jaffna claimed adherence to Protestant Christianity. By 1806, Claudius Buchanan declared Protestantism all but extinct in the region, with a handful clinging to Catholicism and the majority reverting to Hinduism. Miron Winslow noted in 1816 that the northern province of Jaffna contained a handful of Singhalese and European Protestants, one "native Christian preacher," and two British Wesleyan missionaries. Besides these, he wrote, "*the whole district was a wild waste of heathenism.*"[36]

Buchanan publicized the "deplorable" state of Protestantism in Jaffna in his *Christian Researches in Asia*, and the English societies soon undertook missions there. The field offered a wide scope for work, however. The British governor welcomed the Americans. Upon their arrival in the capital city of Colombo in 1816, he gave them possession of the old parish churches and lands at Batticotta and Tillipally, a grant soon followed by six other parishes.

The missionaries immediately established a boys' boarding school at Tillipally, boarding schools being preferred as the most effective means of shielding children from the "influence of heathen society."[37] By 1818, eight stations existed. Seven hundred male pupils also attended village day schools, and many, along with their fathers and brothers, attended Sunday worship. By contrast, in all the stations combined, only about twelve girls and twelve adult women attended Sunday worship in that entire year.[38] The mission continued its strategy of establishing boarding schools for boys, whom they had little difficulty attracting when they began teaching English, a knowledge of which opened doors to "lucrative positions in government offices, plantations, and mercantile houses."[39] Eventually, only converts and graduates of the boarding schools could hold teaching posts in the village schools, but initially, native "heathen" teachers taught at those schools.

The American missionaries also wanted to establish a college with a six-year curriculum. They argued that only through prolonged and intensive instruction on the "evidences of Christianity" (both in Scripture and in nature) would they succeed in prying the Tamil people from Hinduism. One advocate of broad education in the mission schools argued,

> They must learn to bring their credulous belief in everything marvelous to the test of reason, and understand the difference between truth and fable, and think, compare, reflect; things which the great mass of peoples in India never do.... It might easily be shown that so contrary as to fact are the principles of Geology, Natural Philosophy, and Astronomy, as laid down in their sacred books, that even a superficial acquaintance with these branches of science would explode their systems, and materially affect the credit of the books which contain them.[40]

Undermining the Brahmins' teaching was seen as essential to undercutting the system of caste:

> It was the Hindu assertion that maintenance of caste status was incompatible with conversion and the realization that it was caste rather than faith or intellectual conviction which restrained some from seeking baptism which led the missionaries to develop a critique of caste and a dual strategy for its overthrow: a running battle with the caste system as a whole in the belief that this was a central element in the total engagement with idolatry, and the complete exclusion of observances based on caste from the indigenous church.[41]

Thus, the missionaries viewed caste as the principal obstacle both to conversion and to progress toward civilization.[42] Mission schools afforded an opportunity to attack caste not only through the curriculum, but also through the structure of the schools themselves—that is, by refusing to allow caste distinctions in the classroom and dormitory. The missionaries "believed it to be entirely impossible to fulfill the ethical demands of Christian faith or to build up a true church if caste practices were maintained."[43] Their strategy thus included an "attack on the whole interlocking complex" of Hinduism.[44] The British colonial government refused to grant permission for the proposed college and theological seminary, however. Instead, the missionaries enlarged the boarding school at Batticotta into Central High School for the boys of the province and offered in it much the same curriculum that they would have offered at a college.

Great resistance to the idea of girls' education prevailed on the part of the Hindu residents of Jaffna. True to missionary assumptions that Hindus permitted only the "dancing girls" (i.e., "prostitutes" to the missionaries) associated with the temples to learn to read, the missionaries found upon their arrival in 1816 "only three respectable females in Jaffna...able to read and write."[45] Missionary wives persisted in their attempts to get at least a few girls in school, and some girls boarded as early as 1818.

On 8 June 1819, Miron and Harriet Winslow, with three other missionary couples, departed Boston. They arrived at Colombo in late December and shortly thereafter reported to their station at Oodooville.

One of the first things the newly arrived missionary wives did was to tour two of the Wesleyan missionary schools. Harriet noted in a letter on 16 January 1820 that she found the schools promising and was "much gratified by their appearance." Nevertheless, she gently criticized the skill of the teachers. "When I see missionaries, habituated to the use of words beyond the comprehension of the ignorant, attempting to instruct children," she wrote, "I am more and more convinced that females should be employed among the heathen."[46] Harriet thus expressed her belief that the nurturing qualities of women that naturally fitted them for motherhood also made them natural teachers.

Harriet embarked on her efforts for girls' education almost immediately. Not long after the Winslows arrived at Oodooville in 1820, two little girls began to loiter about their house, peeking in the windows and then running away. Harriet gradually persuaded them to stay for short periods by offering them fruit. She then began teaching them to sew and finally persuaded them to learn to read. After about six months, she asked their parents to let them come and live with her: "They however could not think of having their children 'lose caste' by eating on our premises, and there was 'no custom' for girls to be instructed. The father of one of them was the keeper of a devil's temple next door to us; a very bad man. The mother was little better."[47] This passage indicated Harriet's assessment of the condition of Tamil girls generally. Their parents, being "heathen," could not be good parents; therefore, she was justified in her efforts to get them to give up their daughters. Their main opposition, as far as she could see, consisted in their devotion to caste—not their natural affection for their daughters. Finally, the parents simply could not see a reason for girls to be taught anything. They did, however, permit the girls to continue coming by day, and Harriet gradually acquired boarding scholars from among the daughters of the native Christians. Eventually, one of the two day students pleaded with her father to let her go to the boarding school. He agreed on the condition that Harriet promise to find a husband for her when she reached marriageable age.

In October 1821, Harriet was able to report to Mrs. Payson, secretary of the Maternal Association in Portland, Maine, that

> In obtaining female children to instruct, we have much reason for thankfulness that of late we have had some success. "Females have no custom to learn," is the universal excuse, and generally it has more weight than all we can urge in favor of what would prepare them for usefulness and happiness. We consider every female child added to our number as a great acquisition, on account of her subsequent influence, and of the strength of prejudice and custom against females being instructed.[48]

By April 1823, she noted that "several schools for girls only have lately been established in the mission, which shows a great change in the feelings of the people. Heretofore they have strongly opposed every thing like learning in females."[49]

The missionaries established a central boarding school for girls at Oodooville in September of 1823. Missionary wives at each of the stations had instructed a small number of girls, sixteen of whom were among the twenty-two in the first class of the boarding school. The missionaries designed the boarding school "to take girls away from the heathen influences of their homes, and so provide suitable companions for the graduates of the Batticotta Seminary."[50] Responsibility for the school fell to Harriet Winslow, a charge she welcomed with some trepidation. She wrote in September 1823,

> It is agreed to have the Female Central School here. I feel that it is a great object; but how can I undertake it while so unfaithful to my present charge? Yet I wish to do all I can; and perhaps this is in answer to the prayer, "Lord, what wilt thou have me to do?" I have used this petition more frequently of late than formerly. If it is the will of God that the school should come here, may we be prepared by his Spirit to enter on the work with right hearts, feeling our helplessness and entire dependence on him.[51]

Harriet later wrote of her students, "We are training them up to be christian teachers, and wives for our native assistants. Three of those who are hopefully pious are now teaching girls' schools, and they do much better with them than men. The benefits visible to the people are already such that we have now *many more girls brought to us than we can receive*, and we could obtain almost any number."[52] For the first twenty years of the school's existence, in fact, the missionaries considered it necessary to have the girls stay in the boarding school (which they generally entered between the ages of six and twelve) until they married Christian husbands from the boys' Central High School or Batticotta Seminary. The mission provided their clothing and board and gave them a dowry of twenty-five dollars if they married "with the approval of the mission."[53] Miron Winslow noted that "furnish[ing] suitable partners for the native preachers" was, in fact, a "leading object" of girls' education. "It was considered of great importance that they should marry educated and especially christian wives," he wrote. "If not, they would probably form unscriptural connections with the heathen, which would injure their usefulness and perhaps destroy their souls."[54] Furthermore, while the missionaries intended their own families to serve as living illustrations of the effects of the gospel, they recognized that *indigenous* Christian families would send a more powerful message.

In 1822, for example, a young man who had been living with the Richards missionary family converted and decided that he wanted a well-educated Christian woman for a wife. He chose a young woman who had attended a village school for girls taught by one of the missionary wives. She had been one of the best students and had made a profession of faith and entered into full communion in the church. She was, however, "of comparatively low caste and with scarcely half the dowry he might receive with a heathen wife." Nevertheless, citing the advantage of her education, he broke caste and married her against "popular sentiment." He further offended his family and friends, according to the missionaries, by adopting the virtually unheard of practice of eating his meals in her company. "The immediate effect was so favorable," Rufus Anderson later recorded, "that three girls of high caste from the village where [the girl] lived applied for admission to the school."[55] Anderson, with this statement, demonstrated the underlying assumption of nineteenth-century missionaries that Hindu women had only to see the effect of Christianity on their status and value in the eyes of men to desire conversion. Winslow reported proudly that before his wife, Harriet, died in 1833, twelve of her female students had married Christian husbands: "They were settled among idolaters, where they had opportunity, as christian wives and christian mothers, to exhibit a pleasing contrast with heathen families, and to show the loveliness of domestic virtue in the midst of abounding vice. One such example in a dark heathen neighborhood is like a star on the thick brow of night."[56]

When Harriet died in 1833, another missionary couple, the Spauldings, took over. Marking the evolution in thinking, both about teaching as a women's vocation and about the role of single women in missions, Eliza Agnew joined them in 1837. Together, the three oversaw the Central Girls' Boarding School at Oodooville for more than thirty-five years. In 1846, the mission stopped providing a dowry, and a few years after that began to limit the term of residence. By 1850, the mission began to charge some of the more affluent students for a portion of their board. Even with such changes, however, the school continued to receive more applicants than they could admit. The pupils came from all castes except the highest and lowest, but distinctions of caste were not recognized within the school. The school experienced modest success. In its first eighteen years, a total of 295 students had attended. That the school's primary value to the mission was as an agency of conversion is evidenced by Rufus Anderson's pleasure in reporting that, of those 295 students, 175 "became church members, and not more than twelve of these dishonored their profession."[57] To demonstrate further the role of the boarding schools in evangelizing young people, Anderson offered a number of statistics. For example, in an "awakening" at the Jaffna stations in the winter of 1824–1825, the missionaries recorded forty-one conversions, "of whom thirty-six belonged to the boarding schools. "[58] By July of 1831, a total of 204 people had received communion in the board's Protestant churches, of whom 117 attended the boarding schools and thirty served as native teachers.[59] Anderson concluded his discussion of the boarding schools by noting that in all of "the visitations of divine grace previous to 1835,...the favoring circumstances of the boarding-schools were powerful auxiliaries to the preaching of the Gospel, and consequently the revivals stand connected both with preaching and with education as instrumental causes."[60] The early efforts of Harriet Lathrop Winslow at the Girls' Central Boarding School at Batticotta, in the northern Jaffna province of Ceylon, eventually resulted in one of the more widespread networks of mission schools in Asia, and one of the more enduring schools for girls, demonstrating for an American audience the efficacy of the educational strategy in missions.

As the role of mission schools for girls expanded and the number of those schools multiplied, mission boards began to see the expediency of adding some judiciously chosen single women to the ranks of missionaries to take charge of those schools. Several factors motivated this gradual shift, which began in the 1830s and became a solidly entrenched practice by the 1860s. For one thing, there was a growing sense that missionary wives, like Harriet Winslow, were working themselves into early graves. Also, the sheer numbers of children waiting for instruction on the one hand, and the persistence of single women applying to the boards on the other, made the employment of single women seem like a providential provision rather than a mere human (and therefore suspect) innovation. Mary Lyon declared, "It is my humble opinion that the leadings of Providence should be decisive to justify our encouraging an unmarried female to go on a foreign mission."[61] Furthermore, the trend toward employing single women as teachers on the mission field paralleled the growing acceptance of teaching as a suitable vocation for single women in the United States. Fidelia Fiske, a single woman who embarked on a career as a missionary teacher in Persia in 1843, provides an instructive example of that trend.

The circumstances surrounding ABCFM missions to the Nestorian population of Persia differed markedly from those among the Hindu population in India and Ceylon.[62] The board sent Eli Smith and Harrison Dwight to survey the Persian field in the early 1830s. They concluded that "large bodies of nominal Christians" existed throughout the region, requiring only Protestantizing to revive their "spiritual life" and shed "a flood of light [that] would illumine the Turkish empire and shine far up into Central Asia." To evangelicals of the early nineteenth century, the collapse of Islam ranked with the fall of Catholicism and the conversion of the Jews as the three major events that would precede the advent of the millennium. The board believed that direct evangelization of Muslims by Westerners would effect little, however. In their view, God was going to use the instrumentality of the "Oriental church" to evangelize the Muslims: "We may not hope for the conversion of the Mohammedans, unless true Christianity be exemplified before them by the Oriental Churches. To them the native Christians represent the Christian religion, and they see they are no better than themselves. They think them worse; and therefore the Moslem believes the Koran to be more excellent than the Bible."[63]

Their research led the board to establish the Nestorian mission in 1833. Justin Perkins was the first missionary. Asahel and Judith Grant joined Perkins in 1835. The missionaries began a boarding school for boys and young men in 1836, along with several village day schools. Attempts to attract girls to the village schools were fruitless. Judith Grant began the work among Nestorian women by teaching her "female domestics" to read. Through visiting and conversation, she tried gradually "to interest mothers in the education of their daughters." Finally, on 12 March 1838, she began a girls' school with four pupils.[64] Judith, however, died in January of 1839 at age twenty-five, less than a year after commencing her work for the education of Nestorian women. Even though other missionary wives tried to keep the effort going, fewer than sixty of over five hundred pupils in the mission schools were girls in 1841. That year, however, Perkins went to the United States with a Nestorian bishop, Mar Yohannan, and succeeded in recruiting Fidelia Fiske to go to Persia and carry forward the educational work for girls.

Fidelia Fiske was born near the village of Shelburne in western Massachusetts, the fourth of six daughters of Rufus and Hannah Fiske. She came from devout Congregational stock. Her Fiske ancestors had first arrived in North America during the Puritan Great Migration of the 1630s. Her uncle, Pliny Fiske, departed the United States in 1819 to serve as the ABCFM's first missionary to Palestine. Because of that family connection, the nascent foreign missions movement became a "daily topic of conversation" in her home from the time she was three years old, and her life was in many ways steeped in that cause.[65] Her mother taught her to read, using not only the Bible, but also the popular Congregational magazine the *Missionary Herald.* She often entertained herself as a child by pretending that she was a missionary, drawing information for her imagined scenarios from her Uncle Pliny's letters. When she was eleven, a missionary to Greece visited in her family's home. When he took his departure, he patted her on the head and told her that when she grew up, she ought to follow in her uncle's footsteps and go out to "teach the heathen the gospel."[66] Years later, as a student at Mount Holyoke, she shared a room with the daughter of a missionary to Hawaii. Visiting missionaries made frequent stops at Mount Holyoke. Fidelia recorded having heard "Mr. Parker, from China, Mr. Thurston, from the Sandwich Islands, Mrs. Butler, from the Choctaws, [and] Mr. Perkins, accompanied by Mar Yohannan, from Persia."[67]

Fidelia benefited greatly from the revolution in women's education during the first third of the nineteenth century. She attended the village school from age four to twelve and showed both an aptitude and a taste for learning. The compiler of her memoir noted that she "learned with great facility" and "early manifested a disposition to learn *thoroughly* whatever was assigned her."[68] She loved to read; in addition to the Bible and the *Missionary Herald*, she had read the *Memoir of Henry Martyn* (a noted British missionary to India), Cotton Mather's *Magnalia Christi Americani*, and Timothy Dwight's *Theology* (twice) by the time she was eight years old. She also manifested a strong sense of "self-reliance," usually choosing to puzzle out for herself those things that she did not understand.[69]

Fidelia's conversion occurred over a period of seven years, beginning when she was eight years old. She later recalled having an "agitated and burdened heart" as a result of conversations with a visiting minister. She "wept" much and "earnestly" longed for salvation. Her older sister's conversion at age eleven while a student at Mary Lyon's Buckland school made "an indelible impression" on Fidelia's mind. Two years later, a Sunday school teacher implored her students to give their hearts to Jesus. Fidelia could not and carried the "burden" for months. She characterized that period as one of rebellion against God as unjust in his condemnation. This began the process of "humbling" her pride and bringing her to the conviction that God's wrath was not unjust, but that she deserved it. She then despaired of God's mercy because of a conviction that she did not deserve it. Then, and only then, did she discover a willingness "to accept the terms of mercy." Fidelia made her public profession of faith on 12 July 1831, at age fifteen. By her own account, the outward evidence of her salvation occurred in a newfound "usefulness" in fulfilling Christian duty: seeking her friends' conversion and teaching Sunday school.[70]

From 1833 to 1839, Fidelia taught in the local school while living at home. She spent two terms at private academies furthering her own education. The pivotal moment of her life occurred in the fall of 1839 when she entered Mount Holyoke Female Seminary. Late in the spring of 1840, a typhoid fever epidemic struck the school. Fidelia became ill shortly after arriving home for the summer vacation. Her father and sister caught the disease from her and died; she very nearly died herself. She long remembered that period in the "valley of the shadow" as a time when she learned compassion for the sick and suffering and when she "gained vivid impressions in regard to the reality of the invisible world," which inspired her with a great concern for the "dying multitudes." She considered her illness a school in which God prepared her for the work she would later do in Persia.[71] Her career became a means of sanctifying her affliction: making valuable use of the deaths of her father and sister and of her own suffering.

Fidelia returned to Mount Holyoke for her senior year in the fall of 1841, graduating in August 1842. She returned to South Hadley that October to join the Mount Holyoke faculty. During her six-week vacation, she read ABCFM missionary Justin Perkins's book, *Eight Years Residence in Persia*, not realizing that in a few months she would be on a ship with Perkins headed for Persia herself. That autumn, Mary Lyon, founder and principal of Mount Holyoke, attended the annual meeting of the ABCFM at Norwich, Connecticut. She came back convinced that her seminary should renew its dedication to the cause of missions. Her efforts in that respect ended up costing her six of twelve teachers, including Fidelia Fiske, who went abroad as missionaries.[72] To inspire the students in their support of the cause, Lyon brought a steady stream of missionaries to the school to speak. On 16 January 1843, Justin Perkins came to South Hadley with Mar Yohannan in hopes of finding teachers for the female seminary at Oroomiah, Persia. On the evening of his arrival, Lyon announced at evening prayers that Dr. Perkins needed two teachers and asked anyone who was interested to give her a note privately. She got forty responses and met that same evening with Perkins to evaluate them. Most of the note-writers had emphasized their qualifications. Fidelia, however, had only written, "If counted worthy, I should be willing to go." Her humble attitude, along with Lyon's strong recommendation, led Perkins to extend an offer to her.

The compiler of her memoir, interestingly, felt it necessary to assure his audience that Fidelia's desire to be a missionary was no mere response to impending spinsterhood: "How much this secretly cherished hope of being a missionary had to do with the reasons which led her to decline a proposal to become the wife of a New England pastor, it is scarcely pertinent to inquire. Certain it is that the want of an eligible offer of marriage was not among the motives that predisposed her to a missionary life."[73] Fidelia encountered fierce opposition from her family. During her period of indecision, Perkins wrote to Lyon, "I do hope Miss Fiske will go and help plant a Holyoke in Oroomiah. We shall justly consider it the loveliest plant of the East—'The Rose of Sharon.'" Fidelia, with Mary Lyon's help, persisted and finally won her family's approval. By early March, she was on board a ship. In mid-June, she arrived at her place of service in Oroomiah.[74]

Even before the opportunity to go to Persia presented itself, Fidelia evidenced her preconceptions about the Nestorians among whom she would serve. In particular, she adopted the missionary practice of seeing in dirtiness and poverty a symbol of all that was physically and spiritually "degrading" and "oppressive" in "Oriental" culture—of the people's need both for salvation and for social redemption. Upon reading Justin Perkins' account of the mission in Persia, prior to assuming her post at Mount Holyoke, she recorded in her journal, "How I should love to teach those little children! It would be just such employment as I should like, to go out into the streets and pick them up and comb their hair, and wash their faces."[75] Less than a year later, she described some Nestorians coming out to meet her as she approached their town:

> As we came in, the hill that overlooks the village was literally covered with men, women and children. Their tattered garments and great filthiness showed their extremely degraded condition. Yet their willingness to hear inspires us with the hope that something may be done to raise them to the ranks of "freemen in Christ Jesus." When we reached the dwelling of the bishop, we found it, like those about it, a miserable hut of mud.[76]

If the filth and poverty of the people spoke volumes of their need for salvation, the condition of the women particularly marked them as a heathen people. A letter to her brother and sister encapsulated virtually all of the tropes then in circulation regarding "Oriental" women—forbidden to learn to read, employed in heavy agricultural labor, forced to marry very young, and forbidden to take meals with their husbands:

> Oh, could you see these poor females, as they are, you would be thankful that you have a sister to spare them! None of them read, and few of them have any correct ideas of eternity, or the God to whom they are accountable. Their days are spent in those labors, which, in our country, are performed by the other sex alone. To the fields they carry their little ones, as they engage in their work.... At night they return to their homes, milk their cows, prepare supper for their husbands, and then eat alone. To eat with their husband is the height of indelicacy in their view. They marry very young; often at the age of eighteen they are the mothers of two or three children. To be the mother of sons is considered a great blessing, but of daughters a great misfortune.[77]

Fidelia considered it a "sadly significant fact that the language of the Nestorians contained no words corresponding to home and wife, the nearest approach to them being house and woman."[78] Men considered women "drudges and slaves," subjecting them to regular beatings.[79] Women commonly lied and used profanity, Fidelia maintained, and often revealed their "degradation" by engaging in fisticuffs, pulling hair, and throwing stones and rotten eggs at each other to settle their quarrels. "You say, and justly, other women than these were 'last at the cross and first at the sepulchre,'" she wrote to a friend, referring to the widely held belief that the Nestorians were one of the lost tribes of Israel, descended from early Christian converts from Judaism. "But *those* may once have been like *these*." Fidelia thus suggested that an acquaintance with the redeeming power of the cross and the resurrection would elevate those animal-like Nestorian women to the level of virtue held by the female devotees who stayed with Jesus when all of the male disciples had run away out of fear and despair.

Fidelia viewed her life's work as helping "to raise these poor females to the place which their Maker designed should be theirs."[80] The ABCFM and the missionaries in Persia considered boarding schools the most effective method, hence Fidelia's presence as one of the few single women then employed by the board. Upon their arrival in Persia in 1833, the first missionaries had found only one woman who could read. They had opened three day schools by 1836, but could not get girls to attend. On 12 March 1838, through her "indefatigable zeal," Judith Grant had opened a girls' school with four children. When she died the following January, several male missionaries and their wives sustained the school, but the pupils did not advance very far. The school had only day students, all living with their own families. With such an arrangement, "comparatively little could be done, especially for the moral improvement of girls who were still, more than half the time, breathing the tainted atmosphere in which they were nurtured."[81]

By September 1843, within a few months of her arrival in Persia, Fidelia was meeting regularly to read with a small group of young girls. She wanted to transform the day school into a boarding school where the children could receive "the continuous and exclusive care and training of the teachers."[82] The Nestorians, however, found the idea of educating their daughters "repugnant," according to Fidelia. They feared that being away from heavy work in the fields and vineyards for several years would render them unfit for such work. Even the fathers studying in the mission seminary refused to give up their daughters for education, saying that it was unnecessary because girls could not serve as priests or deacons and therefore had no need to read. Furthermore, they feared that educating their daughters would render them unmarriageable. Most Nestorian girls were betrothed by the age of twelve and for several years prior to that had to devote a considerable amount of time to preparing household linens and clothing in anticipation of marriage.[83] Setting obstacles aside, however, the governing committee of the mission voted to approve the proposed girls' boarding school and set aside funds to support six pupils. Fidelia's first task—finding six pupils—had commenced.

With the help of Mar Yohannan, Fidelia ultimately succeeded, and the Female Seminary at Oroomiah was born. She based her program and method of instruction on Mount Holyoke's, making due allowance for the younger ages and relative lack of preparation of her students. She did not intend completely to remove them from their culture. They did not have beds but instead made up pallets on the floor after their own custom. Fidelia made new clothing for each pupil, since their own was usually ragged and infested with fleas and lice. She made it, however, after the "native fashion." "They eat with their hands," she wrote, "as knives and forks cannot be obtained in this country, and we have no reason to suppose they will ever have them after leaving us."[84] She nevertheless clearly intended the girls' boarding school experience to transform their lives spiritually, morally, intellectually, and physically. The curriculum included the basics: reading, writing, and arithmetic, with the Bible as primary text. The first lessons the pupils received, however, focused on personal hygiene, and Fidelia designed their daily routine to instill "habits of neatness and industry which will fit them for usefulness."[85] Like their Mount Holyoke counterparts, they helped with the domestic chores and also received basic instruction in sewing and knitting. Fidelia also decided that her young charges were devoid of consciences, so she set about teaching them right from wrong, especially focusing on the importance of truthfulness and the sinfulness of lying. She gradually introduced the Mount Holyoke system of giving a daily personal account of oneself, only on a much more basic scale. She focused on asking direct questions with easily verifiable answers, such as "Did you comb your hair today?" and "Were you late for prayers?"[86]

That Fidelia succeeded in her goal of recreating Mount Holyoke for the benefit of Nestorian girls is evident in her description of the first revival that occurred in the school at Oroomiah just over two years after its inception. It bore a remarkable resemblance to a revival that had occurred at Mount Holyoke during her first year there, in 1839–1840. That revival in South Hadley began on an appointed day of prayer with an intense spirit of prayer on the part of the students, along with a desire for solitude. Those who were "indulging hope" of salvation were invited to a special private prayer meeting in Mary Lyon's private quarters. All exhibited great anxiety for their souls, accompanied by much solemnity and weeping. "The number of hopeful conversions," wrote Fidelia's biographer, "was about thirty.... Amid the delightful scenes of such a revival, Miss Fiske was taking practical lessons which were to be invaluable to her in similar scenes, on missionary ground, in which she was to become so important a part."[87] The first of those "similar scenes" occurred in January of 1846 and continued for two months. As with the Mount Holyoke revival, the one at Oroomiah began on an appointed day of prayer. Several of the girls exhibited an unusually strong desire to be alone to pray. Fidelia allowed those who seemed under conviction to seclude themselves. The boarding school, not being supplied with an adequate number of closets like a good New England house, lacked space for privacy. Two of the pupils went so far as to retire to the "wood cellar," where they stacked wood to make "closets" for themselves.[88] As Mary Lyon had done before, Fidelia invited those who were "deeply affected" to join her in private meetings, where she "sought to show them the wickedness of their hearts, their utter alienation from God, and their need of a change of heart, and thus lead them to the sinner's only Friend." More than half the school was affected (perhaps a dozen students).[89] Even though the students left for a week of vacation in March, they returned manifesting the same spirit of solemnity. They were very quiet on their return, except for those who "burst into tears as they again met their companions." "The closets were immediately filled with those praying souls," Fidelia wrote a friend and fellow teacher at Mount Holyoke, noting that each closet had a line of girls three or four deep waiting for a turn to have private prayer. The boarding school revival had exactly the effect that the mission had hoped such an event would have on the larger community, for several of the girls' mothers also experienced conversion.[90]

The revival and its corresponding conversions confirmed for Fidelia Fiske her belief in the transforming power of the gospel and the importance of formal education in conveying that gospel to untutored minds. "The permanent effect of the revival in the general deportment of the scholars was marked and gratifying," she later recalled. The students lost their coarse and temperamental natures and became "gentle, affectionate, and tractable." Incidents involving theft and lying virtually disappeared. Fidelia's long struggle to instill a conscience into each girl seemed suddenly to take effect, for, according to her, "great tenderness of conscience was manifested, sins of which they had not been suspected were confessed, stolen articles were restored." Furthermore, even their intellectual development improved. Their ability to learn "seemed greatly quickened by grace in the heart. They had better lessons, wrote better compositions, and were in all respects better scholars, strikingly illustrating the power of the gospel, when received by faith, to elevate and improve the whole character and life."[91]

Fidelia Fiske's ministry at the head of the Female Boarding School at Oroomiah continued until 1858, when ill health forced her to return to the United States. Her own account of the work for Nestorian women, together with the memoir of her life, appeared at a propitious time, however. Those accounts, together with the body of missionary literature on "Oriental" women amassed over a half-century, within a decade proved influential in transforming the entire foreign missions movement into one dominated by single women and by strategies focused on social institutions such as schools and hospitals rather than primarily evangelistic enterprises.

6

"The Healing of The Nations"
Women's Medical Mission In The "Orient"

In 1877, eighty-nine-year-old Sarah Josepha Hale closed her lengthy career as editor of *Godey's Lady's Book* (arguably the most popular women's magazine in the United States in the nineteenth century) with this reminiscence:

> The first medical college for women in the world was founded in Philadelphia in 1850. I had often heard how strong was the gratitude and respect felt by the natives of India for men whose medical skill enabled them to alleviate their sufferings, and what an opportunity was thus afforded for the teaching of the Gospel. This suggested to me the idea of educating young women in medical knowledge to be sent as missionaries to the women of Heathendom.[1]

Hale pioneered in drawing the connection between women as physicians and women as missionaries. In 1851, she founded the Ladies Medical Missionary Society (LMMS) in Philadelphia and formulated an argument in favor of women receiving medical education in order to serve the foreign mission movement, most notably in Asia. Although she did not see the fruits of her labor until Methodist physician Clara Swain went to India in 1869, Hale's efforts on behalf of the LMMS laid the foundation for what became a major part of the women's foreign mission movement in the late nineteenth and early twentieth centuries.

Sarah Josepha Buell was born in 1788 in New Hampshire and received her education at home alongside her older brother, Horatio, until he left for Dartmouth. One of her biographers wrote that "it was a matter of regret to both that the accident of sex should exclude her from college."[2] During his summer vacations, Horatio came home and taught Sarah what he had learned. She taught school from 1806 until her marriage to David Hale in 1813. David Hale, an attorney, was also self-educated. They continued their studies together in their evenings at home until his sudden death from pneumonia in 1822. At the age of thirty-four, Sarah found herself a widow with five young children to support. After a brief (and unsuccessful) attempt at the millinery trade, Hale turned to writing. With the backing of some of her husband's friends, she published a volume of poetry and her first novel, *Northwood.* The novel became a bestseller in the United States and also enjoyed popularity in Great Britain. On the strength of its success, she received an offer in 1828 to edit the new *American Ladies Magazine*, headquartered in Boston. She held that position until 1836, when the magazine merged with Louis Godey's Philadelphia-based *Lady's Book* to form *Godey's Lady's Book*. From 1837 until 1877, she edited *Godey's Lady's Book*. Under her editorship, the magazine gained a national circulation and achieved great popularity. In its first year of publication, 1837, it had a circulation of 10,000; by 1860, that number had reached 150,000.[3]

Hale and publisher Louis Godey created and sustained the magazine's popularity by studiously avoiding discussion of sectional controversies. Although Hale used her "Editor's Table" as a platform from which to champion many reforms, she maintained silence on the subject of slavery. Popular (but abolitionist) writers such as Sarah Jane Clarke Lippincott quietly disappeared from the magazine's pages by 1850. Reading it in the 1860s, one would not know that the Civil War was underway.[4] Hale also fiercely opposed the movement for women's suffrage and served as principal architect and purveyor of what historians have called the "cult of domesticity."[5] Despite (or perhaps because of) her cultural conservatism, however, Hale frequently devoted her monthly column to issues related to the condition and status of women. Her own experiences—educating herself, teaching, and then having to support five young children—led her, early in her editorial career, to embrace the cause of education for girls and young women and argue in favor of transforming teaching into a women's profession. In the 1840s, she began to devote some of her energies to decrying the sickliness of women and calling for health and dress reforms to remedy that evil. Then, inspired by Elizabeth Blackwell's graduation from Geneva (NY) Medical College in 1848 and the founding of the Woman's Medical College of Pennsylvania in Philadelphia the following year, Hale added women's medical education to the list of causes that she championed from her "Editor's Table."[6] Her advocacy of women's medical education arose from a logical combination of her interest in women's education generally, in health reform, and in another favorite cause—Protestant foreign missions.

Historians of women and antebellum reform movements have tapped into *Godey's* in general and the "Editor's Table" in particular for their rich source material on benevolent activity, women's education, and the cult of domesticity.[7] Historians of missions have occasionally briefly noted Hale's support for women's medical missions.[8] Regina Morantz-Sanchez, a historian of medicine, has used Hale's columns to develop a nuanced understanding of the social context out of which the more conservative advocates of women's medical education emerged. She points out that Hale supported medical education for women "for the purpose of preparing them for missionary work."[9] No one, however, has explored how and why Hale developed her advocacy of women's medical education within the context of the foreigns mission movement. Combining the two allowed her to support the idea of vocational ministry for women and contributed substantially to the formulation of the idea of "woman's work for woman" that gained such prominence at the peak of the women's foreign missions movement in the late nineteenth century.

It is by now a truism among historians of women that middle-class white women in antebellum America were elevated by the various organs of bourgeois culture—sermons, tracts, advice manuals, novels, magazines, and consolation literature—to the status of "angels in the house." The ideal woman protected the home, made it clean and comfortable, nurtured children, and purified the men in her household from the contaminating influences of the political and economic marketplaces. *Godey's Lady's Book* is often cited as one of the chief purveyors of the "cult of true womanhood," its pages replete with such direct assertions as "woman…is the appointed guardian of whatsoever is good, pure and lovely in manners and morals."[10] Indirectly, every issue of the magazine buttressed that belief with articles, poetry, illustrations, reviews, and even brief quotes used as filler. Hale brought her belief in the purifying moral influence of women into the service of her argument in favor of opening the field of medicine to women by using the pages of her magazine to demonstrate a connection between the physical nature and the spiritual nature. According to Hale, women's inherently moral and spiritual nature fitted them to serve as physicians for other women and for children.

While historians of women and medicine have appropriated Hale's discourse in service of their particular interests, they have effectively extracted that discourse from the contexts in which Hale herself constructed it. Historians of women have portrayed the "angel in the house" as an ideal designed primarily by men to contain women within certain bounds and maintain social order—to keep women in their subordinate (and thus oppressed) places. Morantz-Sanchez and other historians of women in medicine have demonstrated that opponents of women's medical education used the image of the "angel in the house" as a primary reason for their opposition. Both the social order and the public virtue of the male citizenry hinged on the purifying moral influence of the woman in the home. Women who entered the public sphere by engaging in a profession such as medicine would themselves become contaminated and therefore could not fulfill their necessary social role. More radical advocates of women's medical education challenged that ethos at its root; that is, they denied the validity of the "angel in the house" and thus attacked the social order—hence the moniker "radical." Conservative advocates embraced the cultural values reflected by the metaphor, but used it to emphasize the nurturing and healing qualities that, in their view, made women eminently qualified to be doctors (and, later, professional nurses).[11]

Hale fit into the latter model because she linked the practice of medicine with the cultural ideal of the "angel in the house." Hale viewed the professional practice of medicine by women as a legitimate form of vocational ministry. She developed her arguments in favor of medical education for women specifically within the context of the Protestant deaconess and foreign missions movements. Furthermore, she did not view the "angel in the house" as simply a white, middle-class, cultural ideal to which American girls and women should aspire. Hale continued the by then well-established tradition of viewing women in Christian cultures as holding a high status that derived expressly from the tenets of Christianity. Furthermore, she also continued the practice of illustrating and reinforcing that point by using the unconverted "Oriental" woman as a point of negative comparison. Conversion to Christianity, however, would confer on the "Oriental" woman the same elevated status that her Western Christian counterparts held.

Hale supported her position favoring women's entry into the medical profession by drawing connections between physical and spiritual ailments. She argued that God and nature intended women to be "preservers"—preservers of home and moral purity and, by extension, preservers of health. Women needed medical education, she argued, to "fit" them "for their duties; one of the most important is to be the guardians of health as they are of morals."[12] Hale consistently connected physical health, treated through medical science, and moral/spiritual health, treated through religious faith. How can women understand the importance of "preserving health" and the means of doing so, she asked, unless "they know their own structure, their own nature, the laws of health, and the penalties of transgression?"[13] Furthermore, "as the *preserver*, women...will excel in the preventive department...and will bring about a renovation of the general health, and doubtless, a prolongation of human life."[14] The language of law, transgression, penalty and renovation evoked the image of a Protestant universe governed by spiritual laws of sin, punishment, and redemption.

Hale drew the connection between religion and medicine more expressly in quoting Frederika Bremer: "In the old times, the physician was also the priest and consecrated to holy mysteries." She went on to point out that the ancient physician Aesculapius supposedly spawned a "holy race," including a daughter named Hygeia, the "Goddess of Health." She then proclaimed that Hygeia "must be recalled to earth, she must have some room given to her, and justice done to her, if she is to present the earth with a new Hippocrates."[15] Hale also repeatedly used the image of the "ministering angel" to represent women in their healing capacity and to emphasize the religious nature of the art of healing.[16] Discussing the water cure, for example, she pointed out that "an angel from heaven took charge of the pool of Bethesda; an angel of earth ought to have charge of the pools for water cure."[17] In Jewish tradition, an angel watched over the pool of Bethesda in Jerusalem. Occasionally, the angel would stir the waters and the first person to enter the pool after that would receive healing for whatever malady ailed him. The Gospel of John relates an account of Jesus miraculously healing a lame man who had been waiting by the pool for thirty-eight years.[18] Hale's judicious reference to this familiar Bible story served a two-fold purpose. She connected women with the act of healing through her use of the word "angel," and she gave biblical authority to the spiritual nature of the healing arts through the oblique reference to the healing ministry of Jesus.

Further evidence that Hale viewed the practice of medicine by women as an essentially ministerial vocation appeared in her interest in the emerging Protestant deaconess movement in Europe.[19] This movement combined several of her interests: the need of educated women of all classes for meaningful vocational choices, the unique spiritual nature of women, and the suitability of women for medical work in a mission setting. The nineteenth-century movement to reintroduce deaconesses in Protestant churches on a large scale began in the town of Kaiserswerth in Rhenish Westphalia in 1833.[20] In 1831–1832, Lutheran minister Thomas Fliedner toured England and the Netherlands to raise money for his work as a Protestant Bible Society missionary in the Catholic community of Kaiserswerth. In London, he observed the work of prison reformer Elizabeth Fry, while in the Netherlands he had some contact with the deaconesses of the Mennonite churches. As part of his work for the Bible Society, Fliedner served as Protestant chaplain for a women's prison in Düsseldorf. He found that discharged female convicts rarely had a place to go or a means of earning a living, so they often ended up back in prison. He began a refuge for such women in the summerhouse in his back yard and began to train women to work with former prisoners and to train the former prisoners for some type of work. From that effort, he established in 1836 the Rhenish Westphalian Deaconess Society. The refuge in his backyard became a training institute where Protestant women of all classes could enter upon vocational ministries of nursing, midwifery, teaching, caring for orphans, and other types of charitable work. The first deaconess trained at Kaiserswerth was a physician's daughter who had trained under her father and subsequently instructed others in "nursing and hospital duties."[21] By mid-century, the movement had evolved into two orders of deaconesses, one for nursing and one for teaching.[22] The healing ministries—nursing, midwifery, and related hospital work—soon achieved dominance.

Because the role of deaconess was considered a full-time vocation, only single women and widows were eligible. Unlike Catholic sisterhoods and later high-church Anglican sisterhoods, however, Protestant deaconesses did not take vows for life; they generally made a five-year commitment to "service for Jesus' sake."[23] In exchange for their commitment, they received training, room and board, travel expenses to their field of labor, and a modest stipend for purchasing their uniforms—"plain, distinctive attire" consisting of dark blue dresses, blue aprons, and white caps and collars.[24] While training, they lived in a "mother-house" where they roomed in pairs and shared their meals. The Kaiserswerth Institute and other mother-houses maintained programs of Bible study, private devotion, and group worship. Upon completing their training they went often in pairs or small groups to work in hospitals, schools, and orphanages in Europe and in the Near East and India.[25] By the mid-nineteenth century, deaconess institutions had become the primary source for trained nurses on the continent and in England. In the latter third of the nineteenth century, some missionary societies also began sending single women to the deaconess institutions to train as nurses or teachers before sending them abroad to foreign stations. The Church of England Zenana Society, for example, sent women to the Mildmay Institution in London for medical training.[26] Furthermore, as American mission boards began sending single women as medical missionaries, they drew on the deaconess house model to address the main problems encountered earlier by single women missionaries abroad—being an outsider in someone else's household and conflicts with missionary wives over roles. Deaconess institutions proved that a group of single women could establish a home that could serve a socially redeeming role comparable to that of a traditional household headed by a father and maintained by an "angel in the house."

Accounts of the deaconess movement captivated Sarah Josepha Hale. In 1852, she ran an article by Frederika Bremer describing a "Visit to the Protestant Sisters of Mercy at Kaiserswerth."[27] Bremer pointed out that while most of the women training at Kaiserswerth came from the lower classes, the work for which they trained was eminently suitable for educated and pious Christian women of the middle and upper classes. She illustrated her point by focusing her description on "Miss T." Miss T. had "resigned all the pleasures which wealth and a respectable position could obtain for her" in order to become a deaconess.[28] Bremer painted a rosy portrait of Miss T.'s health, happiness, piety, and usefulness. Her language brought to mind the image of the "angel in the house." Miss T. was a "harmonious being" with a "beaming countenance."[29] With a graceful figure and a light step, "she seemed, as it were, borne upon invisible wings."[30] In fact, each time Bremer encountered her, she was "always borne aloft on the same invisible wings: all her movements, words, and glances seemed inspired by I know not what gay and elevating harmony."[31] This angel, however, was not a wife and mother presiding over the domestic hearth. She was a single woman, a trained nurse working in what was considered a professional Christian ministry.

That Hale selected this particular account of Kaiserswerth with the audience of *Godey's Lady's Book* in mind is evidenced by the concluding passage:

> And in this is the home, the sphere of operation, in which the poor and the mean of the world may become esteemed, noble, and useful members of the community; and not merely the unemployed of the lower, but those of the higher class.... There is everywhere a superfluity of the unemployed, even in the higher regions of society; and if they here become servants, they at the same time are elevated to *high-born* in the kingdom of God, and even in the judgment of the world; for, although the world may ridicule and blame that which appears eccentric in these respects, it always secretly esteems them.[32]

Four months later, Hale followed up Bremer's account and reiterated the suitability of the role of deaconess for the single, educated, middle- or upper-class woman. "WOMEN NEED EMPLOYMENT," she wrote. "Yes, women need a wider sphere of employment for their tastes, talents, and the affections. Then they would not invent delusions. Give them something to do which men consider important, and, if the education of the women has been at all judicious, see if their work be not done well." It was God, she wrote, who implanted within women "that thirst for action, useful action." She then offered evidence from the New Testament and from Christian history to justify re-establishing the diaconate of women in Protestant churches.[33]

The following spring, Hale returned to this theme. Arguing that "the present century is to be most extraordinary in its developments of the real position women ought to hold in the world" and that those developments would "prove what the influence, intelligence, and moral power of the sex can effect on the character of society," she listed as her first example the establishment of training schools for Protestant deaconesses. American churches should re-establish the diaconate of women, she maintained, because the "industrial excitement and pursuits of American men" made it extremely difficult to recruit men for the ministry. Deaconesses could relieve ministers of the responsibility for visiting the sick, thus freeing up the time of the ministers for preaching and restoring to women their "apostolic office." She further demonstrated the extent to which she connected the deaconess movement with the foreign mission movement and both of them with the cause of medical education for women by noting that while Americans had few deaconesses *at home*, they could "challenge the world for examples of love, patience, and usefulness" that would rival American women serving as missionaries in foreign lands. She immediately followed that statement with a letter from a female missionary in China, an account of medical education for women in the United States, and a brief report of the "doings" of the LMMS. She thus described in a single editorial column an entire framework of opportunity for women that incorporated spiritual mission, vocational ministry, and professional medical practice.[34]

Arguments in favor of women as teachers had often been couched in terms of their roles as mothers.[35] Hale incorporated that theme into her own discourse about women teachers and then transplanted the same argument to serve the cause of women's medical education. She frequently set aside the question of whether women ought to practice medicine professionally in order to argue in favor of medical education as suitable for all women because of their destinies as mothers. Under the heading of "self-evident propositions" she asserted that "mothers should know the best means of preserving the health of their children."[36] Medicine, she claimed, was actually "the study of the laws of life and health" and fell to the sphere of women because God had "delegated" to women the care and nurturing of children:

> That it would be very useful and conducive to the health and happiness of families, if the mothers of families, and women in general, were familiar with the principal doctrines of anatomy, physiology, and pathology, so as to understand, to some degree, the organization, functions, and diseases of the human system, there cannot be any doubt.... Her knowledge of medicine cannot be detrimental to society.[37]

Regarding the ability of women to study medicine, she noted that since God had "placed her at the fountain of life, given into her care the new-born child," one certainly could suppose that God had also provided the "capacity to learn how the child should be ordered."[38]

While Hale believed that all women possessed the ability to study medicine and would benefit from medical knowledge in their domestic responsibilities, she also maintained that the relationship of women to children justified medical careers for women. Announcing the plan of the Woman's Medical College of Pennsylvania to open a children's hospital, she noted that a woman physician would supervise it:

> To woman's care the little "drooping buds" will be given. Woman is gifted with insight to understand the nature of children. God has endowed her for this mission: and when she is encouraged to cultivate her gifts, and permitted to exercise them in treating the diseases of women and children, the world will see a marked improvement in the health of our people.[39]

Hale regularly published the writings of male physicians who shared her views. One such article by Dr. William M. Cornell, titled "Woman the True Physician," maintained that since women spent so much more time with children, they were more attuned to their needs and complaints than men and could thus serve more effectively as their physicians.[40] Dr. John Stainback Wilson, a regular contributor to the magazine's "Health Department," agreed that all women would benefit from medical education for carrying out the most important of their domestic duties: "the mental, moral, and physical education of children." He nevertheless recognized that circumstances would not allow for all or even most women to pursue such education. Those who did have the opportunity, therefore, should avail themselves of it and become physicians to consult with other women and help them fulfill their responsibility to preserve the health of their children.[41]

Hale also viewed the special relationship between women and children as an important reason for training women as medical missionaries. The preamble to the constitution of the LMMS opened with the words, "Believing that God, in committing the care of the young especially to woman, imposes on her the duty of preparing herself, in the best possible manner, for her important vocations, among which are the care of her own health, the physical well-being of her children, and tendence on the sick, suffering, and helpless."[42] In her "Appeal to American Christians" to support the LMMS in affording medical training to missionary wives and "pious unmarried ladies," she particularly noted the importance of vaccinating for small pox among the "people of the East." American missionaries in Siam, she reported, had bemoaned the "thousands of children...swept away by this disease." Fear and ignorance on the part of both the children and their parents presumably prevented them from agreeing to vaccination, but "female physicians could win their way among these poor children much easier than doctors of the other sex." Women physicians would gain access to the "homes and harems" where the women of "India, China, and Turkey" were supposed to live. Access to women would yield access to children; then the missionary side of the medical missionary could come into play and sow in the "hearts of children" the "good seed" of the gospel.[43] The Reverend Harrison Dwight, missionary of the ABCFM at

Constantinople, reiterated that point. Dwight wrote to Hale expressing his approval of her plan and pointed out that a woman who possessed the "love and zeal of Christ" combined with professional medical education would "gain access where the missionary never can go, and access, too, to that portion of the community which greatly influences all the rest; for even in Turkey,...as everywhere else, it is true that those who stamp the character of the nursery stamp the character of the nation."[44]

Hale, like many other conservative reformers, used a perceived threat to the moral purity of women—"meddlesome man-midwifery"—as her primary justification for supporting women's medical education. Until the mid-eighteenth century, midwifery had been primarily the domain of women. Historian Jane Donegan has noted that the shift from female midwifery to male obstetrical practice was "directly related to the evolution of midwifery from an art to a science" in the mid-eighteenth century.[45] With the development of forceps and other obstetrical instruments and their control by the university-educated, male physicians began to assume a larger share of that practice, primarily among middle- and upper-class families.[46] Obstetrical practice was not only profitable in itself but brought entire families into the astute physician's practice. Physicians thus used the promise of safer and easier childbirth to acquire obstetrical practice. The male orthodox medical community carefully guarded the technology of forceps, arguing that only those who had acquired advanced medical training in female anatomy and the mechanics of childbirth should use them. In their efforts to develop a reputation for safe and easy deliveries, however, physicians often interfered far more than necessary, sometimes with devastating results. By the 1840s a backlash had grown against "meddlesome man-midwifery," opening up the potential for women to receive formal medical education and enter into professional practice.[47]

As we have already seen, however, the three decades preceding the Civil War also marked the apex of what historians have termed the "cult of true womanhood." Hale and other advocates of restoring midwifery to women emphasized with horror the image of the preservers of the nation's moral virtue having to submit themselves to the indignity of undergoing gynecological examinations or having their babies delivered by men:

> Now, we ask those who are strenuous advocates of "woman's sphere," to examine and see if man is not "out of his sphere" when acting as *midwife!*... Is the faithful husband satisfied that his beloved and delicate wife should be subjected to the power, influence, and *confidence* of any other man besides himself? Is a young man made any purer or holier from having received the degree "Doctor of Medicine?" Would American husbands and fathers permit men of any other profession or pursuit to have the familiar intercourse with their wives and daughters which "the Faculty" are now privileged to hold?[48]

Obstetrics was a branch of medicine that the male physician simply "'ought not to practice.'" [49] Some opponents of "man-midwifery" favored restoring childbirth to female midwives and providing them with appropriate (but limited) medical education. Many, however, argued that women should be able to train in medical school as "physicians for their own sex" and that the entire practice of women's medicine should be turned over to women physicians.[50]

Hale led opponents of man-midwifery in arguing not just that women should resume traditional modes of practicing midwifery, but that women should receive professional medical education to fill the role. She frequently used the pages of *Godey's Lady's Book* as a platform for her cause, arguing first and foremost that the practice of "man-midwifery" was "unscriptural and unnatural."[51] Hale published an article by Samuel Gregory, one of the leading public spokesmen in favor of women's medical education, in which he argued that "Heaven and Nature" had "designed" women for the role of midwife just as it had designed them as mothers.[52] Hale pointed out that the Bible mentioned only women in connection with the role of midwife and thus provided scriptural authority for her view. One could see that the practice of midwifery by women was "natural" in the fact that "presiding over the nativity of mankind has devolved upon women in all ages from the days of the 'Hebrew midwives' to the present time; and in all nations, with trifling exception, and those chiefly of a recent date."[53]

Those "trifling exceptions" included France, England, and the United States in the previous one hundred years. Hale forcefully illustrated her view that man-midwifery was "unscriptural and unnatural" in her account of the origin of the practice. It originated, she said, in the court of Louis XIV, who supposedly arranged for his physician to attend his mistress, Madame La Valiére, in childbirth. Though the doctor was blindfolded "to envelop the affair in greater mystery," word nevertheless got out, the British and French aristocracy began aping the practice, and its popularity filtered down to the middle classes.[54] Thus, its supposed origins in the delivery of an illegitimate child to the mistress of the Catholic French king clearly tainted the validity of the practice of man-midwifery in the view of Hale and her Protestant, republican readers.

Another argument for training women as physicians for "their own sex" lay in their presumed "native delicacy and modesty." The unwillingness of women to "divulge their symptoms" to male physicians or to submit to embarrassing physical examinations had resulted in a physically "degenerate" generation of women.[55] Such women became prey to "quackery" and to the ineptitude of "ignorant and...superstitious old women."[56] Women would much more readily confide in a physician of their own sex; thus, disease could be arrested early in its course and debility or premature death avoided. John Stainback Wilson wrote,

> Besides the mental capacity, the manual dexterity, and moral fitness of woman, we contend that she has a great advantage over man in diagnosticating disease...because she has a *feeling knowledge*. If we mistake not, there is an old saw which runs thus: "Seeing is believing, but *feeling* is *knowing*." Who will pretend to say that a woman is not more competent than the opposite sex to comprehend the diagnostic value of certain symptoms and sensations originating in the feminine constitution when she has *felt* those sensations which are peculiar to her as a woman, and which render her such an enigma to those who have only an intellectual or theoretical knowledge of her peculiarities in health and disease?[57]

Wilson was not merely arguing that women could better diagnose and treat gynecological complaints or oversee childbirth because they presumably would have personal experience of both. After all, he and others advocated medicine as a particularly appropriate profession for unmarried women. By coining the phrase "feeling knowledge," Wilson was feminizing medical practice at a more essential level. Two leading arguments *against* women doctors were that practicing medicine required great physical and emotional strength and that it required scientific knowledge. A major procedure in childbirth, turning a breach, required great strength, for example. Furthermore, effective anesthesia had not yet been developed. At a time when even minor surgical procedures such as setting bones and suturing cuts required the ability to steel oneself against the patient's pain and to work very quickly, a procedure such as a caesarean section would prove daunting. Finally, opponents presumed that the increasing scientific content of medical education posed a significant barrier to women, who supposedly did not have the rational faculties to master such subjects as anatomy and physiology or the technical skills to use forceps or other surgical tools. Wilson, however, drew from older ideas of medicine as a healing art. At a time when scientific medicine had not yet produced effective therapies or overcome the barrier of pain in surgery, popular attitudes remained somewhat malleable. Many still found the ancient notion of healing as an art appealing and persuasive. Just as sectarians successfully capitalized on such sentiments to undercut the authority of orthodox physicians, so the likes of Wilson and Hale drew upon those same sentiments to justify training women as medical professionals.

Medicine as the art of healing demanded a radically different sort of knowledge from medicine as a mechanical science. Wilson called it "feeling knowledge" to emphasize it as intuitive and rooted in sympathy and compassion. Scientific medicine, by contrast, was rational and dispassionate—unfeeling. It is important to note that Wilson only claimed the effectiveness of "feeling knowledge" for women physicians and their patients. He did not mention "feeling knowledge" as a possibility for male physicians or suggest its necessity for male patients. "Feeling knowledge" was a strictly feminine quality. If it occurred to Wilson or Hale that male physicians *could* have such knowledge and use it on female patients, they did not discuss the possibility. In fact, such an image hearkens back to Hale's condemnation of the "familiar intercourse" that occurred between the male doctor and his female patient.

Advocates of women's medical education did not dismiss the value of scientific knowledge, nor did they concede that women were incapable of obtaining such knowledge. Hale recognized that the shift from traditional midwifery to male obstetrical practice had occurred as a result of scientific advances in the previous one hundred years, the benefits of which had been confined to those able to receive a university education. Since universities barred them from formal medical education, female midwives had not been able to offer the same promise of safer and easier childbirth. Hale quoted from the Sixth Annual Report of the Female Medical Education Society of Boston:

> Medical schools have been open to males only; the light of advancing science, and the improvements effected by professional skill and experience, have been confined to them; women, though with superior natural adaptations for acquiring and using this knowledge, have been left in ignorance, and have thus become helpless, and almost entirely dependent on men for aid. The present state of things, then, is a modern innovation, brought about by the force of circumstances, and will give place to old and approved customs when women have equal advantages with men in acquiring medical knowledge and professional skill.[58]

Hale and Wilson did, however, assign scientific knowledge a position of lower relative importance—effective medical *practice* consisted of success in healing, and one could achieve success only by exercising intuition and compassion. In a letter to the ABCFM, Hale noted that despite teaching a thoroughly scientific curriculum, the faculty of the Woman's Medical College of Pennsylvania were "fully aware that Science alone can never prepare a woman for her important duties." She enclosed in that letter the latest announcement of the Woman's Medical College, showing their commitment to incorporating religious principles into the medical curriculum. Hale maintained that the presence of "pious female missionaries" pursuing medical degrees in the college raised the moral tone of the whole institution and would thus prove beneficial for "those women who become physicians at home." She further hoped that a similar purifying effect would take place within the medical profession at large as a result of the presence of women physicians. "Medical Science wants Christianizing—this can never be done while it remains solely in the hands of men," she wrote to the board.[59]

The language Hale used to describe the circumstances of American women who suffered because of their reluctance to consult male physicians for gynecological complaints bore a remarkable resemblance to the language she used to describe the situation of "Oriental" women in the *zenanas* and harems of the East. Her reports of the LMMS strikingly juxtaposed the "poor suffering" women of America, who were embarrassed to consult male physicians, with the "poor, suffering women of heathendom," whose seclusion precluded access by male physicians.[60] Women, however, might enter those quarters freely: "Men can never gain access to the homes and harems where the women and children of the Eastern nations dwell. If those poor, ignorant ones are healed and taught, it must be done by pious Christian women."[61] Women physicians, in particular, would find welcome because "'the people have a superstitious reverence for those who have a knowledge of diseases and their remedies; and although we could not honestly wish to foster this feeling, yet while it exists it may be turned to good account.'"[62] Not only did "all heathen people have a high reverence for medical knowledge," but "the bosom of the sufferer," Hale believed, provided fertile ground for the gospel.[63] Thus, while the *zenanas* and harems of the East were both the source and the evidence of "Oriental" women's degradation, they nevertheless provided a feminine space into which women missionary doctors could enter wielding both scientific authority and spiritual power. In a sense, people such as Hale who sought to return the experience of childbirth to an exclusively female sphere were trying to create a similar space within the homes of American women.

Almost one quarter of the original "Appeal" on behalf of the LMMS addressed the issue of midwifery. Hale maintained that the reluctance of women to confide in male doctors forced them to resort to the purveyors of patent medicines ("poisonous nostrums"). When it came to matters relating to "knowledge of the laws of health," American women were just as "ignorant" and "superstitious" as their heathen sisters. But in both cases, knowledge offered the cure: "Quackery would be swept away as superstitious notions are when people are enlightened." In the case of the "heathen," the very sight of educated female physicians working among them would "greatly raise the sex in the estimation of those nations."[64]

Hale regarded obstetrical care as the primary medical need of "Oriental" women. She emphasized that male doctors *could not* enter the "harems and *zenanas* of the East," but read in the light of her condemnation of man-midwifery in America, one realizes that she believed men also *should not* enter that space. The birthing room was sacred, inviolable, feminine space into which men should not trespass, symbolizing reverence and esteem for the "angel of the house." Islamic and Hindu societies had, in Hale's view, perverted the concept of inviolable feminine space by creating harems and *zenanas* that imprisoned women and represented in a physical way their oppression in those societies. The ultimate evidence of that crime appeared in what took place behind the *purdah* during childbirth. The laboring woman (often depicted as a "child mother") was presumed to endure her sufferings alone or with the assistance only of an "ignorant and superstitious midwife." In Christian societies, by contrast, a woman's assistants marshaled care, concern, and effective aid in the birthing room, usually a couple's bedchamber that became a space literally separate and controlled by women only during this event. The bedchamber at all other times represented monogamous, companionate marriage—in the view of American observers like Hale, yet another example of the superior position that women held in Christian societies.

Hale was by no means alone in justifying medical education for women on the grounds that their role as moral purifiers of society both made it necessary to protect that purity from contamination by male doctors and uniquely qualified them as healers. She did, however, lead the way in constructing those arguments in terms of the need of the foreign mission movement for women doctors to extend that protection to the women of "Oriental" lands and through their influence to uplift those women from their "degraded" and "oppressed" status into positions comparable to those of their Christian sisters in the West. In doing so, she linked the discourse of "woman's work for woman" to a broader, ongoing conversation about the efficacy of medical missions in general for accomplishing the ultimate goal of converting the "heathen" world to Protestant Christianity. She was also a leader in moving beyond mere discussion or *ad hoc* responses to specific needs by attempting to formulate an institutional approach to the concept of medical missions.

Nineteenth-century advocates of medical missions pointed to several instances in the previous one hundred and fifty years in which Protestants had justified sending doctors as missionaries along with evangelists by citing the link between the "teaching and healing" ministries of Jesus and the apostles.[65] Soon after it was established in 1701, for example, the Society for the Propagation of the Gospel in Foreign Parts received a bequest to found a college to train men in both medicine and theology concurrently. The society never carried out that plan, but it nevertheless indicated a "recognition of the principle of medical missions."[66] German and Danish Protestants commissioned doctors as missionaries to both the West and the East Indies in the 1730s.[67] Dr. John Thomas accompanied William Carey to India in 1793; the Baptists' first convert was a Hindu man whose injured arm Thomas treated. The ABCFM sent John Scudder to India in 1819 as its first medical missionary. By the mid-1830s, Scudder had colleagues in Persia (Asahel Grant), Siam (Dan Bradley), and China (Peter Parker).[68] By 1849, forty physicians served American and British Protestant missionary societies: twenty-six Americans, twelve Britons, one Turk, and one Arab.[69]

Most missionaries, regardless of whether they had received medical training, found themselves called upon to practice medicine in a lay capacity. This was especially true of missionary wives and daughters, who often tended the sick and served as midwives in mission compounds and in native Christian communities. Their reputations sometimes produced new converts to Christianity. Annie Ryder Gracey, a Methodist missionary in India in the 1860s, wrote that "every missionary's wife finds that much time must be given to attendance on the sick and dispensing medicines."[70] Judith Grant, wife of Dr. Asahel Grant of the ABCFM mission in Persia, was one examplar of the missionary as lay healer. Judith had been raised by her uncle and aunt, William and Sobrina Campbell, of Cherry Valley, New York. William was a physician; early in her marriage, Sobrina, wanting to be useful to him, read his medical books, made frequent visits to the sick, and acquired some reputation for her medical expertise. She "imbibed deeply of the missionary spirit" and inculcated within Judith a love of missions from early childhood.[71]

Dr. Campbell directed Judith's early education. She completed her studies at an academy in Brooklyn, excelling in languages and mathematics.[72] In 1835, at age twenty-one, Judith fulfilled the wishes of her adoptive mother by marrying missionary Asahel Grant, one of the first physicians sent out by the ABCFM.[73] She also followed in Sobrina Campbell's footsteps by educating herself as a lay medical practitioner. Judith spent the brief four years between her marriage and her death serving with Asahel in Oroomiah, Persia. Her knowledge of medicine "was considerable, and in the necessary absence of her husband, she...in a good degree supplied his place as physician.... How like mercy's angel have we beheld her hastening from house to house and room to room in the mission, when several of us have been sick at the same time!"[74] Judith quickly mastered Turkish, ancient Syriac, and the vernacular dialect of the Nestorians; she impressed the Nestorian bishops with her ability to read Greek and Latin.[75] She taught English in the mission's seminary, taught in a girls' school, visited and instructed the native women in their homes, gave birth to a son and twin daughters, and cared for three orphans, "nor did her nursery and fireside ever give indication of confusion."[76]

Judith Grant epitomized the ideal of the missionary wife and the "moral mother," as Reverend Justin Perkins of the ABCFM mission at Oroomiah, Persia, demonstrated by his eulogy upon her death in 1839 at the age of twenty-five:

> Her situation, as the wife of a physician, opened before her a very extensive acquaintance, both among the Mohammedans, and the native Christians;—and the ardour with which she entered into their interests, enlightening their dark minds, or administering relief to their sufferings, secured the affections of all who knew her. Whether imparting instruction to the bishops, priests, deacons, and the Mohammedan Meerza, or teaching the ignorant of her own sex, and endeavouring to raise them from their deep degradation; whether visiting the harems of the rich and great, entering the cottage of the poor and wretched, or imparting relief to suffering, and joy to the disconsolate around her own domestic fireside; her characteristic

> ardour in doing good, and her affectionate concern for the happiness of others, won the confidence and opened the hearts of all who came within the reach of her influence.[77]

What is important about her experience for the sake of this study, however, is that one of the duties for which her colleagues esteemed her was her skill as a lay medical practitioner. Judith represented the early nineteenth-century paradigm in which medical missions were carried out by persons not trained as physicians, but whose work as missionaries forced them to engage in the healing arts to the best of their ability. Judith's husband and his colleagues, Drs. Scudder, Parker, and Bradley, were exceptional among missionaries in possessing professional medical degrees. The lot of nursing the sick most often fell to the wives of missionaries, for, in Persia as in America, that role was viewed as an integral part of the domestic life of a married woman. Within a dozen years of Judith's death, however, medical education for women became a reality, and the possibility of developing new avenues of missionary service for women as physicians to women and children presented itself to Sarah Josepha Hale.

Through much of the first half of the century, the missionary man or woman serving as lay healer remained the norm, but the very demand for their services pointed to the need for fully trained medical personnel. Furthermore, anecdotal evidence about the experiences of Grant, Scudder, Bradley, and Parker, along with tales of the famous British missionary doctor and explorer David Livingstone, suggested that physicians could effectively break new ground in places where foreigners were viewed with suspicion and fear. Rufus Anderson, looking back at the end of his long career as secretary of the ABCFM, wrote,

> In the early stage of a mission, the value of a pious physician is most apparent. With the exaggerated conceptions usually entertained of the temporal blessings he is able to confer, he is welcomed by all classes from the first. Every door is opened, every man and woman is accessible. The good-will thus awakened is more or less shared by his fellow missionaries and is thus likely to be all the sooner confirmed by a spiritual appreciation of the Gospel.[78]

Peter Parker's work in China seemed particularly to provide evidence for such speculation. When he arrived in Canton in 1834, the movements of foreigners were strictly confined to the commercial factories along the waterfront. Technically, foreigners were not permitted to have contact with the Chinese, but in reality the boundaries between the Chinese and the Westerners were quite fluid in the busy port. Parker took advantage of those circumstances to create opportunities for interacting with the Cantonese. In June of 1835, he established an "ophthalmic hospital" because opthalmia and cataracts particularly plagued the Chinese residents of Canton. Soon, people were forming lines in the evening in hopes of receiving treatment the next day.[79] Within two weeks of setting up practice, Parker had seen 240 patients.[80]

Parker's astounding success at establishing inroads "in a land in which previous contacts between local citizens and Protestant missionaries had been rare" and his remarkable ability to create his own publicity produced quite a stir in Canton, Great Britain, and the United States.[81] The Western community in Canton, under the leadership of Parker and his evangelist colleague Elijah Coleman Bridgman, organized the Medical Missionary Society in China in 1838 to provide financial and organizational support for medical missions.[82] When the Opium War broke out in 1839, Parker had to flee the country temporarily, so he took advantage of the opportunity to tour Great Britain and the United States and promote the cause of medical missions. A group of physicians in Edinburgh responded by forming the Edinburgh Medical Missionary Society in 1843, the first such society to form in the West.[83] While a similar society did not form in the United States, Parker still found much support, notwithstanding the severe financial crisis gripping the nation at the time. A committee formed for the purpose in Boston raised $5,000 for the work in China. In his report to the society in China, Parker particularly noted the response of women in both Great Britain and the United States. "Benevolent ladies" in London began to make "systematic efforts" to collect funds, which they channeled through the London Missionary Society. He personally received the donations of a number of individual women, along with £20 from a Ladies Chinese Medical Missionary Association in Hackney. A Ladies' Chinese Association in Philadelphia collected $330, and Miss Ann Rutter of

Framingham, Massachusetts, left the Medical Missionary Society in China a bequest of $200. Parker remarked that in both countries, "it was the importance of the plan of this Society, as calculated to introduce the blessings of the gospel into China, that most powerfully influenced these truly devoted Christian ladies."[84]

It was within this context of efforts to systematize both the theory and practice of medical missions that Sarah Josepha Hale established the LMMS in 1852. The LMMS had a three-fold purpose: to support the work of the Woman's Medical College of Pennsylvania, to "give kindly encouragement to those females who are engaged in medical studies," and to provide financial support to women who sought a medical education and intended to use it on a mission field.[85] The LMMS sponsored the studies of three women at the Woman's Medical College of Pennsylvania: Elizabeth G. Shattuck (Baptist), Emmeline Horton (Presbyterian), and Mary J. Thayer (Congregational), who had previously served the ABCFM as a missionary teacher among the Tuscaroras and whom the board's secretary recommended to Hale.[86] All of them completed their degrees, but none became missionaries. Shattuck had hoped to go to Burma, but died of a fever caught in the hospital where she worked before ever getting the opportunity. Horton married; she and her husband were about to go abroad to a mission field when he became ill and suffered permanent disability She eventually became a professor at the Woman's Medical College. Thayer returned to her former position in the Tuscarora tribe.

The LMMS apparently did not make any further attempts at educating women to serve as medical missionaries. When the Woman's Union Missionary Society (WUMS) formed in 1860, a Philadelphia branch soon followed. Hale merged the LMMS with that branch and became its president. In 1869, the call for women medical missionaries was renewed in a letter from Mrs. D. W. Thomas, a Methodist missionary at Bareilly, India. The Thomases ran an orphanage, and a "native gentleman" had suggested the practicality of offering medical training, probably in midwifery, to some of the young women who had grown up and received their education in the institution. A woman physician could conduct such training and still "find plenty of practice among the native Christians and Zenana women in the city." Mrs.

Thomas wrote to Annie Ryder Gracey, a former colleague in India who was then residing in Philadelphia, asking if she would place a request for a "Doctress" before the Philadelphia branch of the WUMS. She did so, and as Hale was still the organization's president, the suggestion received "hearty and enthusiastic support."[87]

With the WUMS offering financial backing, Gracey applied to the Woman's Medical College for a suitable candidate. Clara Swain, a Methodist, accepted the offer, but by that time (still 1869) Methodist women had formed their own denominational mission board. Swain chose to go out under the auspices of her denomination, and in November 1869 she sailed from New York with Isabella Thoburn, another single missionary. Clara Swain offered a marked contrast to her earlier counterpart, Judith Grant. Grant epitomized the early nineteenth-century wife and mother whose efforts as a self-educated lay healer were part of her domestic responsibilities. Although she considered herself called to missions at an early age and although both the ABCFM and her fellow missionaries highly valued her work, that role came to her by way of her husband's appointment rather than her own. She was in her grave by the age of twenty-five. Swain, on the other hand, began teaching school in 1855 at age twenty-one. Eight years later she embarked on three years of practical medical training at the Castile Sanitarium in New York before entering the full three-year course of medical study at the Woman's Medical College of Pennsylvania. Graduating in 1869 at the age of thirty-five, Swain received a denominational mission appointment in her own right as a physician. She served as staff physician for the Methodist orphanage in Bareilly and taught a medical class for Indian women. She also engaged in medical practice among the women of the city, seeing 1,225 patients at the mission house and visiting 250 patients at home in her first year. She negotiated a gift of forty acres from the Nawab of Rampore and oversaw the construction of a women's hospital and dispensary, which she then superintended for many years. Swain was an archetype of the professional medical missionary of the late nineteenth century.[88] By 1890, British and Scottish missionary societies supported twenty-six women physicians, while their American counterparts sponsored fifty. Most, if not all of the women, served in Asia.

In 1870, inspired by Swain's departure, Sarah Josepha Hale reflected back on her own unsuccessful efforts in behalf of women's medical missions in the 1850s. Hale suggested that while "public opinion seemed warmly favorable," the ABCFM and other missionary boards resisted on the grounds that "the heathen people…were not ready for such an innovation."[89] In an article written on her retirement at the age of ninety in 1877, she contradicted herself by claiming that "public opinion was not yet ripe" for the support of women missionary doctors in the 1850s. She further maintained that at that time, "the experiment of sending single women as missionaries was an untried one, and it was feared that troubles might arise which would prejudice the mission cause."[90] In truth, the "experiment of sending single women" was by no means "untried," as earlier chapters of this study have demonstrated. Furthermore, in regard to her own efforts, Hale seems to have been mistaken in her recollection that missionary boards specifically opposed women medical missionaries. In fact, in a letter to the ABCFM in 1852, she stated that a "gentleman" had called to tell her that the board wanted "to send one of their female missionaries here to attend the medical lectures in the Female College in this City [Philadelphia]."[91] That woman was apparently Mary Thayer, who served in the board's mission to the Tuscarora. The other two women who received medical degrees with the support of the LMMS also came with the recommendations of their denominations (Baptist and Presbyterian) and would have served under the authority of those denominations had not the death of one woman and the disability of the other's husband intervened.

Some hesitation regarding the place of single women on foreign fields does seem to have troubled Rufus Anderson, who, as secretary of the ABCFM, was perhaps the most influential mission leader on the domestic scene. In 1835, when missionary David Abeel proposed a plan to send single women to China as teachers, Anderson had opposed. But his opposition was not to the *idea* of single women missionaries. Instead, he said that experience had shown that conflicts tended to arise when a single woman was placed in a mission family *unless* she was related to them or already on intimate terms of friendship. Under those circumstances, he thought "our Committee would cheerfully consent to the experiment being made." His real concern, however, seemed to be financial, for he lamented the tendency of women at home to put all their support behind special efforts directed to women abroad.[92] Even more important in explaining Anderson's lack of enthusiasm regarding women medical missionaries, however, was his ambivalence toward medical missions generally. The board's instructions to Peter Parker in 1834 emphasized that "the character of a physician and a man of science respected as they are, and useful as they may be in evangelizing China, you will never suffer to supersede or interfere with your character of a teacher of religion."[93] In 1838, responding to an inquiry by the secretary of the London Missionary Society about the ABCFM's assessment of their medical missions, Anderson wrote of the venture in quite negative terms. He said that hospitals and dispensaries were expensive operations and were "not within the proper range of missionary societies." Where they existed, as with Dr. Parker's hospital in Canton, the funds came from sources outside of the board. In fact, he wrote, such institutions gave medical work "too much prominence in the mission" and created expectations on the part of other missionaries that they would be stationed near a board physician and thus made them unwilling to pioneer new work. In short, he summed up by stating that "it would not be strange if we should discontinue, in great measure, the practice of sending out physicians."[94]

Anderson's ambivalence toward medical missions was characteristic of his attitude toward any activity that threatened to supplant the centrality of evangelism and church-planting. He recognized that medical and educational missions could produce visible and reportable (even dramatic) results that offered specific objects for financial charity, in contrast to the painfully slow process of making conversions, establishing churches, and training indigenous clergy and lay leadership. He and other mission purists, such as Francis Wayland of the American Baptist Missionary Union (ABMU) and Henry Venn of the Church Missionary Society in Great Britain, stubbornly resisted the inexorable tug of institutionalized social missions throughout the mid-nineteenth century.[95] The disappointing response that Sarah Josepha Hale received for her efforts to organize women's medical missions must be understood in this context, later claims of prejudice against women notwithstanding.

By the late nineteenth century, the development of antisepsis and anesthesia, along with the discoveries collectively known as the bacteriological revolution, began dramatically to transform the rhetoric, if not the reality, of medical practice. Even mission apologists began to discuss medical missions in scientific terms. The very act of developing a systematic theory for medical missions indicates the degree to which scientific discourse shaped the thinking of people not primarily engaged in scientific endeavor. The major works of medical mission apologetics, John Lowe's *Medical Missions: Their Place and Power* (1886) and John Rutter Williamson's *The Healing of the Nations* (1899), began to speak of Western medical and scientific advances as some of the blessings of Christian civilization that should be shared with supposedly backward, heathen cultures. Simultaneously, however, most of Sarah Josepha Hale's arguments relating to the relationship between women's purifying role in society, their suitability for the medical profession, and the relationship of each of those factors to missions continued, often parallel with scientific arguments, in the writings of late nineteenth-century apologists for the women's foreign missions movement.

Writers continued to characterize medicine as an art of physical healing closely akin to spiritual healing, drawing on the examples of Jesus and his apostles. In 1885, the American Medical Missionary Society formed in Chicago to support the medical education of men and women who desired to go out as missionaries. They published a tract that same year titled "A Great Field for Women," which maintained that women, as well as men, should emulate the example of Jesus, for the people of his day had "received healing from His hands and the Gospel from his lips." Furthermore, Jesus, in his "Great Commission," had commanded not only that Christians go forth to preach the gospel, but that they "heal the sick." The "professional acquisition" of the woman medical missionary was a "key" that would literally "unlock the doors" of the harems and *zenanas* that physically imprisoned the women of the East. While the missionary's medical skill worked the desired physical remedy, successful treatment would dismantle the "suspicion" and "hostility" that served as inivisible "walls of partition" dividing the Western Christian woman from the "Oriental" woman:

> The medical woman's presence is an influence, her word is a power. She is hailed as a friend. Her benefactions have opened the way, not only for her, but also for her message. She can speak to their benighted souls of Jesus and his salvation. And to her speech her profession ministers, for there is an impressive harmony between preaching and healing: there is a natural transition from the fact of sickness to that of sin; of physical remedies to that of spiritual grace; of an earthly physician to the Heavenly One.

Medical skill thus allowed missionary women to breach the "Oriental" woman's physical seclusion, but, more importantly, physical access prepared for and symbolized the emotional and intellectual access that the missionary gained.[96]

John Lowe's *Medical Missions: Their Place and Power* served for many years as the standard apologetic for medical missions. Lowe, like Hale and others before him, pointed to the example of Jesus and his apostles as the principal justification for medical missions.[97] In elaborating the role of women in medical missions he noted that the "condition of women in heathen lands" had been so widely discussed that he did not need to engage in a lengthy account. One could safely assume that the women of India were "debased and neglected" and that their condition was representative of women throughout the "Orient" and "indeed of all lands on which the Gospel has not shed its Christianizing and humanizing influence." Only a woman missionary could hope to reach a "heathen" woman; a woman doctor had the best opportunity, for "while ministering relief to the suffering body" she could "thereby gain an entrance for the Gospel into the hearts and homes of her patients."[98]

Annie Ryder Gracey, in her 1888 history of women's medical missions in the Methodist Episcopal Church, also noted the biblical precedent whereby Jesus and his apostles linked their "teaching and healing" ministries.[99] She pointed out that missionaries in India had come to recognize the importance of having women medical missionaries: "They realized that through this medium the homes of the people might become open to the reception of the gospel and confidence secured."[100] Likewise, celebrated British traveler Isabella Bird Bishop addressed the Woman's Congress of Missions at the World's Columbian Exposition in Chicago in 1893, also claiming the authority of Jesus when she wrote, "The true missionary-doctor witnesses by his life-work to Christ the Healer, and is an epistle of Christ, translating Christ's love and teaching into object lessons which all can understand." The medical missionary woman had "opportunities which fall to the lot of no other of awaking a sense of the disease of sin."[101]

The pivotal role of women in the redemption of society continued to hold a prominent place in the writings of mission apologists about midwifery and motherhood. While Hale only alluded to the presumed "barbarities" of "Oriental" midwifery, her successors elaborated on the subject. Annie Ryder Gracey, for example, noted that Methodist Clara Swain established the first "medical class for native women" in India in 1869 at the request of a "native gentleman" who wanted to see native women trained in midwifery: "He was very earnest in picturing the suffering that often ensues from the malpractice of the ignorant, superstitious native midwives."[102] Isabella Bird Bishop remarked to her audience in Chicago that "to our medical sisters is the special honor given to enter the domestic Bastiles of the East with healing and light, and to make an end by their skilled and beneficent methods of the barbarous practices of native midwifery, and of the many remediable sufferings of their own sex."[103] Those "barbarous practices," according to Bishop and others, included placing a wooden plank across the abdomen of a woman in labor and having the midwives' assistants sit or jump on either end of the plank in order to hasten the birth. Bishop reported visiting an American mission hospital in northern India and seeing nine patients, five of whom had suffered broken ribs and internal injuries from that practice. Another writer, John Rutter Williamson, described the Hindu process for the ceremonial purification of the postpartum mother and the infant. In his account, the two could not be bathed, were deprived of food and fire for four days, and were left alone in their own filth in a bed of rags on the floor. If the two survived the ordeal, on the fifth day they were bathed, the room was cleaned, and the mother was given an uncooked mixture of graham flour and brown sugar as her only meal.[104]

Williamson went on to excuse his use of such gruesome details by noting that his was no mere story of "cruelty or immorality." Rather, such practices evidenced the level of moral depravity and corruption that abounded in heathen lands. Williamson hearkened back to Hale's estimation of the public importance of motherhood when he wrote, "It is of imperial importance. If the home is blasted the national unit of strength is destroyed and there is moral decadence."[105] Similarly, the American Medical Missionary Society in 1885 echoed the language of Harrison Dwight thirty years earlier: "These women, as they become mothers, stamp their character on their children. If these mothers were converted to Christ, the next generation in pagan lands would be Christian."[106]

However limited Hale's immediate results in the area of women's medical missions might have seemed, late nineteenth-century apologists not only indirectly echoed her sentiments; many of them recognized her influential role and praised her pathbreaking efforts. Annie Ryder Gracey, both in her history of Methodist women and missions and in an address given before the Woman's Congress of Missions in 1893, credited Hale as the "pioneer" in women's medical missions.[107] Isabel Hart dedicated her 1879 book *Historical Sketches of Woman's Missionary Societies in America and England* "to the memory of Sarah J. Hale, the able exponent of Woman's best rights—to culture and service—the beautiful illustration of her truest gifts and highest graces; the conceiver and earnest advocate of Woman's Medical Work."[108]

7

"A Modern Uprising of Women"

Institutionalizing the Women's Missionary Movement

By the latter third of the nineteenth century, the work of women missionaries had given rise to the catchphrase "woman's work for woman." The concept of "woman's work for woman" grew explicitly out of the context of missions to the "Orient," where it was presumed that women were oppressed and hidden from the public eye. Only Western Christian women, it was believed, could hope to gain access to their counterparts and through them reach present and future generations for Christ. The ideal of "woman's work for woman" in the "Orient" gradually developed among American women from the time they first began sending money to William Carey's mission soon after the turn of the nineteenth century.

In 1835, David Abeel, a Dutch Reformed minister working among the Chinese in Bangkok under the auspices of the ABCFM, tried and failed to get American women to organize across denominational lines in order to institutionalize the concept of "woman's work for woman." Such an organization would differ from the multitude of women's missionary societies dotting the American landscape in three ways. First, its leaders would seek a national, interdenominational membership. Second, they would directly employ single women for missionary careers. Third, they would raise funds specifically to support those women's work.

Abeel's ecumenical hope never received widespread support in the first half of the nineteenth century, but an interdenominational Woman's Union Missionary Society (WUMS) did emerge in 1861. By 1875, furthermore, women missionaries had expanded their work and consolidated their support at home to the point that the leading Protestant denominations in the North and West—Congregational, Baptist, Presbyterian, Methodist—all had women's boards that selected single women as missionaries and raised money for their support. Southern women, laboring under heavier financial burdens, nevertheless followed suit in the next decade and a half. R. Pierce Beaver notes that in the decades immediately following the Civil War, "the extensive employment of single women and widows radically changed the proportion of the sexes in the missionary staff."[1] Beaver cited a 1933 study titled *The Health and Turnover of Missionaries*, which stated that "in 1830, like animals entering the Ark, missionaries went to the field in paris: for each man on the field there was nearly one woman. In 1880, for each man there were one and one-third women; in 1929, for each man their were 2.02 women. Expressed in percentages, the missionary personnel was female to the extent of 49 percent in 1830, 57 percent in 1880, and 67 percent in 1929."[2]

What happened to bring about such a radical transformation of one of the largest religious movements of the nineteenth century?[3] Late nineteenth-century participant-observers often maintained that denominational women's boards had their roots in the involvement of northern women in the Civil War.[4] Modern-day scholars have generally followed suit, minimizing or ignoring the widespread involvement of women prior to the war. Virtually all current commentators have located the origin of the ideal of "woman's work for woman" in the wake of the war effort.[5] Previous chapters of this study countered such interpretations by pointing out the importance of early nineteenth-century images of missionary women juxtaposed against images of

"Oriental" women that popular missionary memoirs and magazines transmitted and circulated among an avid evangelical readership. By 1860, American Protestant women began to marshal more than a half-century's worth of accumulated tropes about "Oriental" womanhood to create an imperative for a more elaborate, formalized, and professionalized institutional expression of the ideal of "woman's work for woman."

In 1833, David Abeel left his field of service because of ill health. His physician prescribed a sea journey, so in the autumn he set out for England. He spent the following winter and spring touring England and Scotland, promoting the cause of missions in general and of "female education in China and the surrounding countries" in particular.[6] His efforts culminated with the founding of the Society for Promoting Female Education in the East (SPFEE) in London in July 1834. He departed soon thereafter for the United States. During the winter and spring of 1835, he traveled up and down the East Coast, speaking again on behalf of both the broader evangelical mission and the importance of education for girls and women of the East. In New York City, Abeel found a receptive audience for his plea that the women of the United States unite across denominational lines to form an organization that would send single women to southern, central, and eastern Asia to serve as teachers in the missions of the existing boards.

Sarah Doremus spearheaded the effort to form an American version of the SPFEE. Doremus had long engaged her energies in the benevolent and reform movements of her day. She was, in a sense, born to the work of evangelical philanthropy. As a six-year-old growing up in New York City in the opening years of the nineteenth century, she had accompanied her mother, Elisa Haines, to meetings at the home of the legendary reformer Isabella Graham to pray and raise support for the nascent foreign missions movement.[7] In 1821, she married Thomas C. Doremus, a wealthy merchant who "supplied with princely liberality the means of sustaining" his wife's charitable work.[8] That work included tract societies, Sunday schools, prison church services, charity industrial societies giving work to poor women, a children's hospital, a women's hospital, a home for aged women, and a school for Italian immigrants. In fact, Doremus's activities outside of her home were so astoundingly numerous that her memorialist felt compelled to assure readers that she had not neglected her domestic responsibilities in prosecuting them:

> With all her world-wide usefulness, it is particularly sweet to recognise that her home was the scene of her tenderest cares. No outside duty was undertaken until that first claim had been faithfully discharged. The mind that could have ruled a kingdom gave its best energies to the ordering and beautifying of that dearest realm of a true woman.[9]

Doremus remained a "true woman" despite possessing a masculine intellect and administrative abilities that might otherwise have entitled her to a position of political leadership. Instead, she directed her considerable abilities first toward the work of maintaining a model home and second toward works of charity acceptable for their religious emphasis and their focus on women and children.

Since Doremus engaged so profusely in charitable work for women on the home front, it is hardly surprising that she became an early advocate for giving institutional expression to that same philosophy within the context of foreign missions. She was, in fact, most renowned for her labors in behalf of that cause. Early in her married life, her home became a waystation for American and British missionaries passing through the port of New York: "She refreshed them as only she could, and as she so often cared for the weary, wayworn pilgrims to the Celestial City. Surely her home must have ever seemed to them the Palace Beautiful."[10] In 1828, following the Turkish invasion of Greece, she organized a relief effort in behalf of Greek women.[11] Although herself a lifelong member of the Dutch Reformed communion, she founded a society to support the Baptist mission at Grand Ligne, Canada. Her fellow Dutch Reformed communicant, David Abeel, thus sowed on fertile ground when he issued his plea in behalf of "Oriental" women at a meeting with Sarah Doremus in attendance.

The time for interdenominational work for women had not yet arrived, however. Most later sources state that Doremus's first effort collapsed under the opposition of the existing denominational boards, especially the ABCFM and its foreign secretary, Rufus Anderson. Rufus Anderson did, in fact, object to the formation of such a society. His objection, however, stemmed from a growing resistance to the trend in the 1830s of people supporting pet projects instead of the broad work of evangelization, rather than from opposition to women's involvement *per se*. Exhorting Abeel to throw his efforts behind the "general" work of the ABCFM rather than drumming up support for special causes, Anderson wrote in the summer of 1835,

> I feel concerned and even alarmed when I see the growing disposition in the community to run into *specific* charities. Each auxiliary wants its particular mission or missionary; there is a strong tendency to form associations for the support of particular local schools, or particular teachers, or for patronizing a particular description of the work.... How desirable that the good ladies in New York, who are far from being babes to the business of missions to the heathen, would use their efforts and give their money to the general object. There is no need of their forming associations to *support* particular females. *We* will send out all who ought to go, if *they will give for the* general object all they ought to give: and at the same time we shall always be obliged by their efforts to look up and recommend suitable persons.[12]

Anderson thus expressed his recognition of the women's expertise in raising funds for missions, his desire that they should continue doing so, his support for sending women as missionaries, and his willingness to receive recommendations as to "suitable persons" from the women in New York. It is clear, however, that intense competition existed for benevolent dollars; local missionary auxiliaries increasingly diverted funds away from denominational coffers and toward specific efforts and institutions. The growing interest in medical missions provided a case in point. As previously noted, Anderson expressed regret that Peter Parker's medical work in China garnered so much attention. Anderson believed that an emphasis on girls' education, like the emphasis on medical missions, would lead to an increasing focus on establishing institutions whose main purpose was *not* evangelization and the cost for which was so great that the indigenous peoples served by those institutions would never be able to sustain them themselves but would always remain dependent upon Western benevolence.[13]

One area of service that women developed during the 1850s, however, was clearly evangelistic in its purpose and did not involve institution-building. *Zenana* visitation—the practice of women missionaries visiting upper-caste Hindu women in their private quarters to share the Christian gospel with them—seemed a model of appropriate female evangelism. The practice of systematic *zenana* visitation began in Bengal, apparently by British Baptists at Serampore and Calcutta.[14] The Baptist missionaries at Serampore, like missionaries of other denominations in India, found their work confined primarily to the low-caste and out-caste. Caste was not just a function of the Hindu religion; it was woven into the very fabric of Bengali society. To become a Christian meant more than just giving up Hinduism; it meant losing caste and therefore losing everything. Thus, the missionaries found their earliest success among those who had little or nothing to lose. They always wanted, however, to make converts among the Brahmins. Only the upper castes could "alter national feeling." Win the upper echelons of society, so the wisdom went, and the rest of society would soon follow.[15] Missionary wives had a particular interest in Bengali women of the Brahmin and other high castes, for those women supposedly were secluded in the *zenana*—the segregated part of the high-caste Hindu home in which women lived and to which men from outside the family could never gain admittance. By the 1830s and 1840s, British and American evangelical missionaries increasingly characterized *zenanas* as prisons and Hindu women as slaves. To them, the incarcerated women of the *zenana* epitomized the oppression of all women in non-Christian societies. British and American evangelicals also firmly believed that in India, as elsewhere in the world, women were the agents of spiritual and moral redemption. If missionaries could win Brahmin women to Christianity, those women would in turn win their own children, and within a few generations the Christian gospel would transform India and free her captive daughters. The difficulty, of course, lay in entering the *zenana* in the first place. High-caste women would not or could not leave their *zenanas*, so "the only way to influence them, by secular and Bible education alike, was to send Christian ladies to teach them in their homes."[16]

Despite the number of missionary wives and daughters laboring in India, however, it was mid-century before the first western Christian women finally entered a *zenana*. British Baptist missionaries Elizabeth Sale and Marianne Lewis led the way, and their efforts greatly influenced American women who followed in their footsteps. In 1866, while on furlough in England, Lewis wrote "A Plea for *Zenanas*," which gained wide circulation among evangelicals in England and the United States. Her purpose, she wrote, was "to awaken as widely as possible the concern of English ladies for their less favoured, yet most interesting, Indian sisters." She began by contrasting the "home" of an English nuclear family with the "dwelling place" inhabited by the "aggregation of families" that comprised the typical upper-caste Hindu household. Lewis described the separate women's quarters in the Hindu "dwelling" as "dreary, ill-lighted, ill-ventilated, and miserably-furnished rooms, so constructed that…their inmates may see as little as possible of the outer world."[17] Women could not leave their quarters "unguarded" and then only for special occasions such as temple feasts. "Monotony" and "indolence" ruled the lives of Hindu upper-caste women, wrote Marianne, for, not having companionate marriages, they rarely spoke with their husbands, nor were they allowed to learn to read or to do needlework. "The survey of such jewels as they may possess, the care of their little ones, and the discussion of family gossip" comprised their only activities.[18]

A system of "deference and subordination," she wrote, governed relationships between the men of the family; the position of her husband determined a woman's status among the women. Since the practice of polygamy prevailed, a woman's age and the number of sons she produced established her status among the wives of her husband.[19] Widows, especially young girls who had been widowed before reaching child-bearing age, were objects of contempt within the household. To emphasize the plight of widows, Lewis mentioned *sati*, the practice of burning a widow on her husband's funeral pyre. Though *sati* had been officially abolished in the early 1830s and rarely occurred by the time she was writing, Lewis knew that over the course of the previous half-century it had become a powerful symbol, in the Western mind, of the oppression of Hindu women. "In former times," she wrote, "it was customary to burn [widows] with the dead bodies of their husbands, and many a poor creature, with the knowledge of the misery that would inevitably be her portion in life, willingly accepted the fearful alternative." She further suggested that young widows were "so...desolate and hopeless [that] in numerous instances they fall an easy prey to the seductive arts of wicked men, and abandon the dwellings in which they cannot find a *home*."[20] Thus, in the minds of Baptist missionaries, seclusion did not protect high-caste Hindu girls and women because they had mere walls around them. "True" protection derived only from the human relationships that comprised the Christian "home."

Marianne Lewis went on to inform her readers that since the inception of *zenana* visiting by Elizabeth Sale in 1854, the work had been carried on by missionary wives and daughters in a voluntary capacity and in addition to their numerous other responsibilities. The "demand for instruction," however, was rapidly increasing, and the time had come for Baptists to appoint and support "ladies exclusively devoted to this work."[21] By way of establishing precedent for this suggestion, she pointed out that during the previous decade, the Church Missionary Society, the Scottish Free Church, and the American WUMS had begun to support single women in full-time *zenana* work based on the model established by Elizabeth Sale.

The WUMS to which Marianne Lewis referred represented the fulfillment of Sarah Doremus's dream of answering David Abeel's 1835 appeal on behalf of "Oriental" women. Twenty-five years after Doremus's first attempt to organize women across denominational lines, she finally succeeded. One of the organizations in which she was involved was the New York Female Bible Society. In the spring of 1860, Ellen Huntly Bullard Mason, an American Baptist missionary in Tounghoo, Burma, on furlough, spoke before that group about her dream of establishing a women's society based on the British SPFEE to "send Bible Readers to the *Zenanas* of India."[22] Sarah Doremus joined in the conversation and told of her efforts twenty-five years earlier when David Abeel had issued a similar plea. The two began to plan a renewed effort and quickly enlisted the ready support of such prominent local clergymen as Richard Storrs and Henry Ward Beecher.

Ellen Huntly Bullard Mason is an extremely important, if ironic, figure for understanding the success of American women in organizing an interdenominational women's foreign missionary society in 1860 and a telling figure in considering why that success helped to spawn such a dramatic movement in succeeding years. Ellen Huntly was born in New Hampshire in 1817. Her father was a poor, itinerant Baptist minister. Early in life, she imbibed of the ruling passion of the young evangelical women of her day—missions. She recalled in her memoir that "when but nine years old, there seemed to be some propelling power ever pushing me on to Burmah." Her early "companions" were the published accounts of the martyred missionary heroines Harriet Newell and Ann Judson. She amused herself by playing missionary in the woods near her home. "Often," she wrote, "did I turn the old brown and yellow birches into Burmese and Hindu girls. Many a time have I talked till tears came, to these imaginary heathen women."[23] Ellen harbored an intense longing to follow in the steps of Ann Judson by going as a missionary to Burma. She prepared herself by scraping together a respectable education and acquiring some teaching experience, fully intending to join the small but growing ranks of single missionary women. At some point in the early 1840s, however, she met her first husband, Edwin Buxton Bullard, who had also responded to the call of missions. Under appointment by the ABMU, they sailed for Burma on 18 November 1843. Tragically, Edwin died of cholera on 5 April 1847, early in their career. Ellen found herself alone with her young son, but not for long. The previous October, fellow missionary Francis Mason's wife had died after sixteen years of service. It was perhaps inevitable that the two recently widowed missionaries would marry for the sake of Burma.

Late in 1847, the sainted Adoniram Judson joined Francis Mason and Ellen Bullard in matrimony at the Baptist mission in Maulmein, Burma. They served quietly at the Karen mission in Tavoy for six years. In 1853, Francis Mason requested and received permission to establish a new work among the Karens at a place called Tounghoo, which had recently come under the control of the British as a result of the Second Burmese War in 1851–1852. Ellen, enthusiastic for the prospects of work among the women, wanted to establish a girls' school, but, prompted by financial problems, the ABMU had for several years dramatically curtailed its support for schools. Ellen thus turned to the British colonial government which in 1857 provided a plot of land and a grant of money for a building and some equipment in hopes that the Christianization and "civilization" of the Karen tribes would help to consolidate the gains they had made in the war.[24]

Ellen retained her commitment to education for Karen girls in spite of the union's earlier directive to deemphasize education and another policy statement issued in 1859 to the effect that missionary wives no longer owed direct service to the board. Although at least partially a response to the public perception that denominational boards had placed unreasonable demands on missionary wives, Burma missionaries nevertheless objected to the apparent denigration of women's mission work. The board responded by issuing a disclaimer stating that wives *could* do as much as they wished, but they need not feel compelled to work outside of their homes. "The wives are not to be appointed as missionaries," they wrote, "nor in any manner controlled or guided in their duties, but they are supposed to stand, as it regards the Union, behind the broad shield of their husbands, looking to them for advice in their work, so far as they may need any. In a word, they are to be regarded as occupying essentially the position of pastors' wives in this country."[25]

It may have been in response to those directives, which struck at the heart of her work and self-image as a missionary, or perhaps it was only because of chronic illness, but in the spring of 1860, Ellen Mason returned to the United States without her husband for a furlough. She spent her time in the United States in an energetic effort to arouse the women of America to the condition of their "heathen" sisters of the "Orient." In addition to publishing a memoir of her work among the Karens and two pamphlets on the conditions of women in India and Burma, she spent nearly two years traveling about the Northeast, meeting with individuals and ladies' missionary societies to garner their support.

One of the ladies' groups that Ellen Mason addressed that spring was the New York City Female Bible Society. That organization's constitution limited it to work in New York City, but Mason's message struck a chord with Sarah Doremus, one of its leaders. Together, Mason and Doremus began to enlist the support of New York women for an interdenominational society that would financially support single and married women missionaries who sought to address the special needs of their "Oriental sisters." In the fall of 1860, a group of women met in Doremus's parlor to adopt the constitution and bylaws establishing the Woman's Union Missionary Society of America, for Heathen Lands.[26] Branches soon sprang up in Boston and Philadelphia. As the wife of a wealthy and prominent merchant and a veteran of forty years of benevolent and reform activities, Sarah Doremus and her connections proved crucial to the organization's early success. The effort also received material assistance from Sarah Josepha Hale, who headed the Philadelphia branch and took it upon herself to "[make] the Mission known throughout the land" in the pages of *Godey's Lady's Book*.[27]

The first meeting of the WUMS for which records exist took place on 9 January 1861. The object of the meeting, according to the minutes, was to "discuss the practicability of establishing a missionary society where women could work for the evangelization of their heathen sisters." Seeking specifically to pattern their work after that of the British SPFEE, they concentrated their attention on India and Burma and on educational work and *zenana* visiting. They quickly determined primarily to support single women, especially the widows and daughters of missionaries already on the field.[28]

The SPFEE influenced the women who organized the WUMS in a number of ways. The English women's emphasis on establishing and staffing educational institutions and training teachers from among the indigenous peoples of the countries in which the SPFEE operated (primarily India, China, and Turkey) offered a model approach to evangelical educational work among women that American missionaries had found instructive as they began to formalize their educational institutions in the 1830s. The WUMS consciously sought to emulate the approach of the SPFEE in its educational work.

The WUMS also followed the SPFEE's example by seeking a cooperative relationship with existing mission boards and an interdenominational membership. The SPFEE sent missionaries primarily to work with established denominational missions and only after receiving a specific request from missionaries already on the field.

Rosamond Anne Webb, SPFEE officer, responded to questions submitted by the WUMS's Mrs. Wyckoff in a letter dated 9 February 1861. Wyckoff had apparently related the concerns of some that single women missionaries would interfere with already established denominational work. Webb replied that no interference with the work of male missionaries *could* occur because male and female missionaries operated in entirely different spheres of influence. Overlap was simply not possible:

> Women's work cannot be done by *men*; men cannot address girls in school for instruction nor can they obtain access to the secluded women of the zenana nor can they tend the [page torn]. These are women's duties; it is not hers to preach nor to conduct a meeting. Thus if there is but one missionary of either sex at any station, half the work is necessarily left undone. It has been well remarked that while man's work is represented in the parable as that of sowing seed, a field an open public meeting, woman's is typified by another parable as hiding leaven in a mass of meal, a quiet indoor occupation.[29]

Webb went on, however, to note that it was quite possible for a single woman missionary to interfere with the work of a missionary wife. Therefore, the SPFEE had adopted its policy of only placing their missionaries at stations where the denominational missionaries had explicitly requested help. In keeping with its principle of interdenominational cooperation, the SPFEE accepted those requests from all British Protestant missions. Their early minutes demonstrate cooperation with both the Church Missionary Society and the London Missionary Society, for example.[30] In her letter to Mrs. Wyckoff, Rosamond Webb noted that of the last six requests for missionaries that the SPFEE had granted, one came from Baptist missionaries, two from Presbyterians, and three from representatives of the Church of England. Accordingly, Article 13 of the WUMS's constitution stated that the board would give all (Protestant) denominations equal consideration in making appointments, but that "no lady shall be sent out except to a mission of her own denomination, where she will receive suitable counsel and protection."[31]

The WUMS mimicked the SPFEE's organizational structure by establishing a central committee to oversee day-to-day business and organizing branches and auxiliaries to develop widespread support in the hinterlands of the major metropolitan areas. Women in Boston and Philadelphia soon joined the New York women by forming branches, and eventually auxiliaries arose throughout the Northeast, the Ohio Valley, and the Great Lakes region. A scrapbook for the years 1861 to 1878, for example, contains clippings about the work of the WUMS from more than thirty publications, including the *Boston Daily Globe*, the *New York Times*, the *Chicago Tribune*, the Madison, Wisconsin, *State Journal*, and several national or regional denominational magazines.[32] The primary means for creating and sustaining interest in and support for the WUMS throughout such a wide geographic region thus became its publications—circulars, magazines, and annual reports. In the first decades of the organization's existence, those publications effectively redeployed all of the images of Hindu women that had been in circulation since the early reports of the Serampore Baptists and Claudius Buchanan and used those images to represent the plight of all "Oriental" women. All of the records of the WUMS, published and unpublished, reflected in their rhetoric the extent to which the emotional capital of the concept of "woman's work for woman" drew upon a half-century's accumulation of tropes about "Oriental" womanhood.

First of all, WUMS publications continued the practice of persuading American evangelicals that "Oriental" daughters were "'unwelcomed at their birth.'"[33] One report on China bemoaned the absence of laws against infanticide and noted the "unscrupulous slaughter of infant children, especially daughters." That missionary went on to note her acquaintance with a woman who had admitted to killing nine infant daughters and said missionaries believed that "carts full of dead infants are nightly trundled out of the city of Peking to be thrown into one grave."[34] The Reverend Jared Scudder, a missionary who gave an "Address on the Degradation of Woman in India," maintained that while "the birth of a boy is hailed as the brightest boon,...nothing is dreaded more than the arrival of an infant girl in the family, accounted as she is a present disgrace and a future burden. No impertinent congratulations of friends are waiting to welcome her; only a father's maledictions and a mother's wailing receive the poor little stranger."[35] The low esteem of daughters meant that they would remain uneducated. Scudder repeated the common assertion that only "dancing girls" (i.e., prostitutes) were permitted to read; hence, any young woman who could read would be stigmatized as a wanton "profligate." At the same time, he insisted that the parents of very young Hindu girls permitted them to "roam the streets" unsupervised and unprotected. "I do not exaggerate," he asserted, "when I say that girls of nine or ten years in India are often as conversant with everything impure as grown, mature women of the lowest class in other lands." Hence, he pointed to an inversion of thinking on the part of the Hindu father. That father believed society would brand his daughter an impure woman if he allowed her to receive an education, but since he thus did not permit her to be instructed, she became, in Scudder's view, exactly what her father hoped to prevent. Scudder maintained that Hindu society had a perverted ideal of womanhood. Since a Hindu man did not marry for companionship, but rather to acquire a "good upper servant," to marry an educated woman would invite trouble.[36]

WUMS publications also portrayed the degradation of "Oriental" women by discussing the early marriage of Hindu girls and the consequently pervasive social problem of young widowhood in a society that did not permit remarriage. WUMS writers also took advantage of these discussions to redeploy, by mere mention of the word *sati*, horrific images of young girls burning alive on their husbands' funeral pyres. One circular stated,

> Mere little girls four or five years old, betrothed and married before they have outgrown their baby playthings, if they have seen their husband but once, are widows for life, should he die, and have only the alternative of *suttee* or the equally fearful experience of a comfortless life and a hopeless death.[37]

Jared Scudder maintained that if a young Hindu wife did not commit suicide first, she probably faced early widowhood, "the climax of her misery," and if she sought relief in a second marriage, she became a "*Pariah*, at once a houseless, homeless vagrant."[38] Note that the widow was both "houseless" and "homeless" in Scudder's portrayal. She had no physical dwelling place, and she had no "home"—no protective family or friends, no sphere of usefulness, no social position at all.

The most widely held assumption about Indian women was that their homes were prisons and that they themselves were prisoners at best and slaves at worst. WUMS literature resembled British pieces such as Marianne Lewis's *Plea for Zenanas*, which insisted that women in India did not have homes, but merely occupied dwelling places. One missionary wrote, "Home has no meaning to them because, poor creatures, they have none." She went on to state that she had met women who had never been outside the walls of their rooms in fifty years.[39] The WUMS's circular "What a Pair of Slippers Did for India," a dramatized account of Elizabeth Sale's first entry into a *zenana*, claimed that "*Three-fourths of the women in India are prisoners for life*, in the homes of their husbands, whence they are never allowed to go forth."[40] Other circulars referred to the "neglected prisoners closely guarded in their apartments" and "grated *Zenanas*," bringing up a mental image of prison bars across windows.[41] The 1867 annual report quoted one of the society's first missionaries, Harriet Brittan:

> When I teach in one house I sit up stairs in a little verandah, which is walled all around. Into the verandah a strongly barred window opens, behind which sit the women who are being taught, passing their books and work through the bars. I always think of our Saviour's words, when visting them, "I was in prison when ye came unto me."[42]

Some writers represented the prison-like dwelling places of Indian women by describing both the bareness of their rooms and the inadequacy of their clothing: "Their clothing is scanty and forlorn. Their apartments have almost no furniture, and nothing whatever in the way of ornaments, or even conveniencies."[43] Others sought to highlight their perception of women as virtual slaves of their husbands by examining the "universal contrast between the condition of men and women in India." One missionary's letter, published in the 1866 annual report, described an Indian "gentleman's" apartment as lavishly furnished and richly decorated. His wife, however, locked in her apartment, formed a pathetic figure. She "sat on a dirty mat, which was thrown on a damp stone floor, her hair uncombed, her one article of clothing, a sauree, wretchedly dirty, and the appearance of everything in the bare, miserable little room she lived in, was that of the lowest heathenism."[44]

Finally, WUMS publications continued to emphasize the power of motherhood in the conversion of the world to Christianity. Despite the degraded and oppressed condition of Indian women, "it would be a very false conclusion to suppose that they possess little or no influence," maintained one author. [45] Upper-caste Hindu women acquiesced in the Brahminic traditions because they did not know better. They also passed those traditions along to their young children through explicit instruction and by example. Because (missionaries believed) Hindu women remained secluded and untaught, missionaries faced the task of starting over with each generation and trying to undo what mothers had already instilled in their children's minds. The missionaries thus believed that more than a half-century of efforts to convert their world had stalled because missionaries had made insufficient efforts to reach the most powerful and influential force in Indian society—mothers of the upper castes. The women who organized the WUMS did not merely justify their organization's existence with images of debased "Oriental" womanhood. They also used those images to create an imperative for their work—an imperative that would soon transform the entire foreign missions movement.

That the women who organized the WUMS encountered some opposition is certain. The thought of women shifting their substantial support from the denominations' missionary boards to an ecumenical women's organization must have struck fear into the heart of more than one denominational treasurer. The primary conflict over the WUMS, in fact, seemed to revolve not around the fact that it was a women's organization, but that it was interdenominational and would undercut and dilute (mainly financially) the denominations' efforts in behalf of women. The wife of the corresponding secretary of the New York auxiliary to the ABCFM, for example, attended the 9 January 1861 meeting to organize the WUMS and "made a strong protest against the organization of a new Society, because it would interfere with missionary Boards already established and which were the most successful channels for women's work."[46] Sarah D. Doremus recalled that her mother "rose to reply, saying that it would be a sad thing if Christian women for the second time should be prevented by prejudice or narrow views to attempt a work for our Lord and Master." "Prejudice" and "narrow views" referred not to attitudes toward the work of women, but to blind denominational loyalty. In fact, Doremus, Mason, and their cohorts were attempting to reconfigure evangelical loyalties by placing gender interest above denominational interests. At the same time, they did not want their ecumenical effort to undercut the denominations, so they channeled their workers and funds through the denominational boards. Nevertheless, the potential economic threat to the boards' interests prompted considerable concern.

Ellen Mason, however, seemed to develop an almost paranoid obsession with the idea that the denominational boards were conspiring to stamp out all missionary work by women. She wrote to Sarah Doremus, "I fear we shall be entirely shut out of the field, even Calcutta and Tounghoo. Men will help men and all the men in all the Committees over Christendom and heathen lands have [turned] against us, we cannot move, besides the Collectors [of donations] will be undermined and the whole will be crushed."[47] Ellen's fears notwithstanding, all of the evangelical denominations, while continually debating the *status* of missionary women, had long considered their *work* as central to the evangelization of Asia because they shared the view of women as the moral redeemers of all societies and assumed that "Oriental" women were inaccessible to male missionaries. The WUMS, as noted, did not initially set up new missions, but instead worked in cooperation with established denominational missions. Both the ABCFM and the American Baptists quickly availed themselves of the services of WUMS missionaries, and those women appear to have been warmly received by missionaries already on the field. That approach was in keeping with the American women's desire to model their efforts after those of the SPFEE. Neither the SPFEE nor the WUMS were formed to oppose or subvert existing male-led denominational mission agencies. Rather, they premised their very existence on cooperation with those agencies. The fact that both organizations flourished and survived attested to the willingness of those agencies to cooperate. The first significant business recorded by the WUMS, for example, appeared in their 28 October 1861 minutes. At that meeting they appointed Sarah Marston to work at the Baptist mission in Tounghoo. That appointment required the approval and cooperation of both the ABMU and their missionaries already in the field. They also recorded that the Philadelphia branch had appropriated $50 for Mrs. Gracey of the Methodist mission in northern India to support a female "Native Bible Reader" and $50 for the same purpose to Miss Campbell of the Presbyterian mission in the same region.[48]

While the content of Ellen's response when she encountered opposition seemed inconsistent with the facts of the situation, the tone in which she made that response was startling to say the least. She wrote,

> I very much fear that my own Executive Committee will prevent every ship owner from taking me *with a teacher on board.* Mr. Osgood their Agent has a way of succeeding even with *ladies* to turn them *bitterly* against our undertaking.... Indeed I do not believe half a dozen *Baptists* will hold us at all unless we take some measure to shut their liar mouths.[49]

A response to this letter, addressed to Sarah Doremus, is not extant. It is, perhaps, the earliest written evidence of the irascible nature that would very soon elicit charges that Ellen Mason's mind had come unhinged. In fact, some of the opposition to the WUMS was probably opposition to Ellen Mason personally. That some controversy may have attended her decision even to return to the United States is indicated in the action of the ABMU Executive Committee in 1862 when she applied for the funds to return to Burma. Three hundred dollars was appropriated on the condition that she "indicate her purpose to resume her former relation and cooperate with her husband in the service of the Missionary Union."[50] Even the WUMS received some indication of the ascerbic nature of her personality. For example, the 15 April 1861 minutes recorded the reading of a letter from Mrs. Mason, who was then in Philadelphia helping Sarah Josepha Hale to convert her LMMS into the Philadelphia branch of the WUMS. Mason reported her displeasure that the American Presbyterian board was assuming responsibility for a girls' school in China that had been under the SPFEE. Miss Aldersey had been running the school for many years as a missionary of the SPFEE, but "the increasing infirmities of age" had forced her to give up the work. Mason was angry that a married couple, the Rankins, would be overseeing the work and felt that the WUMS should approach the Presbyterian board about providing a single woman so that the school would remain a woman's domain. Sarah Doremus countered by noting that the work had been transferred according to Aldersey's express wishes and that she rejoiced to see that a denominational board wanted to support girls' educational work.[51]

The WUMS and the ABMU would both soon have reason to suspect that Mason's rhetoric was more than a mere product of personal eccentricity. Preparing to return to her field of labor, Ellen successfully recruited Sara Marston to serve as her assistant for the work among girls and women in Toungoo. On 28 October 1861, the society unanimously approved Sara's application. Having accepted the Baptist Union's demand that she "resume her former relation and cooperate with her husband," Ellen, along with Sara, met with no obstacles when they set sail for Burma in the spring of 1862, arriving in Tounghoo in September. On 23 September, Sara Marston wrote to the society to announce her safe arrival and informed them that

> So far as I am capable of judging, our Woman's Missionary Society meets with universal favor from the Missionaries here, on the field.... My coming was hailed with great joy by them; and since my arrival, I have received nothing but unlimited kindness.... In Calcutta, I met with Presbyterians, and there, my experience was the same as with the Baptists, elsewhere.[52]

She thus explicitly contradicted Ellen Mason's assertions regarding opposition to the WUMS among missionaries already on the field.

Mason quickly busied herself with her own correspondence. In November 1862, shortly after arriving in Burma, Ellen wrote to the British deputy commissioner, Major Lloyd. A brief selection from that letter illustrates the religious opinions that would soon bring upon her charges of insanity:

> Last September I was in Philadelphia.... It was midnight and I sat alone in an upper chamber. Something seemed to speak. There was no

> voice, but it came like a flash: "look down upon the floor." I looked and there was the IVth chapter of Revelation as plain as light woven in the carpet at my feet. It was an English or Dutch carpet of rich design, and that design and the color all spoke out this chapter. I was so much overpowered by it, I called up my son to see it, and neither of us dared afterwards to step on the throne.
>
> The question immediately arose how came the weaver by this pattern. It must have come out of Egypt. I began to look into letters studying out the origin of forms. The result has been this.
>
> 1st. I am convinced that the alphabet was known to Adam and Eve—that the first alphabet is stereotyped in the heavens, and from this all nations have learned...to reckon time. It proves that and that the Solar System is our own Bible, and represents God and the history of man's redemption. It proves that God took upon himself the form of a *world* and covered it with sacred letters, making every rock, mountain, sea, river, and country a shard or chapter. Then the world was made a book lighted up with trees, flowers, grasses, birds, fishes and animals which were created expressly for letters to this *world* Bible.... God has in infinite mercy given me the key to this book, and to my inexpressible joy and surprise...[it is the embroidery on the] Karen dresses.[53]

Mason openly published her views regarding what she called "God language" in English and Karen newspapers in Burma. She detailed those views in lengthy letters to the Executive Committee of the ABMU. She also used money, donated by the WUMS for native Bible readers, to train those readers to propagate her own heterodox religious views.

Within two weeks of her arrival in Burma, Sara Marston wrote to Sarah Doremus a heart-wrenching description of Ellen Mason's teachings and actions. From Sara Marston's point of view, Ellen's behavior had grown increasingly erratic and paranoid; she seems to have subjected Sara herself to intense verbal abuse. Sara wrote, "In the grief of my heart, I must tell you that, had I known her as I now know her, worlds could not have tempted me to be associated with her. Mrs. Mason, in America and upon paper, is a very different being from Mrs. Mason in Burmah and upon her field of operation." Sara's greatest concern was that Mason had "imposed upon" good women in America, and that the money they had worked so hard to raise was being used to promote ideas inimical to the gospel of Jesus.[54]

Needless to say, Ellen Mason's new revelation created quite a stir in Burma and in the United States. The mission at Tounghoo was divided because Francis Mason remained strangely silent on the issue. Two of the other missionaries, Mr. Cross and Mr. Bixby, felt compelled to turn to the British governor and (unsuccessfully) represented Ellen's teachings as designed to stir up Karen nationalism and incite rebellion.[55] The Karen Christians, of whom there were several thousand in Tounghoo, split into two factions—one aligned with Ellen Mason and one opposed. That breach did not heal for over a decade.[56] The ABMU, adhering firmly to their policy that a missionary wife answered only to her husband, repeatedly implored Francis Mason to exercise his authority as "the man, the Christian minister, and the missionary" to stop his wife before she succeeded in undoing what had been such a "remarkable" and "providential" work. He flatly refused, dismissing her writings and teachings as "nonsense" unworthy of all the trouble they were stirring up. The union responded by dismissing him from its employ.[57] Even the WUMS was divided. Sara Marston communicated only with Sarah Doremus at the headquarters in New York. Doremus's effort to handle the situation delicately, without openly exposing Ellen Mason to the women at home, backfired. Mason communicated directly with the Boston and Philadelphia branches, claiming that Sara Marston was a traitor to the cause of "woman's work for woman" and representing herself as the victim of "the bitterest war…to destroy this work."[58] The two branches both demanded Sara's dismissal.[59] Apparently, however, the scandalous news became public in the United States, Ellen's own words became her downfall, and she quietly disappeared from the records of the WUMS after 1863.[60] Sara Marston remained in Burma until forced by ill health to return to the United States in 1865.

Ellen's contemporaries usually described her as having developed an "unbalanced mind."[61] In one of their letters attempting to persuade Francis Mason to action regarding his wife, the Executive Committee of the ABMU wrote that they had "the settled conviction that Mrs. Mason is the subject of mental aberration.… No sane person could speak and write as she has done.… In the judgment of your brethren, Mrs. Mason needs rest, freedom from exhausting labors and such quiet and repose, together with such medical advice as she cannot obtain in Toungoo." They concluded by offering to bear the expense of bringing her back to the United States to undergo treatment.[62] Perhaps those particular individuals did have a "settled conviction" of Ellen's madness; it may have been incomprehensible to them that so devout a Christian as Ellen Mason could have slipped into heterodoxy under any other circumstances. Others, however, seemed to have been giving her the benefit of the doubt. Sara Marston had written from Tounghoo,

> The most of the English people here, think her insane, and many of the natives think her so. I have *tried* to think so. That is the most charitable construction that can be put upon her design.... If it is not insanity, it is something worse. I might as well say what I think. An unhallowed ambition. A desire to be thought something great.[63]

Thus, even some at the time were inclined to think that Ellen Mason was not insane, but apostate; subsequent historians of the Burma mission seemed to agree. When mentioned at all, she was blamed for "leading a number of [Karen] churches into heresy" by her "extravagant teachings."[64] What is remarkable about the entire episode, however, is how little it influenced the subsequent development of the WUMS or women's denominational foreign missions boards. Mason quickly disappeared from the records and almost from the institutional memory of the organization she helped to found. Furthermore, within just a few years, the Baptist men whom she had decried as the inveterate enemies of women's missionary work had welcomed the formation of a denominational women's mission board and enthusiastically embraced the development of "woman's work for woman." Had those denominational leaders borne the antipathy toward women that Mason attributed to them, they could easily have used her example, so readily transformable into the stereotypically "hysterical" woman whose mind came unhinged as a result of venturing beyond her appropriate sphere, to justify restricting the work of missionary wives and excluding single women. In fact, the foreign mission enterprise in general and the Baptist tradition in particular, stemming as it did from the time of the sainted Mary Webb and Ann Judson, had so many examples of strong and effective women workers for the cause that they readily swept aside Ellen Mason and proceeded with the feminization of the entire movement.

In 1872, the report of the Philadelphia branch compared the WUMS to a banyan tree: "Travelers who have seen the luxurious vegetation of India, tell us of the marvellous Banyan tree, whose branches send shoots downwards, which take root and become stems; thus the tree spreads over a great surface and endures for ages." The branches eventually break off and become separate trees and thus the species multiplies. Similarly, the writer noted, the WUMS had sent off branches in the form of the women's mission boards of the Congregational, Methodist, Baptist, and Presbyterian churches. The multiplication of women's mission boards thus offered a sign of health and heralded a bright future for the cause of "woman's work for woman."[65] In January of 1868, Congregational women became the first to organize along denominational lines. Methodist women followed suit the next year, forming the Woman's Foreign Missionary Society (WFMS), which became an official agency of the Methodist Epsicopal Church (MEC) in 1870. Baptist women organized two societies in 1871, one in the East, headquartered in Boston, and one in the West, headquartered in Chicago.[66] Some scholars have attempted to delineate and distinguish among the women's boards in order to determine which became the most autonomous (generally the Methodists win this prize).[67] Each of those boards underwent significant changes within a decade after forming, and relationships with the larger denomination were complex. But at the time of organization—between 1868 and 1871—the denominational women's boards under consideration here had quite similar structures, mainly because they all patterned themselves on the same model, the WUMS. First (and most important for this study), each emphasized the spiritual, physical, and social needs of "Oriental" women to justify their increased involvement in foreign mission work. Each aimed for a "national" membership (that is, coterminous with the geographic extent of the denomination), established a central committee or executive board, adopted an elaborate system of church- or community-based local auxiliaries or branches to involve women at the grassroots, and established a magazine to promote the organization's work and inspire women at the local level to contribute their "mite" to the larger cause. In a departure from the WUMS, each subordinated itself (with some variation in degree) to the male-led, "parent" denominational boards. In all cases, the "parent" board made decisions regarding appointments and expenditures, and all missionary women served under the authority and direction of existing missionary stations.

Some authors have mistakenly portrayed the formation of the women's mission boards as a *separation* from the "parent" boards in an oppositional response to their disfranchisement at the denominational level.[68] In reality, the formation of the denominational women's boards represented an attempt by both women and men to keep the women's influence and money *within* the denominations. Denominational loyalty was extremely important to both women and men. Women indicated this by the eagerness with which they sought to imitate the WUMS by establishing their own boards to cooperate with their own denominations. As noted at the end of the previous chapter, Clara Swain exhibited such denominational loyalty. The WUMS had engaged to send her to India as a missionary doctor, but when Methodist women organized, she immediately expressed her preference to go out under Methodist auspices. The WUMS, while organized with the intention of cooperating with existing boards—a practice that it continued for quite some time—had nevertheless already showed signs of breaking with that resolve by sending three women to China under its own auspices to establish a nondenominational girls' boarding school.[69] Denominational leaders feared that an exodus of women to an ecumenical society would ultimately deplete financial resources and weaken overall enthusiasm for missions, which in all Protestant denominations had traditionally depended heavily upon women's involvement. Even after each of the denominational women's boards formed, male (and some female) leaders expressed anxiety about diluted financial strength, fearing that women would designate all of their funds for women's causes and thus have a negative impact on overall missions funding.

Congregational women, for example, resolved that their organization would raise "extra funds" to support work "for the benefit of the degraded of our sex in Pagan lands." The women had inserted the word "extra" at the insistence of "Mrs. Dr. Anderson" (wife of Rufus Anderson), who feared that women would simply "divert" funds they would have otherwise given for the ABCFM's general work, rather than seeking to "increase the aggregate."[70] When the Methodist WFMS became an agency of the MEC in 1871, denominational officials guarded against such "diversion" of funds by forbidding women to solicit funds at church services or in "promiscuous meetings" (meetings with both men and women present). Instead, Methodist women supported their work by charging annual membership dues.[71] Baptists revealed a similar concern, reminding readers of the 1874 annual report of the ABMU that money given through the women's society should be in addition to regular offerings to the Union.[72]

The women who organized denominational women's mission boards explicitly stated their intention of cooperating with existing "parent" boards. The secretary of the ABCFM, N. G. Clarke, had corresponded early on with one of the women involved in organizing the Woman's Board of Missions. Mrs. Homer Bartlett had requested from him suggestions for such an agency. Clarke responded with a list of seven recommendations. Among them, he suggested that the Woman's Board of Missions recommend candidates and raise funds for their work, but that the ABCFM approve all appointments and that the women go out as missionaries of the ABCFM, which would also handle all of the financial arrangements, coordinate women missionaries' work with existing stations, and receive all of their reports and correspondence. "The Christian ladies of our churches would thus be saved the perplexing details of business to a great extent," Clarke concluded, "while they would have their own missionaries supported by their prayers and contributions, through whom they might feel themselves brought into immediate connection with women of heathen lands." Section Three of the Act of Incorporation of the Woman's Board of Missions essentially enacted that recommendation.[73]

Methodist women in Boston had originally organized in 1869 into a society that, at the recommendation of the secretary of the Methodist board, focused on raising funds, while "leav[ing] the administration of the work to the Board at home and the Mission in India." The WFMS spread rapidly in the form of individual local societies, but the organizational structure proved inadequate and the work uncoordinated, so Methodist women developed a plan modeled after the WUMS and the Congregational women's board, with a central committee and closely coordinated branch societies. At the same time, the women sought a closer relationship with the denominational board and thus submitted their constitution to the General Conference for its approval so that the WFMS could become an official agency of the denomination, with its work auxiliary to the denomination's mission board. The committee assigned to consider the women's proposal stated in its report to the General Conference,

> They propose to act in harmony with the chief missionary instrumentality of the Church, and to assist in the selection of suitable women as teachers and missionaries, who, although devoted to a special work, shall be sent, not to independent fields of labor, but to those under the control of our Parent Missionary Society, and be subject as our missionaries are to the missionary authorities of the church.

The report went on to note that some concern existed over the formation of societies for special purposes, for fear that such efforts would cause the overall purposes of the church to "be frittered away, and divided interests and palpable confusion ensue." The committee responded to those objections by noting that such problems would occur only if work among women represented a "special" work not "comprehended in the plan of our general operations." Reaching women in "heathen" lands, however, very much formed a part of the Methodist plan for world evangelization; therefore, the committee wrote, "so long as our general work is pursued we are not only ready for but solicitous to receive every aid to further it, whether it apply to a particular branch or the work at large."[74]

Baptist women likewise sought advice from the ABMU before organizing. The ABMU suggested that the women focus on raising both enthusiasm and money for the cause of "woman's work for woman," while relegating to the ABMU responsibility for appointing women missionaries, directing their work, and managing and distributing money. The ABMU, for its part, recognized both the increasing demand for women workers and the steady supply of applications from women seeking missionary appointments.[75] Baptist women received their impetus from the women of the First Baptist Church of Newton Centre,

Massachusetts, who organized in February 1871 "for the benefit of women in heathen lands, to act through and in connection with the ABMU." That group of women appointed a committee to issue a circular to churches throughout the Boston area calling on women to organize on a larger scale. The circular noted

> the desire of [the ABMU's] Executive Committee to do every thing possible for the elevation of woman as well as man; of its readiness to employ Christian women as far as practicable in this work; of the urgent need of more laborers at all our stations and in the regions beyond; and of our own duty to co-operate more fully in the great work; we believe the time has come for us to form a society or societies for the special purpose of aiding our missionary Union to do more for the heathen and Christian women in the stations under its care.[76]

The Woman's Baptist Missionary Society subsequently adopted a constitution that acknowledged just such a cooperative purpose by declaring its object as "furnishing support, through the ABMU, to Christian women employed by said Union as Missionaries, native teachers, or Bible readers, together with the facilities needed for their work, such labours being recommended by this Society."[77]

In addition to offering tacit cooperation, male denominational leaders demonstrated active support and enthusiasm for the women's work. That enthusiasm represented, at a pragmatic level, a recognition that women's financial support was crucial to the boards' success. More important, however, men shared with women the belief that, due to the peculiar gender system of the "Orient," only women could successfully evangelize their counterparts in Asia. American evangelicals, men and women alike, continued to share the belief prevalent for nearly a century that religious influence went from wives to husbands and from mothers to children and that therefore evangelizing women was key to evangelizing the world. Furthermore, representatives of each of the societies discussed here repeatedly maintained that new openings existed for women's work, apparently referring to the development of the system of *zenana* visitation in which both the WUMS and several British societies were engaging.

In a letter sanctioning the formation of a Woman's Board of Missions, ABCFM secretary N. G. Clarke wrote that "the time seems to have fully come for new and enlarged efforts to extend the blessings of the gospel to the women of heathen lands" and proceeded to specify work underway in India, Persia, Turkey, and Syria. Referring to the work of four women in "Western Asia," he noted that "by visiting house to house, by inviting the native women to their homes, and attending female prayer meetings, [they] found ready access to the hearts of those who in former years had been utterly neglected." He further reported to the women organizers that he had addressed letters to missionaries in the field to "ascertain what can be done for the women" and determine the human and financial resources needed to prosecute that work. "We shall be glad to see an American Women's Missionary Association, for the spiritual and social elevation of the women in heathen lands," he concluded, "assuming the support of the faithful Christian women now under our direction and greatly enlarging their number."[78] After reading this letter aloud at the organizational meeting on 2 January 1868, Mrs. Albert Bowker, who was presiding, introduced the business of the meeting by commenting on the "300,000,000 women in Asia...waiting for the blessing of the gospel." Mrs. Miron Winslow, a missionary returned from India, elaborated on that comment by noting that those women represented the "great hinderance to the conversion of the men." The "Oriental" woman, according to Mrs. Winslow, was "more supersititious, and she appeal[ed] with the whole force of maternal influence to prevent her sons from becoming Christians and thus disgracing herself."[79]

Methodist women, in a "Memorial of the Woman's Foreign Missionary Society to the General Conference of the Methodist Episcopal Church" issued in 1871, noted that they had received their motive for organizing from the "appalling fact that there are millions of unsaved women in heathen lands who, in consequence of the social customs of their people, can be reached and saved only through the instrumentality of Christian women." Providentially, at the same time that American women awakened to that fact, "a grand revolution of public sentiment with respect to female education was in progress in Asiatic society in consequence of which doors long closed began to open, and Christian women were invited to enter dark homes bearing the light of God's word." Those words echoed the sentiments that the Board of Managers of the Missionary Society of the MEC had expressed the year before upon receiving the WFMS constitution for approval. The men who comprised the committee instructed to study the women's constitution concurred wholeheartedly in the WFMS's purpose. Noting the growth of "so-called *zenana* work," the report went on to recognize that "insuperable barriers" existed between male missionaries and Asian women, but that "female teachers" increasingly could gain access where the men could not. "It seems, therefore, a providential provision," the report concluded in its endorsement, "that, at such a conjuncture, a new and powerful agency should arise in the Church adapted to the exigency of carrying the Gospel and the blessing of education to the women of heathen countries."[80]

In June of 1867, the ABMU issued a circular letter to "their missionaries in Asia" requesting that they express their views "as to how far the interests of the missions may be subserved by the more liberal appointment of female helpers."[81] Missionaries in Burma responded with a plea for more workers, especially teachers, noting that "at a time when few men are offering for this work of missions, the hearts of gifted and cultivated Christian women in every section of the country are being stirred up to it." They went on to recite the contribution of women workers to the Burma mission, concluding that "if one or more Christian women, unencumbered with family and household cares, and free to teach in the schools, distribute tracts, conduct Bible classes, and otherwise aid the work of evangelization, were placed in every mission family, we might reasonably hope to reap great advantages from the plan. Woman, as a teacher, is not an experiment, but is rather God's original ordination."[82] Two years later, the Executive Committee adopted the report of a Special Committee on the Woman's Missionary Society, which expressed confidence that the new organization could be the means of raising up laborers and funds to expand work for "the Christian improvement of women." "We bid them a hearty God speed in the accomplishment of their purpose," the report concluded, "for it is our belief that a Woman's Missionary Society auxiliary to the Union and acting in harmony with it, may double, ere long, the efficiency of our work as a denomination in evangelizing the world."[83]

Why did the denominational women's mission boards form when they did? Clearly, as demonstrated above, the formation of the WUMS provided a strong motivation. The records of each of the new boards, in fact, explicitly indicated the debt owed to the WUMS. Postwar accounts and twentieth-century scholarship, however, have most commonly listed the Civil War itself as the causal factor for the feminization of denominational missions. Just as scholars of women in the Civil War have portrayed that conflict as a catalyst that brought northern women forward to demand a larger role in public life, so have observers and historians of women in missions suggested that the experiences of northern women in supporting the war effort gave them the confidence that they needed to declare their independence from denominational boards and engage in the work of foreign missions on their own terms.[84]

This interpretation, placing nineteenth-century women in opposition to male-led denominations and, by implication, attaching the women's foreign missions movement to the movement for women's political rights, seems to have begun with Helen Barrett Montgomery's classic study *Western Women in Eastern Lands* (1910). Montgomery maintained that, during the war, women "discovered powers of which they themselves and the nation had been quite unconscious" and that it was therefore "no accident that it was the decade following the close of the Civil War that saw the launching of scores of organizations, among them the Missionary Societies."[85] Montgomery's particular interpretation of events stemmed in part from her own role as a feminist and suffragist, as well as missions advocate and Baptist denominational leader. Scholars have generally cited her as the authority on the subject. R. Pierce Beaver, who subtitled his work on women and missions "The First Feminist Movement in America," cited that same passage from Montgomery. Jane Hunter, in her study of American women and Chinese missions in the late nineteenth century, did the same when she maintained that "women's experience with organized work during the Civil War, most historians agree, brought them the confidence to found their own separate sending boards to do together what solitary women had struggled to do alone." Likewise, Joan Jacobs Brumberg used

Montgomery's authority to assert that the "woman's foreign mission crusade...took shape at the close of the Civil War."[86]

Those interpretations derive in part from the tendency of mission leaders to invoke the Civil War experience or military metaphors in the immediate postwar years. They sought to capitalize on patriotic enthusiasm and energy and redirect it into a missionary channel before it had a chance to subside. Those male leaders also praised the roles of women in the war effort and used that precedent to justify their own embrace of an expanded role for women in the work of world evangelization. In 1867, a report to the Executive Committee of the ABMU asserted,

> In the female members of our churches, there is manifestly a large amount of earnest missionary spirit, and it would seem to be wisdom on the part of our organization to avail itself fully of this force for the more effective prosecution of its work among the heathen. After the illustrations furnished in our Civil War of woman's ability to render useful service on a generous scale, it can hardly be expected that such ability will easily fall back into its old channels of usefulness, and do as little as formerly in so great an enterprise as the world's evangelization. Woman has learned her power for good, and her aspirations are towards a higher plane of activity and a larger participation in the executive forth-puttings of this age. May not the hand of God be in all this? And may not these developments be prophetic of His purpose to employ female agency in a larger measure for the benefit of the degraded millions of women and children in pagan lands?[87]

The following year, both the male leaders of the ABCFM and the female leaders of the WUMS issued similar statements, adopting the language of war to describe the work of evangelizing the world. The ABCFM proclaimed that a special place for women existed in the "consecrated host" that was engaged in the great "conflict of the church with heathenism."[88] The WUMS similarly noted the "peculiar place for Christian women in the army of the Lord" and went on to ask, "Shall not her influence here become a power as honored as during our late national contest, when it was said, that the active hearth-blaze kept pace with the camp-fire, the ready fingers with the marching feet, and the rapid needle with the deadly bayonet?"[89]

Women who organized the denominational women's mission boards no doubt felt the significance of their Civil War experiences. The view of the Civil War as somehow socially liberating women from the confinement of the domestic sphere is somewhat unconvincing, however, particularly in regard to the work of foreign missions. As this study has demonstrated, women had long engaged in efforts to support that cause, and an important catalyzing factor, the WUMS, had organized prior to the conflict.[90] Furthermore, after the war, women established mission boards explicitly in cooperation with male denominational leaders, not in opposition to them. Those leaders welcomed the women's efforts, even as they expressed anxiety over the financial arrangements and other logistics entailed by such an expansion of the work, as well as the shifting gender relations within the movement at home and abroad. It was after the war, however, that denominational women adopted the national vision of the WUMS and its complex organizational structure, connecting local branches to a centralized executive board. Women organized themselves in such a way that their work effectively became a department of the larger missions work. The denominations, in fact, began to refer to the "women's department" of work. One can perhaps argue that the Civil War significantly influenced the foreign missions movement, but not primarily by liberating women from their traditional roles. Historians have argued that the Civil War contributed to the "modernization" of the United States by increasing the complexity and efficiency of both the federal government and private industry, creating a more tightly integrated national economy. Likewise, one could argue that those developments had implications for religious culture as well. Denominations reflected changes in the corporate world by developing more complex bureaucratic structures.[91] Developing separate "departments" for women's work reflected that increasing complexity and specialization of function. Mirroring the growing importance of the professions in the postwar economy, women also began to construct a professional identity from the work of missions—they created an elaborate curriculum to educate their constituency, established training schools for their workers, and began recruiting educated, single women in large numbers for careers as missionary teachers, nurses, social workers, and doctors, as well as evangelistic workers. The institutionalization of "woman's work for woman" was, indeed, a very "modern uprising."[92] The underlying premise for the women's work, however, remained the same as at the beginning of the century—rooted in the "social systems of the East" and the plight of the "Oriental" woman.[93]

Conclusion

The WUMS and all of the denominational women's boards focused most of their energy and resources on Asia for the rest of the nineteenth century and well into the twentieth. Methodist women provided the most striking example. Of all the American Protestant denominations, only Methodists had developed their foreign mission effort within the context of Africa rather than Asia, establishing their first overseas mission in Liberia in 1833. Their first woman missionary, a widow by the name of Ann Wilkins, arrived in Liberia in 1837. Financial support for her work came chiefly from the first local Methodist women's missionary society, the Female Missionary Society of New York, established in 1819. Methodists did not enter an Asian mission field until 1847, when they sent a missionary couple to China. But even though the denomination was relatively new to the work of Asian missions, when Methodist women organized a national denomination-wide missionary society in 1869, they did so specifically with India and China in mind.[1] Their monthly publication, *The Heathen Woman's Friend* focused almost exclusively on India and China for at least the first five years of its existence. The Methodist women's board, for example, supported only two missionaries, both in India, in their first year of existence. By 1910, they had 312 missionaries, most in Asia.

As Edwin Munsell Bliss noted in 1893, "the modern uprising of women in behalf of foreign missions had its motive in the social systems of the East... When the degradation and suffering of Asiatic women and the darkness of their future were revealed to the western world, the conscience of Christian women was aroused."[2] That a "great uprising" of women occurred is without question, as indicated by the growth of local auxiliaries affiliated with the denominational women's boards. The northern Woman's Baptist Foreign Missionary Society expanded twenty-fold, from 255 to 5000 auxiliaries, between 1873 and 1909, while Presbyterian women increased the number of their local auxiliaries from "100 in 1870 to 10,869 in 1909." Methodist women's annual contributions were nearing $1 million by 1910.[3] The roots of that "uprising," however, began early in the nineteenth century, not after the Civil War as some have suggested. Its greatest impetus came from the fascination of evangelical women with their "benighted heathen sisters" in the "Orient."

The organization of the Woman's Union Missionary Society proved an important catalyst for Protestant women's engagement in the cause of foreign missions and the Civil War also exerted a complex and multifaceted influence. As the last chapter demonstrated, the formation of the WUMS was an especially important factor not only for women's decisions to form their own mission boards within the major denominations, but also for the denominations' leadership and rank-and-file to support those decisions. The most important factor motivating Protestant women to volunteer their time and money for the mission cause, however, continued to be those images, deeply embedded in evangelical culture through nearly a century of popular mission literature, of the degraded "Oriental" woman whose very life, in this world and the next, depended on her privileged American sisters.

Helen Barrett Montgomery's enormously popular book, *Western Women in Eastern Lands* (1910), demonstrated the extent to which images of oppressed "Oriental" women continued to energize evangelical Protestant American women to support the cause of world missions in the early twentieth century. Part of the United Study of Foreign Missions, an educational curriculum launched by an interdenominational group of women in 1901, *Western Women in Eastern Lands* sold 50,000 copies in six weeks and 100,000 copies in its first year.[4] Its wide availability in reprint form even today means that historians of the women's mission movement commonly cite Montgomery as an authority on the nineteenth-century history of women and missions. That is unfortunate, because Montgomery was no historian. Even though it contains much valuable statistical information difficult to find elsewhere, the book is replete with inaccuracies. Montgomery was a feminist and a suffragist in addition to being a great proponent of evangelical missions and did not hesitate to bring the history of women in missions into the service of her politics and ideology. Her work is the source of the two most common errors among historians today -- that the "great uprising" of women in the cause of foreign missions occurred only after the end of the Civil War and was largely impelled by the war experience and that the women's mission movement was part of a larger feminist political movement.[5]

While *Western Women in Eastern Lands* has limited value as a work of historical scholarship, it is invaluable as a primary source for the cultural history of the evangelical women's mission movement. After surveying the "history" of women's involvement in missions in her first chapter, entitled "What Our Mothers Have Told Us," Montgomery went on to describe in detail the conditions of women in the "Orient" and the efforts of missionary women to ameliorate those conditions and win converts to Christianity. Montgomery effectively redeployed images of the degraded "Oriental" woman that had been around since the first decade of the nineteenth century. She maintained that, while western Christian societies held to the rule "ladies first," "Oriental" societies were governed by the rule "ladies last." Likewise, western Christian women had the luxury of enumerating and pursuing "woman's rights," while their counterparts in the East were barely aware that they suffered from "woman's wrongs." She went on to assert,

> The appeal to the women of England and America was winged by the recital of the intolerable injustices and oppression under which the women of the non-Christian lands spent their lives... . For while there are terrible wrongs against women in our own land, there is this difference: the wrongs of Hindu, Chinese, and Moslem women are buttressed behind the sanctions of religion and are indorsed by the founders of their faith; while in our own land these wrongs flaunt themselves against the spirit and the plain provisions of our religion. If women fully recognized the emancipatory nature of the pure religion of Jesus, the force of the religious missionary arguments would be tremendously strengthened.[6]

Montgomery's words echoed the message that had been central to evangelical missions since their inception at the dawn of the nineteenth century: that the status of women in a society was a fair indicator of the degree to which that society was modern and civilized; and that the "Oriental" religions oppressed, degraded, and enslaved women, but Christianity would liberate them and as a result of their liberation, their influence as Christian wives and mothers would uplift the entirety of Eastern civilization to the standard achieved by the West.

Montgomery then catalogued the "wrongs of woman" in the East. She began in China, describing footbinding and female infanticide as "but symptoms of fundamental errors in the Chinese conception of womanhood and the home." Those practices, she said, were rooted in the teachings of Confucianism and Buddhism, which offered women "no hope of immortality" except being born as a man in a future life.[7] Daughters in China, she argued, were "not desired at birth… and [were] denied the privileges of education. To destroy girl babies at birth," she continued, "was formerly exceedingly common, and not regarded as a crime by the majority." Fathers often would not name their daughters, she explained, merely assigning them a number. When asked about their families, fathers discussed only their sons. Both daughters and wives, according to Montgomery, could be sold into slavery. "The binding of the feet," she concluded, "is but an outward and visible sign of the crippled lives and energies of one-half of the Chinese people."[8]

Montgomery then turned her attention to Muslim women. "The darkest blot upon the prophet Mohammed," she wrote, "is the low appreciation of womanhood that led him to embed in the Koran itself legislation that affronts the intellect and heart of womanhood."[9] Montgomery conceded that Muslim customs regarding women could vary from one culture to another. But she insisted that certain aspects of Muslim treatment of women were the same regardless of geographic location. "All women, except the very poor, are secluded behind barred windows in the harem, and are never seen in public unveiled."[10] Her litany continued: a man could divorce his wife with little or no cause; a man could take multiple wives; boys were educated but girls were not; women were seldom allowed to worship in mosques. Montgomery quoted a "Moslem jurist" to the effect that under Islam, it was unheard of for a man to love his wife.[11]

Montgomery saved her harshest indictment for Hindu treatment of women in India:

> It is in the ancient land of India that we see the deepest degradation of womanhood, a degradation that inheres in the very religious standards of the people. Enforced seclusion, child marriages, perpetual widowhood, may be said to characterize the social life of the women of India. Every one of those disabilities and evils rests on positive teaching of the most venerated scriptures.

Montgomery cited the "most sacred code of Hinduism, the code of Manu" as her authority on the status of Hindu women. She listed first and foremost the "prison-like confinement" of all but the lowest caste women, quoting Manu: "'A woman is not allowed to go out of the house without the consent of her husband; she may not laugh without a veil over her face or look out of a door or a window.'"[12] Montgomery's discussion of the seclusion of women is an excellent example of the practice of collapsing a variety of cultural practices into a single "Oriental" practice. In explaining the terminology, she noted, "The term 'zenana,' strictly speaking, can be applied only to Indian homes; but in popular use it has been made to cover the enforced seclusion of women in zenana, purdah, harem, anpang, and the like, wherever practiced. The extreme form is found in Moslem lands and among the aristocratic portions of Indian society."[13]

From the seclusion of women, Montgomery turned her attention to the "revolting ugliness" of child marriage and the closely related evil of perpetual widowhood.[14] In addition to referencing the Code of Manu on this subject, Montgomery also cited the authority of Pandita Ramabai. Ramabai, the celebrated Hindu widow who had converted to Christianity, found at the meetings of American and British missionary societies a platform from which to advocate for Indian women. Montgomery related Ramabai's testimony that Hindu fathers often contracted marriages for their daughters in infancy and those marriages were sometimes consummated before the age of twelve. Terrible consequences resulted when the child became a widow. Even if the marriage had never been consummated, Hindu custom forbade the widow from ever remarrying, viewing the death of a husband as punishment for the wife's sins in a former life. "A child of three, widowed by the death of her aged husband," Montgomery declared, "is condemned to widowhood, since the remarriage of widows is absolutely abhorrent to all Hindu ideas." That child-widow faced a dismal future: "Because she is accursed she is stripped of her ornaments, her hair shaved, her food restricted to one scant meal a day. Twice in the month she must go without food or water for forty-eight hours. Only one coarse white garment is allowed her, she is debarred from all family feasts, shunned, hated, and made the drudge and slave."[15] Although she did not offer a source for her statistics, Montgomery asserted that in 1901, 14,000 widows under the age of four lived in India and 400,000 under the age of 15.[16]

Also closely related to the evils of child marriage (or any "Oriental" marriage, in Montgomery's view) was the inadequacy of "oriental medical practice," particularly the midwives' "frightful malpractice in childbirth." "The ministering to women is left to ignorant, filthy, and often immoral midwives or 'half-doctors' as they are called in India," wrote Montgomery. "The suffering of mothers at their hands beggars description. Sometimes this aid is denied and the girl-mother is left frightened and alone in her hour of need." Montgomery also discussed "Oriental" women's lack of access to medical care in general because of the practice of forced seclusion. She reiterated the arguments in favor of women medical missionaries that Sarah Josepha Hale had first proposed nearly sixty years earlier.[17]

From child marriage, inadequate medical care, and perpetual widowhood, Montgomery turned her attention to another characteristic of the treatment of Indian and other "Oriental" women that missionaries had been decrying for a century. "As a logical outcome of the doctrines advanced in their sacred scriptures, women are denied education," she stated. "To-day [1910], after a century of educational effort, not one percent of the women of India are able to read and write, and that small fraction is almost wholly Christian."[18] Nevertheless, Montgomery echoed the sentiments of early policy-makers for the ABCFM and other mission agencies by maintaining that educating girls and young women offered the best hope for improving the condition of women in India and the rest of the "Orient": "The education of girls is the quickest method of elevating the home life of the East. These educated girls make better mothers, better wives, better housekeepers, than their untrained sisters." It is unclear whether Montgomery and others saw conversion to Christianity as improving the educational level and social status of women or whether those improvements would demonstrate the value of Christianity and lead to conversion. Whatever the case, educated and elevated female Christian converts were key to evangelizing Asia through their influence on their husbands and children.[19]

In addition to Montgomery's work, other late nineteenth and early twentieth-century mission publications also demonstrated the persistence and pervasiveness of tropes about "Oriental" women. Joan Jacobs Brumberg, in "Zenanas and Girlless Villages: The Ethnology of American Evangelical Women, 1870-1910," examines the late nineteenth-century missionary publications of the (northern) Baptist, Methodist, Presbyterian and Congregationalist denominations, with a particular focus on three publications: the Methodist magazine *Heathen Woman's Friend*, the Presbyterian magazine *Woman's Work for Woman*, and the Congregational magazine *Life and Light for Women*. She also draws heavily on *Western Women in Eastern Lands*. Brumberg studied magazines that Congregationalist, Presbyterian, Baptist, and Methodist women published in the late nineteenth century because, she says, thousands of local auxiliaries throughout the country used them as textbooks for missions education and thus they effectively served as instruments of "self-culture."[20] The magazines enjoyed wide popularity, as did all of the publications emanating from the United Study of Foreign Missions. Those publications all played many variations on the same theme: the oppressed status of women in non-Christian lands, with primary focus on that area of the world traditionally labeled by Westerners the "Orient." Brumberg notes that the literature of women and foreign missions was so widely read that, "by 1900, American women were familiar, if not conversant, with an entire vocabulary that implied the degradation of women."[21]

Examining those publications, Brumberg identifies a number of tropes about "heathen" women that she believes emerged in the context of the development of ethnological studies as a new "science" in the late nineteenth century. Brumberg found the same images, explained in this book as emerging at the close of the eighteenth century, still widely circulating in the latter decades of the nineteenth century. She categorizes women missionaries' descriptions of "Oriental" womanhood as a type of "missionary ethnology" through which missionary women engaged in the practices of "describing, classifying, and interpreting the distinguishing characteristics of other races." Although Brumberg seems unaware that the images she describes date back to the late eighteenth century, her work nevertheless effectively demonstrates that those images which had so long circulated only continued to gain force toward the end of the nineteenth century.

In cataloging those tropes about the degradation of women in other lands, Brumberg includes the seclusion of Hindu and Muslim women, female infanticide, the refusal of the peoples of the "Orient" to educate their daughters, taboos against a woman sharing meals with her husband, the practice of polygamy, child marriage, and the oppression of widows, including images of *sati*.[22] Her conclusion is intriguing, countering as it does the claims of Helen Barrett Montgomery as well as many late twentieth-century historians. Brumberg maintains that American Protestant women, by and large, compared their own social position to that of their "heathen sisters" rather than to that of their American brothers. Hence, they viewed themselves as privileged rather than oppressed and greeted the "feminist political movement" with "skepticism." Furthermore, Brumberg maintains that American Protestant women viewed the perilous condition of "heathen women" as a justification both for American imperialism and for their own involvement in Progressive reform movements in behalf of women and children at home.[23]

Brumberg's research into late nineteenth- and early twentieth-century mission literature further demonstrates the extent to which images of "Oriental women" continued to pervade religious culture in the United States and even reached beyond the realm of the religious and into the realm of the political. One can see an early example of Brumberg's "ethnological mirror" at work in the "Address of Mrs. Palmer Potter, President of the Board of Lady Managers," on the opening of the Woman's Building of the World's Columbian Exposition in Chicago on May 1, 1893. The Woman's Building exhibited the varieties of women's work from around the world. Mrs. Potter's address dealt largely with economic issues, anticipating some of the Progressive concerns that Brumberg discusses. Apparently, some people criticized the Woman's Building exhibits for promoting inappropriate roles for women. Mrs. Potter responded that those critics held a romanticized view of women's lives that did not account for the fact that the majority of the world's women had to work from necessity. Lack of access to work forced women in the "Orient" to desperate measures for survival:

> Our oriental neighbors have seen the logic of the situation far more clearly than we and have been consistent enough to meet it without shrinking from heroic measures when necessary. The question is happily solved in some countries by the practice of polygamy, which allows every man to maintain as many wives as his means permit. In others etiquette requires that a newly made widow be burned on the funeral pyre with her husband's body, while the Chinese take the precaution to drown surplus female children.

Mrs. Potter thus deployed the most emotion-laden imagery from the foreign mission literature of the last century to point out the ways in which "Oriental" societies degraded and oppressed women. She was certainly making a political statement regarding the United States, too, though:

> It would seem that any of these methods is more logical and less cruel than the system we pursue of permitting the entire female population to live, but making it impossible for those born to poverty to maintain themselves in comfort, because they are hampered by a caste feeling almost as strong as that ruling India, which will not permit them to work on equal terms with men. These unhappy members of an inferior class must be content to remain in penury, living on the crumbs that fall from tables spread for those of another and higher caste.[24]

In other words, Americans should not be too smug, for as cruel as "Oriental" practices were, many American women suffered as bad or worse a fate.

A number of contradictory messages emanated from the World's Columbian Exposition. Organizers of the Exposition overtly celebrated the conquest of the western hemisphere and emergence of the European imperial age. They sought to promote the idea of western superiority through vast exhibits relating to science, medicine, and technology. At the same time, they simultaneously attempted to represent the cultures of the colonized world in what they considered a positive way.[25] The Exposition Corporation, chartered by the State of Illinois and recognized by Congress, created a World's Congress Auxiliary "for the purpose of bringing about a series of world's conventions of the leaders in the various departments of human progress, during the exposition season of 1893." Under the Auxiliary, a World's Congress of Religions (sometimes referred to as the Parliament of Religions) was established "to unite all Religion against all Irreligion; to make the Golden Rule the basis of this union; to present to the world... the substantial unity of many religions in the good deeds of the Religious life."[26] A more broadly ecumenical, equalitarian statement could hardly have been issued. And yet, among the many gatherings sponsored by the Congress of Religions were a World's Congress of Missions and a Congress of Woman's Missions, both featuring American Protestant evangelical missionary organizations.

The Midway Plaisance was another site of contrast within the Exposition. It offered exhibits featuring a variety of cultures, with a particular emphasis on the "exotic Orient." A popular souvenir book entitled *Midway Types: A Book of Illustrated Lessons About the People of the Midway Plaisance, World's Fair, 1893* included photographs with the following titles: "Chinese Beauty," "Hindoo Jugglers," "Javanese Beauty," "Simon, a Syrian Musician," "Rosa, The Turkish Dancer," "A Shepherd from Khurdistan," "The Turkish Bride," "Four Dancers from Constantinople," "A Cingalese Dancer," "Three Turkish Musicians," " A Dancer of the Persian Palace," "A Syrian Sheik and His Companion," "An Egyptian Girl," "Syrian Women," "Fatima--An Oriental Type of Beauty," and "A Harem Belle." The same publication, however, noted the inferior status of women in the "Orient." The text accompanying one photograph of Egyptian women maintained, "It goes without saying that in Egypt even now nearly all women are slaves... [living in] degradation and hopeless bondage... If they are no longer subject to the hazards of the highest bidder, they are still the sad, living symbols of a system of drudgery older than the Pyramids." Later, in a section entitled "Representing the Orient," the author stated, "The women of the far east are struggling to obtain an individuality, and an influence in public affairs proportionate to that enjoyed by their sex in England and America." Under the heading "The Hidden Woman," the author included the following account:

> Not all women of foreign lands were seen by Midway eyes. People from Turkey, Persia, Algeria, of a dozen nations, maintained in jealous retirement the women who came as their wives. The latticed windows of many a building in the Oriental quarters hid weary, watching, faces, worn and sad with a seclusion but little less than that of a prison. Take this Algerian woman! Life to her was barren of Joy. If she ventured upon the street she went closely veiled and with a vigilant watcher always at her side. If she remained in her little room it was to see, day after day, the same tiresome objects, while through the open windows came the outcries of careless throngs. To lie upon a divan, to think, to dream, was about all that engrossed her time. She had nothing to live for. To die, in a strange land, was a fate full of unspeakable terrors. Masculine and heavy of feature, devoid of sentiment, barren of education, yet the woman had the softer feelings, the yearnings, the hunger for companionship, that are the ever-pleading accompaniments of her sex. But through the hot summer days and the waning warmth of October she watched and waited and then, in bleak November, still unknown and unseen, still the victim of tyrannical seclusion, she and hers passed out of the Midway and towards a land dear to her because it was home. Chicago she did not see.[27]

Once again, an American commentator used the powerful image of the seclusion of "Oriental" women in an oblique reminder to American women of the privileged position that Christian society conferred upon them. This time, however, the seclusion was rendered more starkly than ever before because it existed right in the middle of a raucous world's fair in the heart of the teaming Midwestern metropolis of Chicago. The "Oriental" woman's "tyrannical seclusion" was so complete, according to the author, that she never saw Chicago even while in the midst of it. Furthermore, she was never seen *by* Chicago either. Because the exotic "Orient" was represented on the Midway Plaisance, the "Hidden Woman" had to be there as well, for, as every moderately well-informed American "knew," the "Orient" was filled with "hidden women."

Today, we no longer speak of the "Orient." We recognize the complexity of the world and pride ourselves on valuing cultural diversity. We would never presume to speak of China, India, and Afghanistan as though their cultural practices are interchangeable. And yet many of the same images of the oppression of "Oriental" women discussed in this book are still pervasive in American society today--perhaps more so than at any other time in recent history. A cross-section of American society, from secular feminists to evangelical Christians to celebrities and politicians, decry the oppression of women in China, India, and the Middle East and advocate for reform. For example, China instituted a one-child policy in the 1970s as a population-control measure. The abandonment of female infants and orphanages overflowing with little girls resulted. In 1991, China liberalized its policies regarding international adoptions in order to alleviate the overcrowding. In 1998, the most recent year for which reliable statistics could be found, US families adopted 4206 Chinese children, 95% of them girls.[28]

A similar devaluing of girls exists in India. Throughout India, a significant sex ratio gap exists, especially among children six and under. According to Indian government statistics, the sex ratio in that age group for the nation is about 970 females for every 1000 males. The number varies widely by region, however. In the Punjab, the ratio is 793 girls for every 1000 boys. Indian commentators cite the "likely role played by the combination of greater neglect of girl children and wider practice of female foeticide based on modern medical techniques to determine the sex of the foetus."[29] The US Agency for International Development (USAID) supports those numbers, noting that "almost twice as many girls die before the age of five as boys." USAID also notes that girls in India have significantly less access to primary education than boys, resulting in a literacy rate of 50% for women in India, compared to a

64% literacy rate for men. Not surprisingly, USAID also reports, "Women are the most disadvantaged members of the Indian population and comprise the largest proportion living in absolute poverty."[30]

Most of the images today, however, emanate from Afghanistan and other Islamic societies in the geographic heart of what was the nineteenth-century "Orient." Western media widely reported on the status of women in Afghanistan under Taliban rule, for example. Between 1994 and 2001, girls' schools were shut down; women had to wear the burqa (a head to toe covering with only a three-inch square opening for the eyes) on pain of severe corporal punishment; a woman was not permitted to laugh or to go into public unaccompanied by her husband or other close family member; the law required windows of homes in which women lived to be painted in order to prevent outsiders from looking in and the women from looking outside; and women could not work, regardless of their profession. Thus, since women could not see male doctors, their access to medical care was severely curtailed and in many areas vanished altogether.[31] Ninety-five percent of women and girls in Afghanistan are illiterate. Western media in September 2003 reported incidents in some parts of Afghanistan in which newly opened girls' primary schools were burned and the girls and their teachers threatened with harm should they attempt to resume the schools. Very few secondary schools for girls exist in Afghanistan.[32] Afghan women attending a September 2003 conference in Kandahar drafted a proposed "women's bill of rights" for the new Afghan constitution. The proposed bill of rights, among other things, ensures that "education for girls would be mandatory through secondary school."[33]

Just like their sisters of the nineteenth century, twenty-first century American women, from radical feminists to evangelical Christians, find motivation in reports of female fetuses aborted for purposes of sex selection (a modern version of female infanticide), female infants abandoned, girls unable to attend school, young girls forced to marry, women with no political rights forced to live in seclusion, and women and girls of all ages deprived of medical care. Images of the oppressed women of the East continue to resonate in American culture, both secular and religious. Secular solutions include systemic social and political reform, initiated and sustained through the actions of the

United Nations and its constituent agencies, through US State Department programs such as USAID, and/or through military action, whether multilateral as in Afghanistan in 2001 or unilateral as in Iraq in 2003. American evangelical Christians support some or all of those approaches, at least in part because they have the potential to clear the way for the resumption of full-scale missionary activity. Most evangelical Christians continue to see conversion to Christianity as both the means of eternal salvation and the ultimate remedy for all earthly oppression. Heather Mercer and Dayna Curry are twenty-first century counterparts to the nineteenth-century women who are the subjects of this book. In the grand tradition of evangelical women's missionary memoirs, they have recounted their experiences in a best-selling book entitled *Prisoners of Hope*.[34] Mercer and Curry were "relief workers" for a Christian agency in Afghanistan in 2001. On August 3 of that year, the Taliban arrested the two women and six of their European colleagues on charges that they were covertly seeking Christian converts (which they now readily concede). When terrorists leveled the World Trade Center in New York on September 11 and the United States declared war on Afghanistan shortly thereafter, the prisoners' situation became even more perilous. Americans were spellbound by the dramatic rescue of the two women by Afghan opposition fighters and US Army Special Forces under cover of night on November 15. In a moment of spectacular irony and potent symbolism, the women aided their deliverers by lighting afire the head-coverings they were required as women to wear.

Notes

Introduction

[1]I use the term "evangelical" to denote a variety of Protestantism emphasizing an intense conversion experience followed by a strong commitment to strict moral living, to personal piety centered on prayer and Bible study, and to evangelism.

[2]Edwin Munsell Bliss, "Woman's Work for Woman," *Encyclopaedia of Missions*, vol. 2 (New York: Funk and Wagnells, 1891), 479.

[3]See, for example, Patricia R. Hill, *The World Their Household: The American Woman's Foreign Mission Movement and Cultural Transformation, 1870–1920* (Ann Arbor: University of Michigan Press, 1985) and Jane Hunter, *The Gospel of Gentility: American Women Missionaries in Turn of the Century China* (New Haven CT: Yale University Press, 1984).

[4]See, for example, Paul A. Cohen, *China and Christianity: The Missionary Movement and the Growth of Chinese Anti-foreignism, 1860–1870* (Cambridge MA: Harvard University Press, 1963); Joseph L. Grabill, *Protestant Diplomacy and the Near East: Missionary Influence on Foreign Policy, 1810–1927* (Minneapolis: University of Minnesota Press, 1971); John King Fairbank, ed. *The Missionary Enterprise in China and America* (Cambridge MA: Harvard University Press, 1974); Kenton J. Clymer, *Protestant Missionaries in the Philippines, 1898–1916: An Inquiry into the American Colonial Mentality* (Urbana: University of Illinois Press, 1986); Torben Christensen and William R. Hutchison, eds., *Missionary Ideologies in the Imperialist Era, 1880–1920* (Copenhagen: Aros, 1982).

[5]For a fine collection of recent studies regarding the cultural influence of the American foreign missions movement within the United States, see Daniel H. Bays and Grant Wacker, eds., *The Foreign Missionary Enterprise at Home: Explorations in North American Cultural History* (Tuscaloosa: University of Alabama Press, 2003).

[6]See Clifton Jackson Phillips, *Protestant America and the Pagan World: The First Half Century of the American Board of Commissioners for Foreign Missions, 1810–1860* (Cambridge MA: East Asian Research Center, Harvard University, 1969); Edward V. Gulick, *Peter Parker and the Opening of China* (Cambridge MA: Harvard University Press, 1973; John A. Andrew III, *Rebuilding the Christian Commonwealth: New England Congregationalists and Foreign Missions* (Lexington: University Press of Kentucky, 1976); William R. Hutchison, *Errand to the World: American Protestant Thought and*

Foreign Missions (Chicago: University of Chicago Press, 1987); and Murray A. Rubinstein, *The Origins of the Anglo-American Missionary Enterprise in China, 1807–1840* (Lanham MD: Scarecrow Press, 1996).

[7]Classic studies of women's roles in the early nineteenth century include Nancy F. Cott, *The Bonds of Womanhood: "Woman's Sphere" in New England, 1780–1835* (New Haven CT: Yale University Press, 1977); Linda K. Kerber, *Women of the Republic: Intellect and Ideology in Revolutionary America* (Chapel Hill: University of North Carolina Press, 1980); Mary Beth Norton, *Liberty's Daughters: The Revolutionary Experience of American Women, 1750–1800* (Boston: Little, Brown, and Co., 1980); Mary P. Ryan, *Cradle of the Middle Class: The Family in Oneida County, New York, 1790–1865* (New York: Cambridge University Press, 1981).

[8]R. Pierce Beaver, *American Protestant Women in World Mission: A History of the First Feminist Movement in North America*, rev. ed. (Grand Rapids MI: Eerdmans, 1980); Joan Jacobs Brumberg, *Mission for Life: The Judson Family and American Evangelical Culture* (New York: New York University Press, 1984); Patricia Grimshaw, *Paths of Duty: American Missionary Wives in Nineteenth-Century Hawaii* (Honolulu: University of Hawaii Press, 1989); Amanda Porterfield, *Mary Lyon and the Mount Holyoke Missionaries* (New York: Oxford University Press, 1997); Dana Lee Robert, *American Women in Mission: A Social History of Their Thought and Practice* (Macon GA: Mercer University Press, 1996); Ruth A. Tucker, *Guardians of the Great Commission: The Story of Women in Modern Missions* (Grand Rapids MI: Academie Books, 1988); Mary Zwiep, *Pilgrim Path: The First Company of Women Missionaries to Hawaii* (Madison: University of Wisconsin Press, 1991).

[9]Billie Melman, *Women's Orients: English Women and the Middle East, 1718–1918: Sexuality, Religion and Work* (Ann Arbor: University of Michigan Press, 1992) 7.

[10]Robert A. Kapp, "Introduction to 'Review Symposium: Edward Said's *Orientalism*,'" *Journal of Asian Studies* 39 (May 1980) 3:481–84.

[11]Christina Klein, *Cold War Orientalism: Asia in the Middlebrow Imagination, 1945–1961* (Berkeley: University of California Press, 2003) 10–11.

[12]The idea that the cultures of the Orient, especially Bible lands, were frozen in time was a virtual truism in both scholarly and popular accounts of the eighteenth and nineteenth centuries. See Edward Said, *Orientalism* (New York: Vintage Books, 1979).

[13]Fuad Sha'ban, *Islam and Arabs in Early American Thought: The Roots of Orientalism in America*, published in association with Duke University Islamic and Arabian Development Studies (Durham, NC: The Acorn Press, 1991) viii. Other explorations of American Orientalism include Hilton Obenzinger, *American Palestine: Melville, Twain, and the Holy Land Mania* (Princeton NJ: Princeton University Press, 1999) and John Kuo Wei Tchen, *New York Before Chinatown: Orientalism and the Shaping of American Culture, 1776–1882* (Baltimore: Johns Hopkins University Press, 1999).

Chapter 1

[1]Late eighteenth- and early nineteenth-century apologists for missions embraced a view of the endtimes that modern scholars refer to as post-millennialism. They believed that God called upon Christians to use "means" to extend the "kingdom of God" throughout the earth by carrying the gospel to all lands through missionaries and through translating the Bible and distributing it around the world. When they had accomplished that task, a 1,000-year period would ensue, marked by the progress of peace and prosperity everywhere. A variety of signs of the times, including the efforts of Christians to organize for missions, marked the beginning of that period. The literal return of Jesus Christ to reign upon the earth would mark the end of the millennium. For the clearest enunciation of the type of millennialism that most influenced early nineteenth-century missions apologists, see David Austin, *The Millennium; or, The Thousand Years of Prosperity, Promised to the Church of God, in the Old Testament and in the New, Shortly to Commence, and to be Carried on to Perfection, Under the Auspices of Him, Who, in the VISION, was Presented to St. JOHN* (Elizabeth Town NJ: Shepard Kollock, 1794). For examples of some of the voluminous scholarship on American millennialism, see Ruth H. Bloch, *Visionary Republic: Millennial Themes in American Thought, 1756–1800* (Cambridge: Cambridge University Press, 1985); James A. de Jong, *As the Waters Cover the Sea: Millennial Expectations in the Rise of Anglo-American Missions, 1640–1810* (J. H. Kok N. V. Kampen, 1970); and James Moorhead, "Between Progress and Apocalypse: A Reassessment of Millennialism in American Religious Thought, 1800–1880," *Journal of American History* 71 (December 1984) 3:524–42.

[2]R. Pierce Beaver, "The Concert of Prayer for Missions: An Early Venture in Ecumenical Action," *Ecumenical Review* 10 (July 1958) 4:425. The classic study of antebellum revivalism is Whitney R. Cross, *The Burned-Over District: The Social and Intellectual History of Enthusiastic Religion in Western New York, 1800–1850* (Ithaca NY: Cornell University Press, 1950). More recent studies include David W. Kling, *A Field of Divine Wonders: The New Divinity and Village Revivals in Northwestern Connecticut, 1792–1822* (University Park: Pennsylvania State University Press, 1993) and Paul K. Conkin, *Cane Ridge: America's Pentecost* (Madison: University of Wisconsin Press, 1990).

[3]For information on the British mission movement, see Brian Stanley, *The Bible and the Flag: Protestant Missions and British Imperialism in the Nineteenth and Twentieth Centuries* (Leicester: Apollos, 1990); James R. Beck, *Dorothy Carey: The Tragic and Untold Story of Mrs. William Carey* (Grand Rapids MI: Baker Book House, 1992); and Timothy George, *Faithful Witness: The Life and Mission of William Carey* (Birmingham AL: New Hope Press, 1991).

[4]R. Pierce Beaver, *American Protestant Women in World Mission: A History of the First Feminist Movement in North America*, rev. ed. (Grand Rapids MI: Eerdmans, 1980); Tucker; and Robert all briefly discuss the formation of mite societies in support of missions. For information on women organizing for benevolent purposes in the early nineteenth century, see Anne M. Boylan, *The Origins of Women's*

Activism: New York and Boston, 1797–1840 (Chapel Hill: University of North Carolina Press, 2002).

[5] Nathanael Emmons, "A Sermon, delivered before the Massachusetts Missionary Society, at their annual meeting in Boston, 27 May 1800," (Charlestown MA: Samuel Etheridge, 1800) 12–20.

[6]Albert L. Vail, *Mary Webb and the Mother Society* (Philadelphia: American Baptist Publication Society, 1914) 18–19.

[7]Ibid., 27.

[8]Ibid., 33; *A Brief Account of the Origin and Progress of the Boston Female Society for Missionary Purposes with Extracts from the Reports of the Society in May, 1817 and 1818* (Boston: Lincoln and Edmands, [1818]).

[9]Luke 21:1–4. For a fuller account of the beginning of mite societies in New England, see Beaver, *American Protestant Women in World Mission*, 13–14.

[10]*Massachusetts Missionary Magazine* 2/1 (June 1804): 41; *Massachusetts Baptist Missionary Magazine* 2/7 (September 1809): 218–19, and 3/2 (June 1811): 41–42; *Connecticut Evangelical Magazine* 4 (October 1804): 147–48.

[11]*Massachusetts Baptist Missionary Magazine* 3/9 (March 1813): 281–84.

[12]*Connecticut Evangelical Magazine* 5/4 (October 1804): 147–48.

[13]*Panoplist* 4/12 (NS) (May 1812): 560.

[14]*Massachusetts Baptist Missionary Magazine* 3/5 (March 1812): 156–57.

[15]*Panoplist* 3/9 (February 1808): 419.

[16]*Massachusetts Missionary Magazine* 5/2 (July 1807): 70–71; *Panoplist* 1/4 (NS) (September 1808): 183–84.

[17]*Massachusetts Baptist Missionary Magazine* 3/3 (September 1811): 92.

[18]*Massachusetts Missionary Magazine* 2/1 (June 1804): 41, and 4/3 (August 1806): 119.

[19]*Massachusetts Baptist Missionary Magazine* 2/9 (March 1810): 282.

[20]*Connecticut Evangelical Magazine* 5/6 (December 1804): 222.

[21]Ibid.; Reuben Puffer, *The Widow's Mite: A Sermon delivered at Boylston, before the Boylston Female Society for the Aid of Foreign Missions, January 8, 1816* (Worcester MA: William Manning, 1816) 11–12.

[22]*Massachusetts Missionary Magazine* 2/1 (June 1804): 41; Puffer, *The Widow's Mite.* A sermon delivered at Boylston, before the Boylston Female Society for the Aid of Foreign Missions, January 8, 1816.

[23][Anonymous], "An Address, written by a female, to the Female Missionary Society, Massachusetts," *Connecticut Evangelical Magazine* 5/2 (August 1804): 73–74.

[24]Mary Webb, "Address of the Female Society, in Boston, to the Female Friends of Zion," Boston, 3 February 1812, *Massachusetts Baptist Missionary Magazine* 3/5 (March 1812): 156–57.

[25]Mary Webb, "An Address from 'the Boston Female Society for Missionary Purposes,' to Females professing godliness," Boston, 7 December 1812, *Massachusetts Baptist Missionary Magazine* 3/9 (March 1813): 282.

[26]Mary Webb, "Grateful Acknowledgment from the Boston Female Society for Missionary Purposes," *Massachusetts Baptist Missionary Magazine* 4/6 (June 1815): 174–76.

[27]*Panoplist* 4/10 (NS) (March 1812): 448.

[28]*Connecticut Evangelical Magazine* 2/7 (July 1809): 275.

[29]William A. Smalley, *Translation as Mission: Bible Translation in the Modern Missions Movement* (Macon GA: Mercer University Press, 1991) 34.

[30]*Connecticut Evangelical Magazine* 4/3 (March 1811): 117 and 5/3 (March 1812): 114.

[31]"Foreign Missionary Society of Boston and Vicinity," *Panoplist* 4/7 (NS) (December 1811): 312–13; "Salem Bible Translation and Foreign Mission Society," *Massachusetts Baptist Missionary Magazine* 3/7 (September 1812): 215–16; "Circular Address, The Savannah Baptist Society for Foreign Missions, to the Inhabitants of Georgia, and the adjacent parts of South Carolina," *Massachusetts Baptist Missionary Magazine* 4/1 (March 1814): 6–7.

[32]*Massachusetts Baptist Missionary Magazine* 3/3 (September 1811): 348–51.

[33]Ibid., 334–35.

[34]Webb, "Grateful Acknowledgment," 176.

[35]Ibid., 174–76.

[36]Catharine Webb, corresponding secretary of the New York Female Missionary Society, to the Baptist Board of Foreign Missions, 1 April 1816, *Massachusetts Baptist Missionary Magazine* 4/10 (June 1816): 14.

[37]*Panoplist* 4/7 (NS) (December 1811): 312–13.

[38]*Massachusetts Baptist Missionary Magazine* 3/3 (September 1811): 88–89.

[39]Jeremiah Evarts, "Memorandum regarding the Memoirs of Harriet Newell," Boston, 19 May 1814, ABC 8.5—Miscellaneous Valuable Documents, 1811–1845; and ABC 40, Papers relating to the memoir of Harriet Newell, Archives of the ABCFM, Houghton Library, Harvard University.

Chapter 2

[1]Joel Hawes, *"A Looking-Glass for Ladies," or the Formation and Excellence of the Female Character: An Address delivered at Hartford on Sunday evening, August 24, 1845, and published at the request of the American Institute for Education* (Boston: William D. Ticknor and Co., 1845).

[2]Barbara Welter, "The Cult of True Womanhood," in Welter, *Dimity Convictions: The American Woman in the Nineteenth Century* (Athens: Ohio University Press, 1976) 21–41.

[3]Hawes, *"A Looking-Glass for Ladies,"* 5. Hawes borrowed the comparison of Proverbs 31 to a mirror from the renowned Bible commentator Matthew Henry.

[4]Mission boards followed the nineteenth-century convention of using the terms "Asia," "Orient," and the "East" interchangeably to designate that region of the world stretching from Palestine to China, bordered on the west by Europe and Mediterranean, on the north by the Black Sea and the Himalayas, on the south by Africa and the Indian Ocean, and on the east by the Pacific.

[5]Joan Jacobs Brumberg, "The Ethnological Mirror: American Evangelical Women and Their Heathen Sisters, 1870–1910," in Barbara J. Harris and JoAnn K. McNamara, eds., *Women and the Structure of Society* (Durham NC: Duke University Press, 1984) 108–28. While Brumberg specifically locates the concept of women's missionary writings as an "ethnological mirror" in the context of late nineteenth-century developments, virtually her entire argument can also apply to the beginning of the foreign missions movement at the turn of the nineteenth century.

[6]Proverbs 31:10, Authorized Version.

[7]Hawes, "*A Looking-Glass for Ladies*," 6–7.

[8]Louisa Hawes, *Memoir of Mrs. Mary E. Van Lennep, Only Daughter of the Rev. Joel Hawes, D.D., and Wife of the Rev. Henry J. Van Lennep, Missionary in Turkey*, 2d ed. (Hartford CT: Belknap and Hamersley, 1848).

[9]H. G. O. Dwight, *Memoir of Mrs. Elizabeth Dwight, Including an Account of the Plague of 1837, by Rev. H. G. O. Dwight, Missionary to Constantinople, With a Sketch of the Life of Mrs. Judith S. Grant, Missionary to Persia* (New York: M. W. Dodd, 1840).

[10]I owe my understanding of the Puritan ritual of "sanctifying affliction" to Joan Hedrick's *Harriet Beecher Stowe: A Life* (New York: Oxford University Press, 1994). In chapter 17, "Crossing the River, 1849–50," Hedrick explores Stowe's response to the death of her youngest son, Charley, and concludes that her grief over that loss was "one of the twin engines of *Uncle Tom's Cabin*" (Hedrick, 201).

[11]Dwight, *Memoir of Mrs. Elizabeth Dwight*, 10–11.

[12]Compiled from Rufus Anderson, *Memorial Volume of the First Fifty Years of the American Board of Commissioners for Foreign Missions* (Boston: The Board, 1861).

[13]Irene Quenzler Brown, "Death, Friendship, and Female Identity During New England's Second Great Awakening," *Journal of Family History* 12/4 (1987): 367–87.

[14]Joanna Bowen Gillespie, "'The Clear Leadings of Providence': Pious Memoirs and the Problems of Self-Realization for Women in the Early Nineteenth Century," *Journal of the Early Republic* 5 (Summer 1985): 217.

[15]James D. Knowles, *Memoir of Ann H. Judson, Missionary to Burmah* (Philadelphia: American Baptist Publication Society, 1835) 10.

[16]Miron Winslow, *Memoir of Mrs. Harriet L. Winslow, Thirteen Years a Member of the American Mission in Ceylon* (New York: American Tract Society, 1840) 5.

[17]Margarette Oliver Woods Lawrence, *Light on the Dark River; or, Memorial to Mrs. Henrietta A. L. Hamlin, Missionary to Turkey* (Boston: Ticknor, Reed, & Fields, 1854) 13.

[18]Gillespie, "'The Clear Leadings of Providence,'" 213.

[19]Hawes, "*A Looking-Glass for Ladies*," 27.

[20]Lawrence, 11. For discussions of parental roles, especially motherhood, see Anne Louise Kuhn, *The Mother's Role in Childhood Education: New England Concepts, 1830–1860* (New Haven CT: Yale University Press, 1947); Ruth H. Bloch, "Ideals in Transition: The Rise of the Moral Mother, 1785–1815," *Feminist Studies* 4/2 (June 1978): 100–26; Richard A. Meckel, "Educating a Ministry of Mothers: Evangelical Maternal Associations, 1815–1860," *Journal of the Early Republic* 2 (Winter 1982): 403–23.

[21]J. B. Jeter, *Memoir of Mrs. Henrietta Shuck, the First American Female Missionary to China* (Boston: Gould, Kendall, and Lincoln, 1846) 14; Daniel Taggert Fiske, *Faith Working by Love, as Exemplified in the Life of Fidelia Fiske* (Boston: Congregational Publishing Society, 1868) 13; Edward W. Hooker, *Memoir of Mrs. Sarah L. Huntington Smith, Late of the American Mission in Syria*, 3d ed. (New York: American Tract Society, 1845) 10.

[22]Knowles, *Memoir of Ann H. Judson*, 14; Winslow, 16; Dwight, *Memoir of Mrs. Elizabeth Dwight*, 135–36.

[23]Hooker, *Memoir of Mrs. Sarah L. Huntington Smith*, 12.

[24]Lawrence, *Light on the Dark River*, 20.

[25]Hawes, *Memoir of Mrs. Mary E. Van Lennep*, 17–18.

[26]Emily Chubbuck Judson, *Memoir of Sarah B. Judson, Member of the American Mission to Burma* (New York: L. Colby and Company, 1848) 8.

[27]A. C. Kendrick, *The Life and Letters of Mrs. Emily C. Judson* (New York: Sheldon & Co., 1860) 10, 16, 23.

[28]Fiske, *Faith Working by Love*, 28.

[29]Knowles, *Memoir of Mrs. Ann H. Judson*, 12, 14.

[30]Leonard Woods, *Memoir of the Life of Mrs. Harriet Newell, Wife of the Rev. Samuel Newell, Missionary to India, Who Died at the Isle of France, November 30, 1812, Aged 19 Years. Extracted from the Third Boston Edition To Which is Annexed a Sermon, Delivered in Boston, September 16, 1813, before the American Board of Commissioners for Foreign Missions, at Their Fourth Annual Meeting, by Timothy Dwight, D.D., L.L.D., President of Yale College* (Lexington KY: Skillman, 1815) 5; Winslow, *Memoir of Mrs. Harriet L. Winslow*, 18; Kendrick, *The Life and Letters of Mrs. Emily C. Judson*, 31–32.

[31]Woods, *Memoir of the Life of Mrs. Harriet Newell*, 4, 6.

[32]William W. Campbell, *A Memoir of Mrs. Judith S. Grant, Late Missionary to Persia* (New York: J. Winchester, 1844) 13; Fiske, *Faith Working by Love*, 28; Hawes, *Memoir of Mrs. Mary E. Van Lennep*, 13.

[33]Hooker, *Memoir of Mrs. Sarah L. Huntington Smith*, 11–12.

[34]Hawes, *Memoir of Mrs. Mary E. Van Lennep*, iv–v.

[35]Hawes, "*A Looking-Glass for Ladies*," 15. Mary Van Lennep studied at Catharine Beecher's Hartford Female Seminary.

[36]Jeter, *Memoir of Mrs. Henrietta Shuck*, 15.

[37]See Kerber; Norton; Kathryn Kish Sklar, *Catharine Beecher: A Study in American Domesticity* (New York: W. W. Norton, 1976); and Elizabeth Alden Green, *Mary Lyon and Mount Holyoke: Opening the Gates* (Hanover NH: University Press of New England, 1979).

[38]Judson, *Memoir of Sarah B. Judson*, 16–17.

[39]Kerber, *Catharine Beecher*, 190–91.

[40]Knowles, *Memoir of Mrs. Ann H. Judson*, 12.

[41]Lawrence, *Light on the Dark River*, 31.

[42]Ibid., 36.

[43]Campbell, *A Memoir of Mrs. Judith S. Grant*, 258, 297.

[44]Judson, *Memoir of Sarah B. Judson*, 56, 59.

[45]Ibid., 16–17.

[46]Lawrence, *Light on the Dark River*, 33.

[47]Campbell, *A Memoir of Mrs. Judith S. Grant*, 13.

[48]William Dean, *Memoir of Mrs. Lucy T. Lord of the Chinese Baptist Mission* (Philadelphia: American Baptist Publication Society, 1854) 44; Judson, *Memoir of Sarah B. Judson*, 37.

[49]Classic studies of the early nineteenth-century revivals collectively known as the Second Great Awakening include Charles R. Keller, *The Second Great Awakening in Connecticut* (New Haven CT: Yale University Press, 1942); Whitney R. Cross, *The Burned-Over District: The Social and Intellectual History of Enthusiastic Religion in Western New York, 1800–1850* (Ithaca NY: Cornell University Press, 1950); Timothy L. Smith, *Revivalism and Social Reform: American Protestantism on the Eve of the Civil War* (Nashville: Abingdon Press, 1957); and Paul E. Johnson, *A Shopkeeper's Millennium: Society and Revivals in Rochester, New York, 1815–1837* (New York: Hill & Wang, 1978). For a more recent treatment, see David W. Kling, *A Field of Divine Wonders: The New Divinity and Village Revivals in Northwestern Connecticut, 1792–1822* (University Park: Pennsylvania State University Press, 1993).

[50]Hooker, *Memoir of Mrs. Sarah L. Huntington Smith*, 3.

[51]Ibid., 12–20.

[52]Winslow, *Memoir of Mrs. Harriet L. Winslow*, 15.

[53]Dwight, *Memoir of Mrs. Elizabeth Dwight*, 135–36.

[54]Winslow, *Memoir of Mrs. Harriet L. Winslow*, 15.

[55]Kendrick, *The Life and Letters of Mrs. Emily C. Judson*, 21.

[56]Knowles, *Memoir of Mrs. Ann H. Judson*, 16, 25.

[57]Lawrence, *Light on the Dark River*, 42–43.

[58]Hawes, *Memoir of Mrs. Mary E. Van Lennep*, 78–79.

[59]Mary Gladding Benjamin, *The Missionary Sisters: A Memorial of Mrs. Seraphina Haynes Everett and Mrs. Harriet Martha Hamlin, Late Missionaries of the ABCFM at Constantinople* (Boston: American Tract Society, 1860) 13.

[60]Kendrick, *The Life and Letters of Mrs. Emily C. Judson*, 22; Dean, *Memoir of Mrs. Lucy T. Lord*, 31.

[61]See Keith Hardman, *Charles Grandison Finney, 1792–1875: Revivalist and Reformer* (Syracuse NY: Syracuse University Press, 1987).

[62]Nancy F. Cott, "Young Women in the Second Great Awakening in New England," in *Placing Women in History*; Susan Juster, "'In a Different Voice': Male and Female Narratives of Religious Conversion in Post-Revolutionary America," *American Quarterly* 41 (March 1989): 34–62; Barbara Welter, "The Feminization of American Religion, 1800–1860," in Welter, *Dimity Convictions*, 83–102.

[63]See Kling, *A Field of Divine Wonders*.

[64]Joseph Conforti, *Jonathan Edwards, Religious Tradition, and American Culture* (Chapel Hill: University of North Carolina Press, 1995); "Jonathan Edwards's Most Popular Work: 'The Life of David Brainerd' and Nineteenth-Century Evangelical Culture," *Church History* 54/2 (1985): 188–201; "David Brainerd and the Nineteenth-Century Missionary Movement," *Journal of the Early Republic* 5 (Fall 1985): 309–29.

[65]Considerable disagreement exists as to whether the New Divinity marked the preservation and continuance of Edwards' theology or represented a significant departure from it. Some question also exists regarding the extent to which "disinterested benevolence" was either "disinterested" or "benevolent." For the purposes of this study, the details of those arguments are unimportant. What is certain and important is that missionary women identified themselves with both Edwards and the leading proponents of the New Divinity and they accepted the ideal of "disinterested benevolence" at face value. For an in-depth discussion of Samuel Hopkins and the New Divinity, see Joseph Conforti, *Samuel Hopkins and the New Divinity Movement: Calvinism, the Congregational Ministry, and Reform in New England Between the Great Awakenings* (Grand Rapids MI: Christian University Press, 1981); William Kern Breitenbach, "New Divinity Theology and the Idea of Moral Accountability" (Ph.D. diss., Yale University, 1978) and "The Consistent Calvinism of the New Divinity Movement," *William and Mary Quarterly* 41/2 (1984): 241–64. For discussions of the influence of the New Divinity on the foreign missions movement, see Oliver Wendell Elsbree, *The Rise of the Missionary Spirit in America, 1790–1815* (Philadelphia: Porcupine Press, 1980; reprint, Williamsport PA: The Williamsport Printing and Binding Co., 1928) and "Samuel Hopkins and His Doctrine of Benevolence," *New England Quarterly* 8 (December 1935): 534–50; R. Pierce Beaver, "Missionary Motivation Through Three Centuries," in Jerald C. Brauer, ed., *Reinterpretation in American Church History* (Chicago: University of Chicago Press, 1968) 113–51 and *American Protestant Women in World Mission: A History of the First Feminist Movement in North America*, rev. ed. (Grand Rapids MI: Eerdmans, 1980); Hutchison, *Errand to the World*; Robert, *American Women in Mission*.

[66]Winslow, *Memoir of Mrs. Harriet L. Winslow*, 38.

[67]Hooker, *Memoir of Mrs. Sarah L. Huntington Smith*, 96–97.

[68]Ibid., 94.

[69]Hawes, *Memoir of Mrs. Mary E. Van Lennep*, 108–109.

[70]Winslow, *Memoir of Mrs. Harriet L. Winslow*, 65; Hooker, *Memoir of Mrs. Sarah L. Huntington Smith*, 97.

[71]For a discussion of the development and role of the Sunday school in American religious culture, see Anne M. Boylan, *Sunday School: The Formation of an American Institution, 1790–1880* (New Haven CT: Yale University Press, 1988).

[72]Benjamin, *The Missionary Sisters*, 20.

[73]Judson, *Memoir of Sarah B. Judson*, 26–27.

[74]Winslow, *Memoir of Mrs. Harriet L. Winslow*, 61–63.

[75]Hooker, *Memoir of Mrs. Sarah L. Huntington Smith*, 94.

[76]Ibid., 115–21.

[77]Knowles, *Memoir of Mrs. Ann H. Judson*, 10.

Chapter 3

[1]Numbers derived from the Library of Congress's *National Union Catalog*.

[2]Claudius Buchanan, *Christian Researches in Asia...To which is added, The Star in the East, a Sermon Preached in the Parish Church of St. James, Bristol, on Sunday, February 26, 1809, with an Appendix, Containing an Account of 200,000 Christians discovered in the sequestered region of Hindostan* (Lexington KY: Thomas T. Skillman, 1813) 65–66.

[3]Hannah More, *Strictures on the Modern System of Female Education: With a View of the Principles and Conduct Prevalent Among Women of Rank and Fortune*, vol. 1, 9th ed. (London: Printed by A. Strahan for T. Cadell, Jun. and W. Davies, 1801) 3.

[4]William Staughton, *The Baptist Mission in India: Containing a Narrative of Its Rise, Progress, and Present Condition. A Statement of the Physical and Moral Character of the Hindoos, Their Cruelties, Tortures and Burnings, with a Very Interesting Description of Bengal, Intended to Animate to Missionary Co-operation* (Philadelphia: Stiles for Hollings & Aitken, 1811) 110–11, 189.

[5]Timothy George, *Faithful Witness: The Life and Mission of William Carey* (Birmingham AL: New Hope Press, 1991); James Beck, *Dorothy Carey: The Tragic and Untold Story of Mrs. William Carey* (Grand Rapids MI: Baker Book House, 1992); Lisa J. Pruitt, "Possessed of a 'Missionary Spirit'?: English Baptist Women and Bengali Missions from Dorothy Carey to the Baptist Zenana Mission, 1792–1914," *American Baptist Quarterly* 17/4 (December 1998): 285–304.

[6]William Carey to the Baptist Missionary Society, 28 December 1796, Baptist Missionary Society Archives (UK), 1792-1914. Microfilm. Nashville, Tennessee: Historical Commission, Southern Baptist Convention, 1991 (BMSA-m).

[7]*Panoplist and Missionary Magazine* 11/4 (April 1815): 118.

[8]Ibid.

[9]For a discussion of the role of the minister's wife, see Leonard I. Sweet, *The Minister's Wife: Her Role in Nineteenth-Century American Evangelicalism* (Philadelphia: Temple University Press, 1983).

[10]*Panoplist and Missionary Magazine* 11/4 (April 1815): 118.

[11]Melville Horne, *Letters on Missions, Addressed to the Protestant Ministers of the British Churches* (Andover MA: Flagg & Gould, 1815) 109–10.

[12]*Panoplist and Missionary Magazine* 11/4 (April 1815): 118.

[13]Ibid., 118–19.

[14]Ibid., 119.

[15]The author of the footnote may well have been Rufus Anderson's father, also named Rufus Anderson. The elder Rufus Anderson (1765–1814) was involved in the formation of the ABCFM, while the younger Rufus Anderson (1796–1880) served as its executive secretary for decades. See Paul William Harris, *Nothing But Christ: Rufus Anderson and the Ideology of Protestant Foreign Missions* (New York: Oxford University Press, 1999).

[16]Robert, *American Women and Missions*, 57–70.

[17]Rufus Anderson, "Introductory Essay on the Marriage of Missionaries," in William Ellis, *Memoir of Mrs. Mary Mercy Ellis, wife of Rev. William Ellis, Missionary*

in the South Seas, and Foreign Secretary of the London Missionary Society (Boston: Crocker & Brewster, 1836) vii–viii.

[18]Ibid., viii.

[19]Ibid.

[20]Ibid., viii–ix.

[21]Ibid., x–xi.

[22]Ibid., xi. Note that the "heathen" is a place as well as a people.

[23]Ibid., xi–xii.

[24]Ibid., xii.

[25]Ibid.

[26]Winslow, *Memoir of Mrs. Harriet L. Winslow*, 273–74.

[27] William Dean, *Memoir of Mrs. Lucy T. Lord of the Chinese Baptist Mission* (Philadelphia: American Baptist Publication Society, 1854) 114–15.

[28]Winslow, *Memoir of Mrs. Harriet L. Winslow*, 255.

[29]Winslow, *Memoir of Mrs. Harriet L. Winslow*, 273–74.

[30] Harrison Dwight, *Memoir of Mrs. Elizabeth B. Dwight, Including an Account of the Plague of 1837, by Rev. H. G. O. Dwight, Missionary to Constantinople, with a Sketch of the life of Mrs. Judith S. Grant, Missionary to Persia* (Boston: American Tract Society, 1860) 156-157.

[31]Winslow, *Memoir of Mrs. Harriet L. Winslow*, 273–74.

[32]Ibid., 384–85.

[33]Lawrence, *Light on the Dark River*, 11–12.

[34]Ibid., 99–100.

[35]Hooker, *Memoir of Mrs. Sarah L. Huntington Smith*, 282–83.

[36]Hooker, *Memoir of Mrs. Sarah L. Huntington Smith*, 296–97.

[37] Winslow, *Memoir of Mrs. Harriet L. Winslow*, 400–403.

[38]Ibid.

[39]Ibid., 265.

[40]Asahel Grant, narrative of a journey over the plain of Mesopotamia to Akra near Nineveh in October of 1839. Appendix to Campbell, *A Memoir of Mrs. Judith S. Grant*, 192–93.

[41]Hooker, *Memoir of Mrs. Sarah L. Huntington Smith*, 373.

[42]Ibid., 186.

[43]Ibid., 303–304.

[44]Dwight, *Memoir of Mrs. Elizabeth B. Dwight*, 198.

[45]Dean, *Memoir of Mrs. Lucy T. Lord*, 172.

[46]Knowles, *Memoir of Ann H. Judson*, 158.

[47]"Report on the meeting to organize the General Convention, held in Philadelphia in May 1814, Address," in *Massachusetts Baptist Missionary Magazine* 3 (September 1814): 72.

[48]Hooker, *Memoir of Mrs. Sarah L. Huntington Smith*, 303–308; Campbell, 125; Knowles, 112; Jeter, 92.

[49]Dwight, *Memoir of Mrs. Elizabeth B. Dwight*, 200.

[50]Hooker, *Memoir of Mrs. Sarah L. Huntington Smith*, 368.

[51]Knowles, *Memoir of Mrs. Ann H. Judson*, 144.

[52]Hooker, *Memoir of Mrs. Sarah L. Huntington Smith*, 275–76, 304.

[53]Campbell, *Memoir of Mrs. Judih S. Grant*, 133.

[54]Lord to the Baptist Church at Delanti, 6 October 1847, Lucy Lord Papers, Mt. Holyoke College Archives, South Hadley, Massachusetts.

[55]Winslow, *A Memoir of Mrs. Harriet L. Winslow*, 165–66.

[56]Ibid., 205–206, 390–91.

[57]Jeter, *Memoir of Mrs. Henrietta Shuck*, 56.

[58]Winslow, *A Memoir of Mrs. Harriet L. Winslow*, 205–206.

[59]Hooker, *Memoir of Mrs. Sarah L. Huntington Smith*, 295–97.

[60]Dwight, *Memoir of Mrs. Elizabeth B. Dwight*, 207–208.

[61]Dwight, *Memoir of Mrs. Elizabeth B. Dwight*, 167–69.

[62]Hooker, *Memoir of Mrs. Sarah L. Huntington Smith*, 296–97, 186. See 1 Peter 3:1–4: "Likewise, ye wives, be in subjection to your own husbands that, if any obey not the word, they also may without the word be won by the behavior of the wives, while they behold your chaste conduct coupled with fear; Whose adorning, let it not be that outward adorning of plaiting the hair, and of wearing of gold, or of putting on apparel, But let it be the hidden man of the heart in that which is not corruptible, even the ornament of a meek and quiet spirit, which is in the sight of God of great price. For after this manner in the old time the holy women also, who trusted in God, adorned themselves, being in subjection unto their own husbands."

[63]Hooker, *Memoir of Mrs. Sarah L. Huntington Smith*, 223.

[64]Adoniram Judson, *Letter to the Female Members of Christian Churches, in the United States of America* (Providence RI: N. H. Brown, 1832) 3–4. According to a note printed on the flyleaf, this letter was published in the *Christian Watchman* and the *Boston Recorder*.

[65]Ibid., 5.

[66]Ibid., 6.

[67]Ibid., 7.

[68]Ibid., 8–11.

[69]Two good overviews of the practice of *sati* are V. N. Datta, *Sati: A Historical, Social and Philosophical Enquiry into the Hindu Rite of Widow Burning* (London: Sangam Books, 1988) and Sakuntala Narasimhan, *Sati: Widow Burning in India* (New York: Doubleday, 1990).

[70]Kenneth Ingham, *Reformers in India, 1793–1833: An Account of the Work of Missions in Behalf of Social Reform* (New York: Octagon, 1973) 44.

[71]Ibid.

[72]Ibid., 45.

[73]Marshman, *The Story of Carey, Marshman, and Ward*, 86–87.

[74]Ingham, *Reformers in India*, 47.

[75]Ibid.

[76]Claudius Buchanan, *The Works of the Rev. Claudius Buchanan, LL.D., Comprising His Christian Researches in Asia..., His Memoir on the Expediency of an Ecclesiastical*

Establishment for British India, and His Star in the East (New York: Whiting and Watson, 1812) 249–50.

[77]"Interesting Sketches of the State of Christianity in India," *Massachusetts Baptist Missionary Magazine* 2/8 (December 1809): 231–32. The *MBMM* printed similar excerpts on a fairly regular basis. See, for example, the article "Horrid Pagan Customs," regarding a 1710 incident in which the Prince of Marava died and forty-seven of his wives burned with his corpse (*MBMM* 3/12 [December 1813]: 355–56).

[78]Letter to the editor from "Beta," *Panoplist* 4/7 (NS) (December 1811): 312–13.

[79]William Ward, *A View of the Idolatry of the Hindoos, Their History, Religion, Manners and Customs, &c., Abridged from his original work in 3 vols. 8vo. Part II in All Religions and Religious Ceremonies, in Two Parts* (Hartford CT: Oliver D. Cook & Sons, 1823) 29–30; Thomas Smith and John O. Choules, *The Origin and History of Missions: Containing Faithful Accounts of the Voyages, Travels, Labors and Successes of the Various Missionaries Who Have been Sent Forth to Evangelize the Heathen; compiled from Authentic Documents; Forming a Complete Missionary Repository...in Two Volumes*, vol. 1 (Boston: Walker, Lincoln, and Edmands, 1832) 207–208, 231–32, 243, 253; and Baron Stow, *A History of the English Baptist Mission to India* (Philadelphia: American Sunday School Union, 1835) 107–108, 161–62, 222–24.

[80]John Scudder, *A Voice From the East to the Young, in a Series of Letters to the Children of the Reformed Protestant Dutch Church of North America* (New York: Board of Publications of the Reformed Protestant Dutch Church, 1859) 46–47.

[81]Ibid., 47–50.

[82]Ibid., 54–55. Scudder also discussed *sati* in his *Letters to Sabbath-School Children on the Condition of the Heathen* (Philadelphia: American Sunday School Union, 1843) 28.

Chapter 4

[1]*Mother's Magazine* (January 1836). Also recounted in Dwight, Dwight, *Memoir of Mrs. Elizabeth B. Dwight*, 162.

[2]Dean, *Memoir of Mrs. Lucy T. Lord*, 182–83.

[3]Jeter, *Memoir of Mrs. Henrietta Shuck*, 128–30.

[4]Ibid., 131–34.

[5]Winslow, *Memoir of Mrs. Harriet L. Winslow*, 423.

[6]Emily Judson, 188.

[7]*Mother's Magazine* (June 1834): 90–91.

[8]Dean, *Memoir of Mrs. Lucy T. Lord*, 222–23.

[9]Ibid., 240.

[10]*The Persian Flower: A Memoir of Judith Grant Perkins, of Oroomiah, Persia* (Boston: American Tract Society, 1853) 30–31.

[11]Bernice J. Lee, "Female Infanticide in China," in Richard W. Guisso and Stanley Johannesen, eds., *Women in China: Current Directions in Historical Scholarship* (Youngstown NY: Philo Press, 1981) 163–77.

[12]Claudius Buchanan, *Works...Memoir on the Expedience of an Ecclesiastical Establishment*, 248.

[13]Conrad Malte Brun, *Universal Geography, or a Description of All the Parts of the World on a New Plan, According to the Great Natural Divisions of the Globe: Accompanied with Analytical, Synoptical, and Elementary Tables, Volume III: Containing the Description of India and Oceanica* (Boston: Wells and Lilly, 1826) 59.

[14]*Massachusetts Baptist Missionary Magazine*, extracted from Cecil's Sermons, III (NS) (September 1811) 3:88–89.

[15]John Scudder, *Letters to Sabbath School Children: On the Condition of the Heathen* (Philadelphia: American Sunday-School Union, 1843) 29–30.

[16]John Scudder, *A Voice from the East to the Young, in a Series of Letters to Children of the Reformed Protestant Dutch Church of North America* (New York: Board of Publications of the Reformed Protestant Dutch Church, 1859) 224–26. Illustration follows page 266.

[17]John Scudder, *An Appeal to Christian Mothers in Behalf of the Heathen* (New York: American Tract Society, 1840) 20–21, 53–55.

[18]Buchanan, *Works...Memoir on the Expediency of an Ecclesiastical Establishment*, 248. Buchanan's accounts of both practices were replicated in the *Massachusetts Baptist Missionary Magazine*.

[19]Ward, *A View of the Idolatry of the Hindoos*, 81.

[20]*Massachusetts Baptist Missionary Magazine* II (December 1809) 8:231–32; Ward, *View*, 81; Buchanan, *Memoir*, 246–47, and *Christian Researches in Asia*, 39; Malte Brun, *Universal Geography*, Volume III, 109–10.

[21]Emily Judson, *Memoir of Mrs. Sarah B. Judson*, 28–29.

[22]Scudder, *Letters to Sabbath School Children*, 18–19. A similar account and the same illustration appeared in Scudder's *A Voice from the East*, 143–46.

[23]*Mother's Magazine* (November 1844): 321–24.

[24]"A Concise View," *Mother's Magazine* I (January 1833) 1:6, 8.

[25]Winslow, *Memoir of Mrs. Harriet L. Winslow*, 237.

[26]Emily Judson, *Memoir of Mrs. Sarah B. Judson*, 178.

[27]Dwight, *Memoir of Mrs. Elizabeth B. Dwight*, 280–81.

[28]Dwight, *Memoir of Mrs. Elizabeth B. Dwight*, 140.

[29]*Mother's Magazine* (June 1835) 95–96.

[30]Asahel Grant, 2 November 1837, *Mother's Magazine* (July 1838): 159–62.

[31]"Future Defenders of the Faith," *Mother's Magazine* (May 1833): 69; "Address of the Maternal Association of the Baptist Church and Society in Utica, to Mothers," *Mother's Magazine* (May 1833): 79.

[32]"The Future Defenders of the Faith," *Mother's Magazine* (July 1833): 99–102.

[33]"The Mother of a Missionary," *Mother's Magazine* (February 1834).

[34]"Children Interested in the Cause of Missions," *Mother's Magazine* (March 1836): 55–56.

[35]"Education for Missionary Labor," *Mother's Magazine* (October 1836): 156–58; continued in March 1837 issue, 55–58.

[36]EIizabeth Dwight to Mrs. H., Constantinople, 4 September 1835, *Mother's Magazine* (January 1836).

[37]Knowles, *Memoir of Mrs. Ann H. Judson*, 273.

[38]Hooker, *Memoir of Mrs. Sarah L. Huntington Smith*, 193–94, 322, 371.

[39]Lucy Lord to Solomon Peck, Ningpo, 2 September 1847, Lord Papers; Dwight, *Memoir of Mrs. Elizabeth B. Dwight*, 211; Campbell, *Memoir of Mrs. Judith S. Grant*, 121; and Jeter, *Memoir of Mrs. Henrietta Shuck*, 95–96, 191, 201–202.

[40]Letter from Mrs. Gutzlaff, China, in response to having been sent a copy of the magazine. *Mother's Magazine* (January 1839): 12–15.

[41]"An Account of Meh Shway-ee, A Burman Slave Girl, Aged Seven Years," *American Baptist Magazine* IX (April 1829) 4:109.

[42]Winslow, *Memoir of Mrs. Harriet L. Winslow*, 212–13, 239, 260, 277–78.

[43]Jeter, *Memoir of Mrs. Henrietta Shuck*, 138–39, 209.

[44]Louisa Hawes, *Memoir of Mrs. Mary E. Van Lennep*, 262–63.

[45]Winslow, *Memoir of Mrs. Harriet L. Winslow*, 281–82, 368–70.

[46]Knowles, *Memoir of Mrs. Ann H. Judson*, 162–63; Emily Judson, *Memoir of Mrs. Sarah B. Judson*, 69, 182; Hooker, *Memoir of Mrs. Sarah L. Huntington Smith*, 225, 265, 267, 380; Dwight, *Memoir of Mrs. Elizabeth B. Dwight*, 280; Campbell, *Memoir of Mrs. Judith S. Grant*, 116; Louisa Hawes, *Memoir of Mrs. Mary E. Van Lennep*, 22.

[47]Hooker, *Memoir of Mrs. Sarah L. Huntington Smith*, 301.

[48]Ibid., 315. Other accounts of visiting as an evangelistic strategy appear in Winslow, *Memoir of Mrs. Harriet L. Winslow*, 210–12, 217–19; Dwight, *Memoir of Mrs. Elizabeth B. Dwight*, 158, 300–301; Campbell, *Memoir of Mrs. Judith S. Grant*, 130, 133–34, 169; Knowles, *Memoir of Mrs. Ann H. Judson*, 153, 169, 181, 214, 217–18; Emily Judson, *Memoir of Mrs. Sarah B. Judson*, 166–67, 170–71; Jeter, *Memoir of Mrs. Henrietta Shuck*, 107, 142–43, 198.

[49]Knowles, 58, 189. Other missionary women who describe native women's prayer meetings included Sarah Boardman Judson, in Emily Judson, 154, 155, 178, 228; Sarah Lanman Smith, in Hooker, 229, 287, 292, 381; Judith Grant, in Campbell, 284; Mary Van Lennep, in Louisa Hawes, 260; Henrietta Shuck, in Jeter, 70; Lucy Lord, in Dean, 185–86.

[50]Emily Judson, *Memoir of Mrs. Sarah B. Judson*,224.

[51]Knowles , *Memoir of Mrs. Ann H. Judson*, 181; Emily Judson, 182–83.

[52]Hooker, *Memoir of Mrs. Sarah L. Huntington Smith*, 294.

[53]Dean, *Memoir of Lucy T. Lord*, 176.

[54]Hooker, *Memoir of Mrs. Sarah L. Huntington Smith*, 294; Dean, *Memoir of Lucy T. Lord*, 196.

Chapter 5

[1]For a history of the changing lives of single women in early America, see Lee Virginia Chambers-Schiller, *Liberty, A Better Husband: Single Women in America, The Generation of 1780–1840* (New Haven CT: Yale University Press, 1984).

[2]Hooker, *Memoir of Mrs. Sarah L. Huntington Smith*, 309–10.

[3]Ibid., 304–305.

[4]Ibid., 306–307.

[5]Ibid., 308–10.

[6]Benjamin Rush, *Thoughts Upon Female Education, Accommodated to the Present State of Society, Manners, and Government in the United States of America. Addressed to the Visitors of the Young Ladies' Academy in Philadelphia, 28 July 1787, At the Close of the Quarterly Examination* (Philadelphia: Prichard and Hall, 1787). For a discussion of "republican motherhood," see Linda K. Kerber, *Women of the Republic.*

[7]Hannah More, *Strictures on the Modern System of Female Education*, vol. 1, 9th ed. (London: n.p., 1801), 66, 3, 63–64.

[8]Ruth H. Bloch, "Ideals in Transition: The Rise of the Moral Mother, 1785–1815," *Feminist Studies* 4 (June 1978) 2:100–26.

[9]More, *Strictures on the Modern System of Female Education*, 3.

[10]William Staughton, *An Address, Delivered October 1807, at Mrs. Rivardi's Seminary, on the Occasion of the Examination of the First and Middle Class* (Philadelphia: Kimber, Conrad & Co., 1807) 6.

[11]Emma Willard, *An Address to the Public, Particularly to the Members of the Legislature of New York, Proposing a Plan for Improving Female Education*, 2d ed. (Middlebury: J. W. Copeland, 1819) 13.

[12]Ibid., 15.

[13]Ibid, 17–25.

[14]Ibid., 27–28.

[15]Ibid., 29–30.

[16]Ibid., 34.

[17]Ibid., 35.

[18]Catharine Beecher, *Suggestions Respecting Improvements in Education, Presented to the Trustees of the Hartford Female Seminary, and Published at Their Request* (Hartford CT: Packard and Butler, 1829) 7. See also Sklar, *Catharine Beecher.*

[19]Beecher, *Suggestions Respecting Improvements in Education*, 9.

[20]Ibid., 24–26.

[21]Ibid., 48–49.

[22]Ibid., 50.

[23]Ibid., 52.

[24]Rebecca was the sister of American Baptist missionary to Burma Ann Hasseltine Judson.

[25][Mary Lyon], *General View of the Principles and Design of the Mt. Holyoke Female Seminary* (N.p.: February 1837) 6. See also Elizabeth Alden Green, *Mary Lyon and Mount Holyoke: Opening the Gates* (Hanover NH: University Press of New England, 1979) and Amanda Porterfield, *Mary Lyon and the Mount Holyoke Missionaries* (New York: Oxford University Press, 1997).

[26][Lyon], *General View*, 1.

[27]Ibid., 17. This is probably a reference to Gordon Hall and Samuel Newell, *The Conversion of the World, or, the Claims of Six Hundred Millions and the Ability and Duty of the Churches Respecting Them* (Andover MA: Flagg & Gould, 1818).

[28][Mary Lyon], *Female Education: Tendencies of the Principles Embraced and the System Adopted in the Mt.Holyoke Female Seminary*, 1.

[29][Lyon], *General View*, 18.

[30][Lyon], *Female Education*, 10.

[31]Green, *Mary Lyon and Mount Holyoke*, 15.

[32]Ibid., 252–54. See also Porterfield, *Mary Lyon and the Mount Holyoke Missionaries*.

[33]Green, *Mary Lyon and Mount Holyoke*, 264.

[34]Rufus Anderson, *History of the Missions of the American Board of Commissioners for Foreign Missions: India* (Boston: Congregational Publishing Society, 1875) 134.

[35]Winslow, *Memoir of Mrs. Harriet L. Winslow*, 191.

[36]Ibid., 191–92.

[37]Anderson, *History...India*, 138.

[38]Ibid., 147.

[39]Ibid., 146.

[40]Ibid., 148.

[41]Duncan B. Forrester, *Caste and Christianity: Attitudes and Policies on Caste of Anglo-Saxon Missions in India* (London: Curzon Press, 1980) 25.

[42]Ibid., 26.

[43]Ibid., 27.

[44]Ibid., 26.

[45]Anderson, *History...India*, 151.

[46]Winslow, *Memoir of Mrs. Harriet L. Winslow*, 185.

[47]Ibid., 334–35.

[48]Ibid., 239.

[49]Ibid., 281–82.

[50]Anderson, *History...India*, 151.

[51]Winslow, *Memoir of Mrs. Harriet L. Winslow*, 288.

[52]Ibid., 337–38.

[53]Anderson, *History...India*, 151.

[54]Winslow, 399.

[55]Anderson, *History...India*, 161.

[56]Winslow, *Memoir of Mrs. Harriet L. Winslow*, 400.

[57]Anderson, *History...India*, 152.

[58]Ibid., 153.

[59]Ibid., 158.

[60]Ibid., 158.

[61]Mary Lyon to Justin Perkins, 6 February 1844, quoted in Fiske, 97.

[62]The use of the term Nestorian is problematic. I retain it for the same reason I retain the term "Oriental": because it was the term that the missionaries who are the subject of this study used. The name derives from a fifth-century bishop, Nestorius, who advocated a christology that viewed Jesus as having two separate identities, one divine and one human. The missionaries used the name "Nestorian" primarily because it was the universally accepted name among Westerners for that particular group of people. The name also bore within it the justification for the mission; the group was Christian, but they were Nestorian Christians; that is, they were unreformed and therefore unredeemed. The use of the term Nestorian has persisted

in the West until the present day (see, for example, *Britannica Online* <http://www.eb.com>). Some disagreement exists over what that group prefers to call themselves and whether they consider the word Nestorian pejorative. One source says that the group prefers to call themselves the Assyrian Orthodox Church (John R. Hinnells, ed., *New Dictionary of Religion* [Oxford: Blackwell Ltd., 1995] 111–12). Another source says that the Nestorian Church exists today as two separate churches: the Assyrian, or East Syrian, Church and the Chaldean Church (Peter Bishop and Michael Darton, eds., *Encyclopedia of World Faiths* [London: Macdonald Orbis, 1987] 84–85). To add to the confusion, *Britannica Online* indicates that "in modern times they are represented by the Church of the East, or Persian Church, usually referred to in the West as the Assyrian, or Nestorian, Church" (*Britannica Online*, s.v. Nestorian). John Joseph maintains that "in spite of its original stigmatic connotation, time has made respectable" the use of the term Nestorian (*The Nestorians and Their Muslim Neighbors* [Princeton: Princeton University Press, 1961] ix). Aziz S. Atiya insists that the term Nestorian was adopted by the group itself in the thirteenth century and was "never objectionable to the members of this sect" (*A History of Eastern Christianity* [South Bend IN: University of Notre Dame Press, 1968] 239n). By contrast, J. F. Coakley states that the term Nestorian is "fiercely rejected...by most members of the church themselves." Coakley uses Church of the East (*The Church of the East and the Church of England: A History of the Archbishop of Canterbury's Assyrian Mission* [Oxford: Clarendon Press, 1992] 4). The choice of terminology is further complicated by the fact that the Nestorians of Oroomiah (Urmia), who are one subject of this chapter, were "received into the communion of the Russian Orthodox Church" in 1898 (*Britannica Online*). Hence, their descendants are not a part of the modern-day Church of the East.

[63]Anderson, *History... Oriental Churches, Vol. I*, 1–2.

[64]Ibid., 179, 184.

[65]Fiske, *Faith Working by Love*, 52.

[66]Ibid., 52–53.

[67]Ibid., 53.

[68]Ibid., 24.

[69]Ibid., 25–27.

[70]Ibid., 31–35.

[71]Ibid., 44–45.

[72]Ibid., 55.

[73]Ibid., 54–55.

[74]Ibid., 57–62.

[75]Ibid., 54.

[76]Ibid., 93–94.

[77]Ibid., 107–108.

[78]Ibid., 120.

[79]Ibid., 121.

[80]Ibid., 113–14.

[81]Ibid., 124.

[82]Ibid., 125.
[83]Ibid., 125–26.
[84]Ibid., 130.
[85]Ibid., 128, 130.
[86]Ibid., 157.
[87]Ibid., 42.
[88]Ibid., 163.
[89]Ibid., 166.
[90]Ibid., 169.
[91]Ibid., 173.

Chapter 6

[1]Sarah Josepha Hale, "Fifty Years of My Literary Life," *Godey's Lady's Book* (*GLB*) (December 1877): 523.

[2]Isabelle Webb Entrikin, *Sarah Josepha Hale and Godey's Lady's Book* (Philadelphia: University of Pennsylvania, 1946) 2–7. See also Ruth E. Finley, *The Lady of Godey's: Sarah Josepha Hale* (New York: Arno Press, 1974; reprint, Philadelphia: Lippincott Company, 1931).

[3]Paul S. Boyer, "Sarah Josepha Buell Hale," in Edward T. James, ed., *Notable American Women, 1607–1950: A Biographical Dictionary*, vol. 2 (Cambridge MA: Belknap Press of Harvard University Press, 1971) 110–14.

[4]Ibid., 111–12.

[5]Welter, "The Cult of True Womanhood, 1820–1860" and "The Feminization of American Religion, 1820–1860"; Bloch, "Ideals in Transition"; Cott, *The Bonds of Womanhood*; Ryan, *Cradle of the Middle Class*; Ann Douglas, *The Feminization of American Culture* (New York: Knopf, 1977).

[6]*GLB* 80 (May 1870): 451–54.

[7]See especially Douglas, *The Feminization of American Culture.*

[8]Helen Barrett Montgomery, *Western Women in Eastern Lands: An Outline Study of Fifty Years of Woman's Work in Foreign Missions* (New York: Macmillan Co., 1910) 126; Beaver, *American Protestant Women in World Mission*, 132. Tucker's *Guardians of the Great Commission*, despite having an entire chapter on medical missions, does not mention Hale's role.

[9]Regina Markell Morantz-Sanchez, *Sympathy and Science: Women Physicians in American Medicine* (New York: Oxford University Press, 1985) 98–99. Morantz-Sanchez also notes that Hale "endorsed the founding of the Woman's Medical College of Pennsylvania" and "participated in a training program for missionaries at the school."

[10]*GLB* 44 (January 1852): 88.

[11]Morantz-Sanchez's *Sympathy and Science* contains an in-depth discussion of the contending parties in this debate. See also Jane B. Donegan, *Women and Men Midwives: Medicine, Morality, and Misogyny in Early America* (Westport CT: Greenwood Press, 1978).

[12]*GLB* 43 (August 1851): 122.

[13]*GLB* 43 (July 1851): 57.

[14]*GLB* 44 (January 1852): 88.

[15]*GLB* 46 (January 1853): 82–83.

[16]*GLB* 43 (July 1851): 57; *GLB* 75 (September 1867): 263–64.

[17]*GLB* 43 (July 1851): 57.

[18]John 5:1-9, King James Version.

[19]Nineteenth-century reformers who sought to establish the office of deaconess (primarily in the Episcopal, Lutheran, and Methodist churches) saw themselves as restoring an ancient role in the church. While in some denominations the diaconate had become a step to an ordained preaching ministry, reformers believed that the diaconate should be a permanent order, either lay or professional, for serving the poor and sick. Professional deacons or deaconesses devoted themselves to full-time service, whereas lay deacons or deaconesses served as volunteers. Both lay and professional deacons and deaconesses received ordination in the sense of being ceremonially set apart for a special work.

[20]Some reformed churches in the Netherlands and Germany had deaconesses in the sixteenth century; see J. C. Wenger, *The Mennonite Church in America* (Scottdale PA: Herald Press, 1966) 279–80 and J. Taylor Hamilton and Kenneth G. Hamilton, *History of the Moravian Church: The Renewed Unitas Fratrem, 1722–1957* (Bethlehem PA: Interprovincial Board of Christian Education, Moravian Church in America, 1967) 102, 342, 345. Background information on deaconesses comes primarily from Jane M. Bancroft, *Deaconesses in Europe and Their Lessons for America. With an Introduction by Edward G. Andrews, D.D., LL.D., Bishop of the Methodist Episcopal Church* (New York: Hunt and Eaton, 1889). See also C. DeSwarte Gifford, ed., *The American Deaconess Movement in the Early Twentieth Century* (1987); Mary Agnes Dougherty, "The Methodist Deaconess: A Case of Religious Feminism," *Methodist History* 21 (1983) 2:90–98; Rosemary S. Keller, "Women and the Nature of Ministry in the United Methodist Tradition," *Methodist History* 22 (1984) 2:99–114; Keller, "Lay Women in the Protestant Tradition," in Keller and Rosemary Radford Ruether, eds., *Women and Religion in America, Volume I: The Nineteenth Century, a Documentary History*; Henry Wheeler, *Deaconesses Ancient and Modern* (New York: Hunt and Eaton, 1889); Julius Disselhoff, *Kaiserswerth: The Deaconess Institution of Rhenish-Westphalia, Its Origin and Fields of Labour* (London: Hatchards, Piccadilly, 1883)

[21]Bancroft, *Deaconesses in Europe and Their Lessons for America*, 63.

[22]Ibid., 80.

[23]Ibid., 79.

[24]Ibid., 82.

[25]Ibid., 84–86.

[26]Ibid., 147.

[27]*GLB* 44 (June 1852): 488–93.

[28]Ibid., 489.

[29]Ibid., 489–90.

[30]Ibid., 490.

[31]Ibid., 491.

[32]Ibid., 492.

[33]*GLB* 45 (October 1852): 389.

[34]*GLB* 46 (May 1853): 465–67.

[35]See Chapter 5.

[36]*GLB* 43 (August 1851): 122; see also *GLB* 44 (January 1852): 88.

[37] *GLB* 48 (July 1854): 80; *GLB* 48 (May 1854): 463.

[38]*GLB* 44 (May 1852): 404–405.

[39]*GLB* 45 (August 1852): 193–94.

[40]*GLB* 46 (January 1853): 82–83.

[41]*GLB* 63 (December 1861): 534–35.

[42]Sarah J. Hale, "An Appeal to American Christians on Behalf of the Ladies' Medical Missionary Society," *GLB* 44 (March 1852): 185.

[43]Ibid., 187.

[44]H. G. O. Dwight, "Letter from Constantinople," 13 May 1852, *GLB* 45 (December 1852): 575. The portion cited was printed again in Sarah Josepha Hale, "Doings of the Ladies' Medical Missionary Society," *GLB* 46 (June 1853): 553.

[45]Donegan, *Women and Men Midwives*, 132.

[46]Ibid., 59–65.

[47]Orthodox physicians were university-educated men trained in long-established traditions of theory and practice. They often used heroic therapeutics, which included bloodletting and purging to extreme. Sectarians came from varied educational backgrounds and practiced gentler, and therefore more popular, therapies such as homeopathy, hydropathy, and botanic medicine. See Regina Morantz-Sanchez's *Sympathy and Science* for a detailed account of the intersecting social forces that contributed to the emergence of women's medical education. Her article "The Female Student Has Arrived: The Rise of the Women's Medical Movement," in Ruth J. Abram, ed., *"Send Us a Lady Physician": Women Doctors in America, 1835–1920* (New York: W. W. Norton, 1985) offers an excellent brief summary.

[48]Hale, "Doings of the Ladies' Medical Missionary Society," 554.

[49]Quoting John Stainback Wilson, *GLB* 49 (November 1854): 464.

[50]Donegan, *Women and Men Midwives*, 141–58.

[51]*GLB* 43 (August 1851): 122.

[52]Samuel Gregory, "Letter to Ladies in favor of Female Physicians for Their Own Sex," published by the Female Medical Education Society of Boston and reprinted in *GLB* 43 (August 1851): 123.

[53]*GLB* 50 (June 1855): 560.

[54]*GLB* 42 (August 1851): 122.

[55]Letter from S. H. Waddell, a "lady" of North Carolina, *GLB* 47 (November 1853): 465–66.

[56]*GLB* 48 (May 1854): 463; *GLB* 47 (December 1853): 554–55.

[57]John Stainback Wilson, "Health Department," *GLB* 48 (February 1854): 175–76.

[58]*GLB* 50 (June 1855): 560.

[59]Sarah Josepha Hale to Rev. S. B. Treat, 15 June 1852, ABC 10 Domestic correspondence received, v. 43, 1846-60, "H," ABCFM.

[60]"Appeal," *GLB* 44 (March 1852): 185.

[61]*GLB* 45 (July 1852): 94–95. Actually, it was not unusual for customs of caste in the stricter Hindu households to bar Christian women from entering the *zenana* as well.

[62]Letter from H. G. O. Dwight, Constantinople, 13 May 1852 *GLB* 45 (December 1852): 575.

[63]"Appeal," *GLB* 44 (March 1852): 185.

[64]Ibid., 187.

[65]Annie Ryder Gracey, *Medical Work of the Woman's Foreign Missionary Society, Methodist Episcopal Church* (Boston: Publication Office of the WFMS, MEC, 1888) 3.

[66]Ibid., 14.

[67]Ibid., 14. See also Christoffer Grundmann, "Proclaiming the Gospel by Healing the Sick? Historical and Theological Annotations on Medical Mission," *International Bulletin of Missionary Research* 14 (July 1990): 120–26. Grundmann says, "But none of this was called *medical missions* nor did one speak of medical missionaries prior to the nineteenth century.... Terms indicating an awareness of medical mission per se, and of a special ministry for the medical missionary first appeared in the middle of the nineteenth century. They denote a new phenomenon in the history of Christianity that is inseparably linked with the heyday of Christian mission activities and to modern medical, surgical, and pharmaceutical achievements" (120).

[68]Phillips, *passim*.

[69]Edwin Munsell Bliss, "Medical Missions," *The Encyclopaedia of Missions*, vol. 2 (New York: Funk and Wagnells, 1891) 49.

[70]Gracey, *Medical Work*, 17.

[71]Justin Perkins, "A Sermon, Delivered to the Members of the Nestorian Mission, January 17, 1839, at the funeral of Mrs. Judith S. Grant, who died at Oroomiah, Persia, January 14, 189," in H. G. O. Dwight, *Memoir of Mrs. Elizabeth B. Dwight, Including an Account of the Plague of 1837, by Rev. H. G. O. Dwight, Missionary to Constantinople, With a Sketch of the Life of Mrs. Judith S. Grant, Missionary to Persia* (New York: M. W. Dodd, 1840) 295.

[72]Dwight, *Memoir of Mrs. Elizabeth B. Dwight*, 258.

[73] See John J. Paul, "Religion and Medicine in South India: The Scudder Medical Missionaries and the Christian Medical College and Hospital, Vellore," *Fides et Historia* 22 (Fall 1990): 16–29; Dorothy J. Scudder, *A Thousand Years in Thy Sight: The Story of the Scudder Missionaries of India* (New York: Vantage Press, 1984); George B. Stevens, *The Life, Letters, and Journals of the Rev. and Hon. Peter Parker, M.D., Missionary, Physician, and Diplomatist* (Boston: Congregational Sunday-School and Publishing Society, 1896); and Gulick.

[74]Perkins, "A Sermon," 301.

[75]Ibid., 316.

[76]Ibid., 300–302.

[77]Ibid., 314–15.

[78]Rufus Anderson, *History of the Missions of the American Board of Commissioners for Foreign Missions to the Oriental Churches*, vol. 1 (Boston: Congregational Publishing Society, 1873) 176–77.

[79]*Report of the Medical Missionary Society in China, Containing an Abstract of Its History and Prospects: And the Report of the Hospital at Macao, for 1841–42, Together with Dr. Parker's Statement of His Proceedings in England and the United States in Behalf of the Society* (Macao: Press of S. Wells Williams, 1843) 4–5.

[80]Gulick, *Peter Parker*, 55.

[81]Ibid., 55, 61.

[82]*Report of the Medical Missionary Society in China*, 5–8.

[83]John Lowe, *Medical Missions: Their Place and Power*, 3d ed. (New York: Fleming H. Revell Co., 1886) 201–202.

[84]*Report of the Medical Missionary Society in China*, 33–36.

[85]Hale, "An Appeal," 185–88.

[86]*GLB* 46 (June 1853): 551–54; *GLB* 80 (May 1870): 451–54.

[87]Gracey, Medical Work, 31–33.

[88]Mrs. Robert Hoskins, *Clara A. Swain, M.D.: First Medical Missionary to the Women of the Orient* (Boston: Publication Office of the WFMS, MEC, 1912) 3–31. See also Frances J. Baker, *First Women Physicians to the Orient* (Boston: Publication Office of the WFMS, MEC, [1904]); Alice Findlay, "A Worthy Woman Who Can Find?: Anna Kay Scott, M.D.," *American Baptist Quarterly* 12 (September 1993): 223–33; Kristin L. Gleeson, "The Stethoscope and the Gospel: Presbyterian Foreign Medical Missions, 1840–1900," *American Presbyterians* 71 (Spring 1993) 1:127–38; Sara W. Tucker, "Opportunities for Women: The Development of Professional Women's Medicine at Canton, China, 1879–1901," *Women's Studies International Forum* 13 (1990) 4:357–68.

[89]*GLB* 80 (May 1870): 453.

[90]*GLB* (December 1877): 523.

[91]Hale to S. B. Treat, 15 June 1852, ABC 10, v. 43, ABCFM.

[92]Anderson to David Abeel, June 1835, ABC 1.0 v. 14, Letters to domestic correspondents, 1835, ABCFM.

[93]Instructions to Peter Parker, ABC 8.1, Instructions to Missionaries, 93–94, ABCFM.

[94]Anderson to Mr. Ellis, Secretary of the London Missionary Society, 9 June 1838; LMS Letters from America, Council on World Missions Archives, School of Oriental and African Studies, University of London.

[95]See William R. Hutchison, *Errand to the World: American Protestant Thought and Foreign Missions* (Chicago: University of Chicago Press, 1987) and Wilbert R. Shenk, *Henry Venn: Missionary Statesman* (Maryknoll NY: Orbis Books, 1983).

[96]Henry Martyn Scudder, *A Great Field for Women* (Chicago: American Medical Missionary Society, 1885) 3–4.

[97]Lowe, *Medical Missions*, vi.

[98]Ibid., 178–83.

[99]Gracey, *Medical Work*, 13.

[100]Ibid., 24.

[101]Isabella Bird Bishop, "Woman and Medical Missions: The Importance of Medical Missions," in E. M. Wherry, comp., *Woman in Missions: Papers and Addresses Presented at the World's Congress of Missions, October 2–4, 1893, in the Hall of Columbus, Chicago* (New York: American Tract Society, 1894) 153–55.

[102]Gracey, *Woman's Medical Work*, 35–36.

[103]Bishop, "Woman and Medical Missions," 155.

[104]Ibid., 148–49; John Rutter Williamson, *The Healing of the Nations: A Treatise on Medical Missions, Statement and Appeal* (New York: Student Volunteer Movement for Foreign Missions, 1899) 17–18.

[105]Williamson, *The Healing of the Nations*, 30.

[106]Scudder, *A Great Field for Women*, 3.

[107]Gracey, *Medical Work* and "Woman's Medical Work in Missions," in Wherry, *Woman in Missions*, 156–74.

[108]Isabel Hart, *Historical Sketches of Woman's Missionary Societies in America and England* (Boston: Mrs. L. H. Daggett, 1879).

Chapter 7

[1]Beaver, *American Protestant Women in World Mission*, 110.

[2]William G. Lennox, *The Health and Turnover of Missionaries* (New York: Foreign Missions Conference of North America, 1933), cited in Beaver, *American Protestant Women in World Missions*, 111.

[3]Hutchison, *Errand to the World*, 1.

[4]See, for example, Gracey, *Medical Work*; Montgomery, *Western Women in Eastern Lands;* and Isabel Hart, *Historical Sketches.*

[5]Hill, Hunter, Robert. Grimshaw, Zwiep, and Brumberg do not discuss "woman's work for woman" as a missions ideology, although they do, of course, discuss women missionaries in the antebellum period. Hutchison and Phillips discuss the early missions movement with little reference to women.

[6]Journal entry, 27 July 1834, in G. R. Williamson, *Memoir of the Rev. David Abeel, D.D., Late Missionary to China* (New York: Robert Carter, 1848; reprint, Wilmington DE: Scholarly Resources, 1972) 140.

[7]"How the Woman's Union Missionary Society Came Into Existence," undated, unsigned typescript, WUMS Archives, Historical File, General, Box 45, Folder 1, Billy Graham Center Archives, Wheaton, Illinois.

[8]*In Memoriam: Being a Brief Sketch of the Life and Labours of the Late Mrs. Thomas C. Doremus, The Beloved and Lamented President of the Woman's Union Missionary Society* (Edinburgh: William Blackwood & Sons, 1877) 4.

[9]Ibid., 11.

[10]Ibid., 7.

[11]Ibid., 7; "How the Woman's Union Missionary Society Came Into Existence," [1].

[12]Rufus Anderson to David Abeel, nd, ABC 1.0 v. 14, Letters to domestic correspondents, 1835, ABCFM. Anderson did note in this same letter that, for "Ultra Ganges" missions (missions in China and southeast Asia), he believed that it was only practical to send single women to mission stations staffed by families with whom they were related or already on an intimate footing of friendship. It is not clear why he placed this particular stricture on this particular field of service, but he cited the experience of the London Missionary Society as communicated to him by its secretary.

[13]Rufus Anderson adhered to a "three self" theory of missions, meaning that the sending agency should encourage the indigenous church to become self-supporting, self-governing, and self-replicating as soon as possible. For a discussion of this philosophy, see Robert, 131–37.

[14]British women, at least, laid claim to having originated the practice.

[15]Mrs. C. B. Lewis of Calcutta, "A Plea for Zenanas," [London, 1866], 13, pamphlet, Historical File, Baptist Zenana Mission Records, Baptist Missionary Society Archives. Because the records of the Baptist Zenana Mission were not included in the microfilm of the Baptist Missionary Society Archives, the author consulted the originals in Oxford. Hereinafter cited BMSA.

[16]Samuel Francis Smith, *Missionary Sketches: A Concise History of the Work of the American Baptist Missionary Union* (Boston: W. G. Corthell, 1879) 79.

[17]"A Plea for Zenanas," 1.

[18]Ibid., 2.

[19]Ibid., 1–2.

[20]Ibid., 2–3.

[21]Ibid., 6.

[22]Sarah D. Doremus [daughter of Sarah Haines Platt Doremus], "What I know about the WUMS," WUMS Archives, Historical File, General, Box 45, Folder 1, Billy Graham Center Archives, Wheaton, Illinois.

[23]Ellen Huntly Bullard Mason, *Great Expectations Realized; or, Civilizing Mountain Men* (Philadelphia: American Baptist Publication Society, 1862) 18–19.

[24]*Minute of the Chief Commissioner of British Burmah, Dated Rangoon, 1st May 1863*, 1. WUMS Archives, Historical File, General, Box 45, Folder 1, Billy Graham Center Archives, Wheaton, Illinois.

[25]Minutes of the Executive Committee of the American Baptist Missionary Union, 20 March 1860, 2–3. American Baptist Historical Society, Valley Forge, Pennsylvania. Hereinafter cited ABMU.

[26]WUMS Archives, Box 1, Folder 1, Board Minute Book, 1861. Typescript note affixed to the flyleaf and signed S. J. Doremus, Corresponding Secretary (Sarah Doremus's daughter) says: "This book contains no records of the business meetings of the WUMS, held in the Fall of 1860, in which its organization was perfected, via; the preparation of the Constitution and Bylaws and the selection of officers." The original constitution and bylaws were rewritten many times in the next few years, and as early as January 1861, the women selected new (or additional) officers. See Board Minutes for 9 January 1861.

[27]Sarah J. Hale to Miss Doremus, 15 March 1861, Correspondence, Box 1, Folder 1, WUMS.

[28]Minutes, 9 January 1861, 15 June 1863, WUMS.

[29]Rosamond Anne Webb to Mrs. Wyckoff, 9 February 1861, Correspondence, Box 1, Folder 1, WUMS.

[30]For examples, see entries for 24 April 1835 and 15 April 1836 in Minutes, vol. 1, SPFEE, Archives of the Church Missionary Society, Heslop Room, Birmingham University Library, Birmingham, UK.

[31]Constitution and bylaws, appended to 1866 Annual Report with separate pagination, 4.

[32]Miscellaneous, Box 49, WUMS.

[33]*Annual Report*, 1869, 4, Box 29, WUMS.

[34]*Annual Report*, 1876, 48-49, Box 29, WUMS.

[35]Jared Scudder, "Address on the Degradation of Woman in India," WUMS *Annual Report*, 1876, 22, Box 29, WUMS.

[36]Scudder, "Address," 4.

[37]"What a Pair of Slippers Did for India," [4]. Nineteenth-century writers used the spelling *suttee*, but *sati* is the currently accepted form.

[38]Scudder, "Address," 25–26.

[39]*Annual Report*, 1868, 7, Box 29 WUMS.

[40]"What a Pair of Slippers Did for India," [3], n.d., Historical File, Pamphlets, Box 45, Folder 6, WUMS.

[41]"To the Christians of America," [1868], Historical File, Pamphlets, Box 45, Folder 6, WUMS.

[42] *Annual Report*, 1867, 8–9, Box 29, WUMS.

[43]"What a Pair of Slippers Did for India," [3].

[44]*Annual Report*, 1866, 7–8, Box 29, WUMS.

[45]"What a Pair of Slippers Did for India," [4].

[46]Minutes, 9 January 1861, WUMS.

[47]Ellen B. Mason to Mrs. Doremus, 16 July 1861, Correspondence, WUMS.

[48]Minutes, 28 October 1861, WUMS.

[49]Ellen B. Mason to Mrs. Doremus, 16 July 1861, Correspondence, WUMS.

[50]Minutes of the Executive Committee, 14 January 1862, ABMU.

[51]Minutes, 15 April 1861, WUMS.

[52]Sara Marston to Miss Doremus, Toungoo, 23 September, 1862, Correspondence, WUMS.

[53]Copy of a letter from Mrs. Ellen B. Mason to Major Lloyd, Deputy Commissioner of Tounghoo, Burma, November 1862, attached to a letter from Sara Marston to Mrs. Doremus, 24 November 1862, Correspondence, WUMS.

[54]Sara Marston to Mrs. Doremus, 4 October 1862, Correspondence, WUMS.

[55]*Minute by the Chief Commissioner of British Burmah, Dated Rangoon, 1st May 1862*, Historical File, WUMS.

[56]Samuel Francis Smith, *Missionary Sketches: A Concise History of the American Baptist Missionary Union* (Boston: W. G. Corthell, 1879) 84–88.

[57]Minutes of the Executive Committee, September 1862–December 1863, ABMU.

[58]Copy of a letter from Ellen B. Mason to the Boston Branch, 24–25 November 1862 and another of 20 December 1862, Correspondence, WUMS.

[59]Minutes of the Board of Managers, April 1863 and 20 March 1865, WUMS.

[60]Doremus, "What I Know about the WUMS."

[61]Ibid.

[62]Letter from the Executive Committee, ABMU, to Francis Mason, recorded in Minutes, 3 March 1863, ABMU.

[63]Sara Marston to Mrs. Doremus, 4 October 1862, Correspondence, WUMS.

[64]G. Winfred Hervey, *The Story of Baptist Missions in Foreign Lands, From the Time of Carey to the Present Date* (St. Louis: Chancy R. Barns, 1885) 401; Samuel Francis Smith, *Missionary Sketches*, 86–87.

[65]"Twelfth Annual Report of the Philadelphia Branch," Appendix to WUMS, *Annual Report*, 1872, I, Box 29, WUMS.

[66]To say that Congregational women organized along denominational lines is not entirely correct, since the women's board organized in 1868 affiliated with the ABCFM, in which some New School Presbyterians still cooperated. The Old School and New School branches of Presbyterianism reunited in 1869, however, and the last Presbyterians left the ABCFM to join the Board of Foreign Missions of the Presbyterian Church in the United States of America, which originated in the Western Foreign Missionary Society established in Pittsburgh in 1833. In the Old School/New School split of 1837, the New School remained with the ABCFM, while the Old School transformed the Western Foreign Missionary Society into their Board of Foreign Missions. Upon reunification, Presbyterian women formed no less than seven regional societies to support the work of foreign missions, the first two in 1870 in Chicago and Philadelphia. See Lois A. Boyd and R. Douglas Brackenridge, *Presbyterian Women in America: Two Centuries of a Quest for Status*, 2d ed. (Westport CT: Greenwood Press, 1996) 9. For untangling the various regional and theological splits and recombinations in American Presbyterianism, see Randall H. Balmer and John R. Fitzmier, *The Presbyterians* (Westport CT: Greenwood Press, 1993). For records of the formation of denominational women's mission boards, see Minutes of the Woman's Board of Missions, 2 January 1868, ABCFM; Appendix 61, "Memorial of the Woman's Foreign Missionary Society," in W. L. Harris and G. W. Woodruff, eds., *Journal of the General Conference of the Methodist Episcopal Church, Held in Brooklyn, N.Y., 1872* (New York: Nelson and Phillips, 1872) 731–38; Minutes of the Executive Committee, 14 March 1871, and Minutes of the Woman's Baptist Missionary Society, 3 April 1871, ABMU.

[67]Hill, Hunter, Robert.

[68]See Joan Jacobs Brumberg, "Zenanas and Girlless Villages: The Ethnology of American Evangelical Women, 1870–1910," *Journal of American History* 69 (1982) 2:347–71; Beaver, Hill, Hunter.

[69]"Guide to the Records of the Woman's Union Missionary Society," n.p., WUMS.

[70]Minutes of the Woman's Board of Missions, 2 January 1868, ABCFM.

[71]Constitution of the WFMS of the MEC, *Journal of the General Conference, 1872*, 734–37.

[72]American Baptist Missionary Union, *Annual Report*, 1874, in "American Baptist Missionary Union: Extracts from Printed Minutes of (1) the Union (2) the Board of Managers, with passages marked which refer to the question of the relation of the Women's Society to the Missionary Union. Prepared in 1909," ABMU.

[73]N. G. Clarke to Mrs. Homer Bartlett, 19 April 1867, recorded in the minutes of the Woman's Board of Missions, 2 January 1868; "Act of Incorporation, Commonwealth of Massachusetts, in the Year One Thousand Eight Hundred and Sixty-Nine," affixed inside cover of volume entitled Minutes of the Woman's Board of Missions, January 1868 to February 1869, ABCFM.

[74]Report of Special Committee in Appendix 61, "Memorial of the Woman's Foreign Missionary Society," *Journal of the General Conference*, 1872, 731–34.

[75]Report of Special Committee on Women's Missionary Societies, Records of the Executive Committee, ABMU, 24 September 1867 and 14 March 1871; "Report on the Missions in Burmah: Call for More Laborers," *Baptist Missionary Magazine* 49 (February 1869) 11:33–43.

[76]Records of the Woman's Missionary Society connected with the Baptist Church at Newton Centre, 7 March 1871, Board of International Ministries Archives.

[77]Mintues of the Woman's Baptist Missionary Society, 3 April 1871, ABMU.

[78]N. G. Clarke to Mrs. Homer Bartlett, et al., 1 January 1868, recorded in the minutes of the Woman's Board of Missions, 2 January 1868, ABCFM.

[79]Minutes, Woman's Board of Missions, 2 January 1868, ABCFM.

[80]Appendix 61, "Memorial of the Woman's Foreign Missionary Society," *Journal of the General Conference of the Methodist Episcopal Church*, 731–34.

[81]Minutes of the Executive Committee, 24 September 1867, ABMU.

[82]"Report on the Mission in Burmah: Call for More Laborers," *The Missionary Magazine* 49 (February 1869) 11:38–41.

[83]Minutes of the Executive Committee, 14 March 1871, ABMU.

[84]The standard work on both northern and southern women's involvement in the Civil War remains Mary Elizabeth Massey, *Bonnet Brigades* (New York: Knopf, 1966). Elizabeth D. Leonard, in *Yankee Women: Gender Battles in the Civil War* (New York: W. W. Norton, 1994), offers a more nuanced interpretation of the consequences of women's involvement in the war effort.

[85]Helen Barrett Montgomery, *Western Women in Eastern Lands: An Outline Study of Fifty Years of Woman's Work in Foreign Missions* (New York: Macmillan Co., 1910) 10.

[86]Beaver, *American Protestant Women in World Mission*, 88; Hunter, 12; Brumberg, "Zenanas and Girlless Villages," 350. All three of these authors quote the same passage from Helen Barrett Montgomery's *Western Women in Eastern Lands*.

[87]Report of a special committee on the application of women to organize a society, Minutes of the Executive Committee, 24 September 1867, ABMU.

[88]"To Christian Women in behalf of their sex in heathen lands," text of a circular letter recorded in Minutes, 6 March 1868, ABCFM.

[89]"To the Christian Women of America," WUMS, 1868, 2.

[90]Recall also that the women who founded the WUMS did so in imitation of the British SPFEE, established in 1834. Another problem with locating the primary catalyst for women's denominational societies in the experiences of the Civil War is that the same process occurred in Great Britain at the same time. British Baptist women, for example, founded the Baptist Zenana Mission in 1867 and also cited the example of the WUMS. See Lisa J. Pruitt, "Possessed of a Missionary Spirit?: British Baptist Women and Bengali Missions in the Nineteenth Century," *American Baptist Quarterly* XVII (December 1998) 4:285–304.

[91]William McGuire King, "Denominational Modernization and Religious Identity: The Case of the Methodist Episcopal Church," *Methodist History* 20 (1982) 2:75–89.

[92]Hill (*The World Their Household*) discusses the professionalization of missions at length. See also Lori Ginzberg *Women and the Work of Benevolence: Morality, Politics and Class in the Nineteenth-Century United States* (New Haven CT: Yale University Press, 1990).

[93]Bliss, "*Woman's Work for Woman,*" 479.

Conclusion

[1]Appendix 61, "Memorial of the Woman's Foreign Missionary Society," 732. See Wade Crawford Barclay, *History of Methodist Missions, Part Two: The Methodist Episcopal Church, 1845-1939: Widening Horizens, 1845-95* (NY: Board of Missions of the Methodist Church, 1957), 139-148.

[2]Edmund Munsell Bliss, "Woman's Work for Woman," in Bliss, ed., *Encyclopedia of Missions* Volume II (New York: Funk and Wagnells, 1891) 479.

[3]Joan Jacobs Brumberg, "Zenanas and Girlless Villages: The Ethnology of American Evangelical Women, 1870-1910," *The Journal of American History* 69 (September 1982): 350-351.

[4]Nancy A. Hardesty, "The Scientific Study of Missions: Textbooks of the Central Committee on the United Study of Foreign Missions," in Daniel H. Bays and Grant Wacker, editors, *The Foreign Missionary Enterprise at Home: Explorations in North American Cultural History* (Tuscaloosa, AL: University of Alabama Press, 2003), 109.

[5]One of the first serious works of historical scholarship about women and mission was R. Pierce Beaver's *American Protestant Women and World Mission: A History of the First Feminist Movement in North America* (Grand Rapids MI: Eerdmans, rev. ed., 1980).

[6]Helen Barrett Montgomery, *Western Women in Eastern Lands: An Outline Study of Fifty Years of Woman's Work in Foreign Missions* (New York: Macmillan Co., 1910) 45.

[7]Ibid.,, 46-47.

[8]Ibid., 48.

[9]Ibid., 52.

[10]Ibid., 53.
[11]Ibid., 54-55.
[12]Ibid., 57.
[13]Ibid., 108-109.
[14]Ibid., 57.
[15]Ibid., 61-62.
[16]Ibid., 62.
[17]Ibid., 117-124.
[18]Ibid., 64.
[19]Ibid., 105-106.
[20]Brumberg, "Zenanas and Girlless Villages," 352.
[21]Ibid., 349.
[22]Ibid., 356-367. Brumberg does not attach any significance to the fact that almost all of the practices she describes in the article were, in the mission literature, specific to the "Orient."
[23]Ibid., 355, 371.
[24]"Address Delivered at the Opening of the Woman's Building, May 1, 1892 [i.e., 1893]," Board of Lady Managers, volume 26, World's Columbian Exposition Collection, Chicago Historical Society.
[25] For accounts of the Chicago exposition see Reid Badger, *The Great American Fair: The World's Columbian Exposition and American Culture* (Chicago: Nelson Hall, 1979) and David F. Burg, *Chicago's White City of 1893* (Louisville, KY: University Press of Kentucky, 1976).
[26] Box 4, Folder 15, World's Columbia Exposition/World's Congress Auxiliary Collection, Harold Washington Library Center, Division of Special Collections, Chicago, Illinois.
[27]*Midway Types: A Book of Illustrated Lessons About the people of the Midway Plaisance, World's Fair, 1893* (Chicago: American Engraving Company, 1894), np. Note the elasticity of the concept of the "Orient" in including both Egypt and Algeria, "Oriental" because they were Muslim.
[28]Cindy Starr, "More Chinese Girls find 'forever homes' in US," *Washington Times* June 22, 1999, E4 [http://www.theadoptionguide.com/complaints/chinalove.html], accessed 9/28/03.
[29]Jayati Ghosh and C. P. Chandrasekhar, "Women in India: A Status Report," *The Hindu Business Line Online Edition*, September 3, 2002, www.thehindubusinessline.com/bline/2002/09/03/stories/
2002090300080900.htm, accessed 9/28/03. Statistics cited are for 2001.
[30]"USAID India: Women's Status," www.usaid.gov/in/programareas/women.htm, accessed 9/28/03.
[31]Nikki Katz, "Women Under the Taliban," http://womenissues.about.com/library/weekly /aa102601a.htm, accessed 9/29/03.
[32]Pamela Constable for the *Washington Post*, "Backlash shutters schools in Afghanistan: Taliban feared in attacks on girls' education," *The Tennessean* (Nashville), Monday, September 15, 2003, 4B.

[33]Carlotta Gall for the *New York Times News Service*, "Advocates, victims gather to draft Afghan women's rights bill," *The Tennessean* (Nashville), Sunday, September 28, 2003, 4A.

[34]Dayna Curry and Heather Mercer, *Prisoners of Hope: The Story of Our Captivity and Freedom in Afghanistan* (NY: Doubleday, 2002).

Bibliography

REPOSITORIES OF UNPUBLISHED PRIMARY SOURCES

Archives of the American Baptist Missionary Union (ABMU), Board of International Ministries, American Baptist Convention, Valley Forge, Pennsylvania

Archives of the American Board of Commissioners for Foreign Missions (ABCFM), Houghton Library, Harvard University, Cambridge, Massachusetts

Archives of the United Methodist Church, Drew University, Madison, New Jersey

Archives of the Woman's Union Missionary Society (WUMS), Collection 379, Billy Graham Center Archives, Wheaton College, Wheaton, Illinois

Baptist Missionary Society Archives (United Kingdom) Microfilm (BMSA-m). Nashville, TN: Historical Commission, Southern Baptist Convention, 1991.

Baptist Zenana Mission Records, Baptist Missionary Society Archives, Regents Park College, Oxford University, Oxford, United Kingdom [not included in Baptist Missionary Society Archives microfilm]

Fidelia Fiske Papers, Mount Holyoke College Archives, South Hadley, Massachusetts

London Missionary Society Archives, School of Oriental and African Studies, University of London

Lucy T. Lord Papers, Mount Holyoke College Archives, South Hadley, Massachusetts

Society for Promoting Female Education in the East, Archives of the Church Missionary Society, Heslop Room, Birmingham University Library, Birmingham, UK

World's Columbian Exposition Collection, Chicago Historical Society, Chicago, Illinois

World's Columbian Exposition Collection, Special Collections Division, Harold Washington Library Center, Chicago, Illinois

PUBLISHED PRIMARY SOURCES—MAGAZINES

American Baptist Magazine, 1817-1829
Connecticut Evangelical Magazine, 1800-1813
Godey's Lady's Book, 1851-1877
The Heathen Woman's Friend, 1870-1874
Massachusetts Baptist Missionary Magazine, 1803-1816
Massachusetts Missionary Magazine, 1804-1812
Missionary Herald, 1842-1850 [continues *Panoplist*]
Mothers Magazine, 1833-1844
New York Missionary Magazine, 1800
Panoplist, 1808-1841 [various subtitles; continued by *Missionary Herald*]]

PUBLISHED PRIMARY SOURCES– MISSIONARY MEMOIRS

Benjamin, Mary Gladding. *The Missionary Sisters: A Memorial of Mrs. Seraphina Haynes Everett and Mrs. Harriet Martha Hamlin, Late Missionaries of the ABCFM at Constantinople.* Boston: American Tract Society, 1860.

Campbell, William W. A *Memoir of Mrs. Judith S. Grant, Late Missionary to Persia.* New York: J. Winchester, 1844.

Carey, Eustace. *Memoir of William Carey, D. D.* Boston: Gould, Kendall, and Lincoln, 1836.

Dean, William. *Memoir of Mrs. Lucy T. Lord of the Chinese Baptist Mission.* Phildadelphia: American Baptist Publication Society, 1854.

Dwight, Rev. H. G. O. *Memoir of Mrs. Elizabeth B. Dwight, Including an Account of the Plague of 1837, by Rev. H.G.O. Dwight, Missionary to Constantinople, With a Sketch of the Life of Mrs. Judith S. Grant, Missionary to Persia.* New York: M. W. Dodd, 1840.

Edwards, Jonathan. *The Life of David Brainerd, Chiefly Extracted from His Diary.* New York: American Tract Society, nd. (Orig. pub. 1747)

Ellis, William. *Memoir of Mrs. Mary Ellis, Wife of Rev. William Ellis, Missionary in the South Seas and Foreign Secretary of the London Missionary Society.* Boston: Crocker& Brewster, 1836.

Fiske, Daniel Taggert. *Faith Working by Love, as Exemplified in the Life of Fidelia Fiske*. Boston: Congregational Publishing Society, 1868.

[Hawes, Louisa]. *Memoir of Mrs. Mary E. Van Lennep, Only Daughter of the Rev. Joel Hawes, D. D., and Wife of the Rev. Henry J Van Lennep, Missionary in Turkey*, 2d ed. Hartford, Conn.: Belknap and Hamersley, 1848.

Hooker, Edward W. *Memoir of Mrs. Sarah L. Huntington Smith, Late of the American Mission in Syria*, 3d ed. New York: American Tract Society, 1845.

Hoskins, Mrs. Robert. *Clara A. Swain, M.D.: First Medical Missionary to the Women of the Orient.* Boston: Publication Office of the Woman's Foreign Missionary Society, Methodist Episcopal Church, 1912.

Jeter, J. B. *Memoir of Mrs. Henrietta Shuck, the First American Female Missionary to China.* Boston: Gould, Kendall, and Lincoln, 1846.

Judson, Ann H. *An Account of the American Baptist Mission to the Burman Empire in a Series of Letters Addressed to a Gentleman in London,* 2d ed. London: Joseph Butterworth and Son, 1827.

Judson, Emily Chubbuck. *Memoir of Sarah B. Judson, Member of the American Mission to Burmah.* New York: L. Colby and Company, 1848.

Kendrick, A. C. *The Life and Letters of Mrs. Emily C. Judson.* New York: Sheldon & Co., 1860.

Knill, Richard. *The Missionary's Wife, or, A Brief Account of Mrs. Loveless, of Madras, the First American Missionary to Foreign Lands.* Philadelphia: Presbyterian Board of Publications, 1839.

Knowles, James D. *Memoir of Ann H. Judson, Missionary to Burmah.* Philadelphia: American Baptist Publication Society, 1835.

Lawrence, Margarette Oliver Woods. *Light on the Dark River; or, Memorial to Mrs. Henrietta A. L. Hamlin, Missionary to Turkey.* Boston: Ticknor, Reed & Fields, 1854.

Mason, Ellen Huntley Bullard. *Great Expectations Realized, or, Civilizing Mountain Men.* Philadelphia: American Baptist Publication Society, 1862.

Memoirs of the Life of Mrs. Harriet Newell Wife of the Rev. Samuel Newell, Missionary to India, Who Died at the Isle of France, November 30, 1812. New York: American Tract Society, nd.

The Persian Flower: A Memoir of Judith Grant Perkins, of Oroomiah, Persia. Boston: American Tract Society, 1853.

Shuck, Henrietta. *Scenes in China: Or, Sketches of the Country, Religion, and Customs of the Chinese*. Philadelphia: American Baptist Publication Society, 1852.

Stevens, George B. *The Life, Letters, and Journals of the Rev. and Hon. Peter Parker, M.D., Missionary, Physician, and Diplomatist.* Boston: Congregational Sunday School and Publishing Society, 1896.

Williamson, G. R. *Memoir of the Rev. David Abeel, D. D., Late Missionary to China.* New York: Robert Carter, 1848. Reprint, Wilmington, Del.: Scholarly Resources, 1972.

Winslow, Miron. *Memoir of Mrs. Harriet L. Winslow, Thirteen Years a Member of the American Mission in Ceylon.* New York: American Tract Society, [1840].

Woods, Leonard. *Memoir of the Life of Harriet Newell, Wife of the Rev. Samuel Newell, Missionary to India, Who Died at the Isle of France, November 30, 1812, Aged 19 Years. Extracted from the Third Boston Edition To Which is Annexed a Sermon, Delivered in Boston, September 16, 1813, before the American Board of Commissioners for Foreign Missions, at Their Fourth Annual Meeting, by Timothy Dwight, D.D., L.L.D., President of Yale College* (Lexington, KY: Skillman, 1815).

Wyeth, Walter. *The Wades: A Memorial.* Philadelphia: By the Author, 1891.

OTHER PUBLISHED PRIMARY SOURCES

Anderson, Rufus. *History of the Missions of the American Board of Commissioners for Foreign Missions: India.* Boston: Congregational Publishing Society, 1875.

_______. *History of the Missions of the American Board of Commissioners for Foreign Missions to the Oriental Churches.* 2 vols. Boston: Congregational Publishing Society, 1873, 1874.

_______. "Introductory Essay on the Marriage of Missionaries. " In William Ellis, *Memoir of Mrs. Mary Ellis, Wife of Rev. William Ellis, Missionary in the South Seas and Foreign Secretary of the London Missionary Society.* Boston: Crocker& Brewster, 1836.

_______. *Memorial Volume of the First Fifty Years of the American Board of Commissioners for Foreign Missions.* Boston: The Board, 1861.

Austin, David. *The Millennium; or, The Thousand Years of Prosperity, Promised to the Church of God, in the Old Testament and the New, Shortly to Commence, and to be Carried on to Perfection, Under the Auspices of Him, Who, In the VISION, Was Presented to ST. JOHN.* Elizabeth Town, N. J.: Shepard Kollock, 1794.

Baker, Frances J. *First Women Physicians to the Orient.* Boston: Woman's Foreign Missionary Society, Methodist Episcopal Church, [1904].

Bancroft, Jane M. *Deaconesses in Europe and Their Lessons for America. With an Introduction by Edward G. Andrews, D. D., LL. D., Bishop of the Methodist Episcopal Church.* New York: Hunt and Eaton, 1889.

Barrows, Elizabeth. *A Memorial of Bradford Academy.* Boston: Congregational Sunday School and Publishing Society, 1870.

Beecher, Catharine. *Suggestions Respecting Improvements in Education, Presented to the Trustees of the Hartford Female Seminary, And Published at Their Request.* Hartford, Conn.: Packard and Butler, 1829.

Bishop, Isabella Bird. "Woman and Medical Missions: The Importance of Medical Missions. " In E. M. Wherry, comp. *Woman in Missions: Papers and Addresses Presented at The World's Congress of Missions, October 2-4, 1893, in the Hall of Columbus, Chicago.* New York: American Tract Society, 1894.

[Blake, Carrie Richardson]. *The Boston Pioneers of the Woman's Union Missionary Society, Nov. 16, 1860 -Nov. 16, 1910: A Memorial.* Boston: Conant & Newhall, 1910.

Bliss, Edwin Munsell, ed. *The Encyclopaedia of Missions.* 2 vols. New York: Funk and Wagnells, 1891.

A Brief Account of the Origin and Progress of the Boston Female Society for Missionary Purposes with Extracts from the Reports of the Society in May, 1817 and 1818." Boston: Lincoln and Edmands, [1818].

Brockett, L. P. *The Story of the Karen Mission in Bassein, 1838-1890.* Philadelphia: American Baptist Publication Society, 1891.

Buchanan, Claudius. *Christian Researches in Asia... To which is added, The Star in the East, a*

Sermon Preached in the Parish Church of St. James, Bristol, on Sunday, February 26, 1809, with an Appendix, Containing an Account of 200,000 Christians discovered in the sequestered region of Hindostan. Lexington, Ky.: Thomas T. Skillman, 1813.

-----------. *The Works of the Rev. Claudius Buchanan, LL.D., Comprising His Christian Researches in Asia... , His Memoir on the Expediency of an Ecclesiastical Establishment for British India, and His Star in the East.* New York: Whiting and Watson, 1812.

Carey, William. *An Enquiry into the Obligations of Christians, To Use Means for the Conversion of the Heathens. In Which the Religious State of the Different Nations of the World, the Success of Former Undertakings, and the Practicability of Further Undertakings, are Considered.* Leicester: Ann Ireland, 1792.

Disselhoff, Julius. *Kaiserswerth: The Deaconess Institution of Rhenish-Westphalia, Its Origin and Fields of Labour.* London: Hatchards, Piccadilly, 1883.

Dwight, Timothy. *Sermon, delivered in Boston, September* 16, 1813, *before the American Boardof Commissioners for Foreign Missions, at their Fourth AnnualMeeting.* Boston: Samuel T. Armstrong, 1813.

Edwards, Jonathan. *An Humble Attempt to Promote Explicit Agreement and Visible Union of*

God's People in Extraordinary Prayer for the Revival of Religion and the Advancement of Christ's Kingdom on Earth, Pursuant to Scripture-Promises and Prophecies concerning the Last Time. Boston: D. Henchman, 1747. In Stephen J. Stein, ed., *The Works of Jonathan Edwards, Vol 5: Apocalyptical Writings.* New Haven: Yale University Press, 1977.

Emmons, Nathanael. *A Sermon delivered before the Massachusetts Missionary Society at Their Annual Meeting in Boston, May 27, 1800.* Charlestown, Mass.: Samuel Etheridge, 1800.

Gammell,William. *A History of American Baptist Missions in Asia, Africa, Europe, and North America, Under the Care of the American Baptist Missionary Union.* Boston: Gould and Lincoln, 1851.

Gracey, Annie Ryder. *Medical Work of the Woman's Foreign Missionary Society, Methodist Episcopal Church.* Boston: Woman's Foreign Missionary Society, Methodist Episcopal Church, 1888.

______. "Women's Medical Work in Missions. " In Rev. E. M. Wherry, compiler, *Women in Missions: Papers and Addresses Presented at the World's Congress of Missions, October 2–4, 1893, in the Hall of Columbus, Chicago.* New York: American Tract Society, 1894.

Hale, Sarah Josepha. "Fifty Years of My Literary Life." *Godey's Lady's Book* (December 1877): 523.

______. "An Appeal to American Christians on Behalf of the Ladies' Medical Missionary Society." *Godey's Lady's Book* 44 (March 1852): 185.

Hall, Gordon and Samuel Newell. *The Conversion of the World, or, the Claims of Six Hundred Millions and the Ability and Duty of the Churches Respecting Them.* Andover, Mass.: Flagg & Gould, 1818.

Hampshire Missionary Society. *A Plan for a Female Association in the County of Hampshire.* Northampton, Mass.: np, 1803.

Harris, W. L. and G. W. Woodruff, eds. *Journal of the General Conference of the Methodist Episcopal Church, Held in Brooklyn, N. Y, 18 72.* New York: Nelson and Phillips, 1872.

Hart, Isabel. *Historical Sketches of Woman's Missionary Societies in America and England.* Boston: Mrs. L. H. Daggett, 1879.

Hawes Joel. *"A Looking-Glass for Ladies," or the Formation and Excellence of the Female Character: An Address Delivered at Hartford on Sunday Evening, August 24, 1845, and published at the Request of the American Institute for Education.* Boston: William D. Ticknor and Co., 1845.

Hervey, G. Winfred. *The Story of Baptist Missions in Foreign Lands, From the Time of Carey to the Present Date.* St. Louis: Chancy R. Barns, 1885.

Horne, Melville. *Letters on Missions, Addressed to the Protestant Ministers of the British Churches.* Andover: Flagg & Gould, 1815.

In Memoriam: Being a Brief Sketch of the Life and Labours of the Late Mrs. Thomas C. Doremus, The Beloved and Lamented President of the Woman's Union Missionary Society. Edinburgh: William Blackwood & Sons, 1877.

Judson, Adoniram. *Letter to the Female Members of the Christian Churches, in the United States of America.* Providence, RI: N. H. Brown, 1832.

Kirby, Jane Welsh. A *View of the Heathen World: And of Light Dispelling the Darkness, with Questions, Adapting it to Sabbath Schools and Juvenile Associations.* Worcester, Mass.: Dorr, Howland and Co., 1834.

Lathrop, Joseph. *A Sermon Delivered to a Charitable Female Association in West - Springfield, May 15, 1810.* Springfield, Mass.: Thomas Dickman, 1810.

Lennox, William G. *The Health and Turnover of Missionaries.* New York: Foreign Missions Conference of North America, 1933.

Lewis, Mrs. C. B. [Marianne]. "A Plea for Zenanas, " n.p. [1866].

Library of Congress. *The National Union Catalog, pre-1956 Imprints: A Cumulative List Representing Library of Congress Printed Cards and Titles Reported by Other American Libraries.* London: Mansell, 1968-1981.

Lowe, John. *Medical Missions: Their Place and Power.* 3d ed., New York: Fleming H. Revell Co., 1886.

[Lyon, Mary]. *General View of the Principles and Design of the Mt. Holyoke Female Seminary.* Np: [February 1837].

_______. *Female Education: Tendencies of the Principles Embraced and the System Adopted in the Mount Holyoke Female Seminary.* N.p: n.d.

Malcom, Howard. *Travels in South-Eastern Asia, Embracing Hindustan, Malaya, Siam, and China; with Notices of Numerous Missionary Stations, and a Full Account of the Burman Empire; with Dissertations, Tables, etc.* 2d ed., 2 vols. in one. Boston: Gould, Kendall, and Lincoln, 1839.

Malte-Brun, Conrad. *Universal Geography, or, a Description of All the Parts of the World, on a New Plan, According to the Great Natural Divisions of the Globe: Accompanied with Analytical, Synoptical, and Elementary Tables. Volume II. - Containing the Description of Asia, with the Exception of India.* Boston: Wells and Lilly, 1826.

----------. *Universal Geography, or, a Description of All the Parts of the World, on a New Plan, According to theGreat Natural Divisions of the Globe: Accompanied with Analytical, Synoptical and Elementary Tables. Volume III: Containing the Description of India and Oceanica.* Boston: Wells and Lilly, 1826.

Marshman, John Clark. *The Story of Carey, Marshman, and Ward, the Serampore Missionaries.* London: Heaton and Sons, 1864.

Mason, John M. *Hope for the Heathen: A Sermon, Preached in the Old Presbyterian Church, Before the New-York Missionary Society at Their Annual Meeting, November 7, 1797.* New York: T & J Swords, 1797.

"Medical Missions." In Edwin Munsell Bliss, ed. *The Encyclopaedia of Missions.* Vol II. New York: Funk and Wagnells, 1891.

Midway Types: A Book of Illustrated Lessons About the People of the Midway Plaisance, World's Fair, 1893. Chicago: American Engraving Company, 1894.

The Missionary Jubilee: An Account of the Fiftieth Anniversary of the America Baptist Missionary Union, at Philadelphia, May 24, 25, and 26, 1864, with Commemorative Papers and Discourses. Rev. ed. New York: Sheldon and Co., 1871.

Montgomery, Helen Barrett. *Western Women in Eastern Lands: An Outline Study of Fifty Years of Woman's Work in Foreign Missions.* New York: Macmillan Co.,1910.

More, Hannah. *Strictures on the Modern System of Female Education: With a View of the Principles and Conduct Prevalent Among Women of Rank and Fortune.* Vol. I. 9th ed. London: Printed by A. Strahan for T. Cadell, Jun. and W. Davies, 1801.

Perkins, Justin. "A Sermon, Delivered to the Members of the Nestorian Mission, January 17, 1839, at the Funeral of Mrs. Judith S. Grant, Who Died at Oroomiah, Persia, January 14, 1839." In H. G. O. Dwight, *Memoir of Mrs.Elizabeth B. Dwight, Including an Account of the Plague of 1837, by Rev. H. G. O. Dwight, Missionary to Constantinople, with a Sketch of the Life of Mrs. Judith S. Grant, Missionary to Persia.* New York: M. W. Dodd, 1840.

Puffer, Reuben. *The Widow's Mite: A Sermon delivered at Boylston, before the Boylston Female Society for the Aid of Foreign Missions, January 8, 1816.* Worcester, MA: William Manning, 1816.

Report of the Medical Missionary Society in China, Containing an Abstract of Its History and Prospects: And the Report of the Hospital at Macao, for 1841-42, Together With Dr. Parker's Statement of His Proceedings in England and the United States in Behalf of the Society. Macao: Press of S. Wells Williams, 1843.

Rush, Benjamin. *Thoughts Upon Female Education, Accommodated to the Present State of Society, Manners, and Government in the United States of America. Addressed to the Visitors of the Young Ladies' Academy in Philadelphia, 28 July 1787, At the Close of the Quarterly Examination.* Philadelphia: Prichard and Hall, 1787.

Sanders, Elizabeth Elkins. *Second Part of a Tract on Missions.* Salem, Mass.: Printed for the Author, 1845

_______.*Tract on Missions.* Salem, Mass.: Printed for the Author, 1846.

Scudder, Henry Martyn. *A Great Field for Women.* Chicago: American Medical Missionary Association, nd.

Scudder, John. *An Appeal to Christian Mothers in Behalf of the Heathen.* New York: American Tract Society, 1840.

_______. *Letters from the East.* Boston: Perkins & Marvin, 1833.

_______. *Letters to Sabbath-School Children: on the Condition of the Heathen.* Philadelphia: American Sunday School Union, 1843.

_______. *The Redeemer's Last Command.* New York: American Tract Society, nd.

_______. *A Voice From the East to the Young, in a Series of Letters to Children of the Reformed Protestant Dutch Church of North America.* New York: Board of Publications of the Reformed Protestant Dutch Church, 1859.

Smith, Ethan. *Daughters of Zion Excelling: A Sermon Preached to the Ladies of the Cent Institution in Hopkinton, New-Hampshire, August 18, 1814.* Concord, NH: George Hough, 1814.

Smith, Samuel Francis. *Missionary Sketches: A Concise History of the Work of the American Baptist Missionary Union.* Boston: W. G. Corthell, 1879.

Smith, Thomas and John O.Choules. *The Origin and History of Missions: Containing Faithful Accounts of the Voyages, Travels, Labors and Successes of the Various Missionaries Who Have been Sent Forth to Evangelize the Heathen; compiled from Authentic Documents; Forming a Complete Missionary Repository... in Two Volumes.* Vol. 1. Boston: Walker, Lincoln, and Edmands, 1832.

Staughton, William. *An Address, Delivered October 1807, at Mrs. Rivardi's Seminary, on the Occasion of the Examination of the First and Middle Class.* Philadelphia: Kimber, Conrad & Co., 1807.

_______. *The Baptist Mission in India: Containing a Narrative of Its Rise, Progress, and Present Condition, A Statement of the Physical and Moral Character of the*

Hindoos, Their Cruelties, Tortures and Burnings, with a Very Interesting Description of Bengal, Intended to Animate to Missionary Co-operation. Philadelphia: Stiles, for Hollings & Aitken, 1811.

Stow, Baron. *A History of the English Baptist Missions to India.* Philadelphia: American Sunday-School Union, 1835.

Tuttle, Sarah. *Conversations on the Burman Mission, by a Lady of New Hampshire.* Boston: Massachusetts Sabbath School Union, 1830.

_______. *Prospective Missions in China.* Boston: Massachusetts Sabbath School Society, 1833.

Ward, William. *A View of the Idolatry of the Hindoos, Their History, Religion, Manners and Customs, &c., Abridged from his original work in 3 vols 8vo.* Part II in Ward, *All Religions and Religious Ceremonies, in Two Parts.* Hartford, Conn.: Oliver D. Cook & Sons, 1823.

Webb, Mary. "An Address from 'the Boston Female Society for Missionary Purposes,' to Females professing godliness," Boston, 7 December 1812. *Massachusetts Baptist Missionary Magazine* 3/9 (March 1813): 282.

_______. "Address of the Female Society, in Boston, to the Female Friends of Zion." Boston, 3 February 1812. *Massachusetts Baptist Missionary Magazine* 3/5 (March 1812): 156-57.

_______. "Grateful Acknowledgment from the Boston Female Society for Missionary Purposes." *Massachusetts Baptist Missionary Magazine* 4/6 (June 1815): 174-76.

Wheeler, Henry. *Deaconesses Ancient and Modern.* New York: Hunt and Eaton, 1889.

Willard, Emma. *An Address to the Public, Particularly to the Members of the Legislature of New York, Proposing a Plan for Improving Female Education.* 2d ed. Middlebury: J. W. Copeland, 1819.

Williamson, John Rutter. *The Healing of the Nations: A Treatise on Medical Missions, Statement and Appeal.* New York: Student Volunteer Movement for Foreign Missions, 1899.

Woman's Missionary Association of the Baptist Missionary Society. *Jubilee, 18671917: Fifty Years' Work Among Women in the Far East.* London: The Carey Press, 1917.

"Woman's Work for Woman." In Edwin Munsell Bliss, *Encyclopedia of Missions.* Vol. II, 479-523. New York: Funk and Wagnells, 1891.

Woods, Leonard. *A Sermon Delivered at the Tabernacle in Salem, Feb. 6, 1812, on Occasion of the Ordination of the Rev. Messrs. Samuel Newell, A. M; Adoniram Judson, A. M.; Samuel Nott, A. M; Gordon Hall, A. M; and Luther Rice, A. B.; Missionaries to the Heathen in Asia.* Boston: Samuel T. Armstrong, 1812. In R. Pierce Beaver, ed. *Pioneers in Mission: The Early Missionary Ordination Sermons, Charges, and Instructions: A Source Book on the Rise of American Missions to the Heathen.* Grand Rapids: Eerdmans, 1966.

Yonge, Charlotte M. *Pioneers and Founders.* New York: Macmillan, 1871.

SECONDARY SOURCES

Andrew, John A., III. *Rebuilding the Christian Commonwealth: New England Congregationalists and Foreign Missions.* Lexington, KY: University Press of Kentucky, 1976.

Atiya, Aziz S. *A History of Eastern Christianity*. South Bend IN: University of Notre Dame Press, 1968.

Badger, Reid. *The Great American Fair: The World's Columbian Exposition and American Culture*. Chicago: Nelson Hall, 1979.

Bagal, Jogesh Chandra. *Women's Education in Eastern India: The First Phase.* Calcutta: The World Press, 1956.

Balmer, Randall H. and John R, Fitzmier. *The Presbyterians.* Westport, Conn.: Greenwood Press, 1993.

Banner, Lois W. "Religion and Reform in the Early Republic: The Role of Youth." *American Quarterly* 23 (1971) 5: 677-695.

Barclay, Wade Crawford. *History of Methodist Missions, Part Two:The Methodist Episcopal Church, 1845-1939: Widening Horizons, 1845-1895.* New York: Board of Missions of the Methodist Church, 1957.

Bays, Daniel H. and Grant Wacker, editors. *The Foreign Missionary Enterprise at Home: Explorations in North American Cultural History*. Tuscaloosa AL: University of Alabama Press, 2003.

Beaver, R. Pierce. *American Protestant Women in World Mission: A History of the First Feminist Movement in North America.* Grand Rapids, MI: Eerdmans, rev. ed., 1980.

______. "The Concert of Prayer for Missions: An Early Venture in Ecumenical Action." *Ecumenical Review* X (July 1958) 4: 420-427.

______. "Missionary Motivation Through Three Centuries. " In *Reinterpretation in American Church History.* Jerald C. Brauer, ed. Chicago: University of Chicago Press, 1968.

______. *Pioneers in Mission: The Early Missionary Ordination Sermons, Charges, and Instructions: A Source Book on the Rise of American Missions to the Heathen.* Grand Rapids, MI: Eerdmans, 1966.

Beck, James R. *Dorothy Carey: The Tragic and Untold Story of Mrs. William Carey.* Grand Rapids, Mich.: Baker Book House, 1992.

Bishop, Peter and Michael Darton, eds. *Encyclopedia of World Faiths*. London: Macdonald Orbis, 1987.

Blake, C. Fred. "Foot-binding in Neo-Confucian China and the Appropriation of Female Labor." *Signs: Journal of Women in Culture and Society* 19 (1994) 3: 676-712.

Bloch, Ruth H. "Ideals in Transition: The Rise of the Moral Mother, 1785-1815," *Feminist Studies* 4 (June 1978) 2: 100-126.

______. *Visionary Republic: Millennial Themes in American Thought, 1756-1800*. Cambridge: Cambridge University Press, 1985.

Bowie, Fiona, Deborah Kirkwood and Shirley Ardener, eds. *Women and Missions, Past and Present: Anthropological and Historical Perceptions*. Providence, RI: Berg, 1993.

Boyd, Lois A. and R. Douglas Brackenridge. *Presbyterian Women in America: Two Centuries of a Quest for Status*. 2d ed. Westport, Conn.: Greenwood Press, 1996.

Boyer, Paul. "Sarah Josepha Hale. " In *Notable American Women, 1607-1950*, Edward T. James, editor. Cambridge, MA: Belknap Press of Harvard University Press, 1971.

Boylan, Anne M. *The Origins of Women's Activism: New York and Boston, 1797-1840*. Chapel Hill: University of North Carolina Press, 2002.

______. *Sunday School: The Formation of an American Institution, 1790–1880*. New Haven: Yale University Press, 1988.

________. "Women in Groups: An Analysis of Women's Benevolent Organizations in New York and Boston, 1797-1840. " *Journal of American History* 71 (Dec 1984) 3: 497-523.

Brackney, William H. "The General Missionary Convention of the Baptist Denomination, 1814-1845: An American Metaphor." *Baptist History and Heritage* 24 (1989) 3: 13-23.

Breitenbach, William Kern. "The Consistent Calvinism of the New Divinity Movement." *William and Mary Quarterly* 41 (1984) 2: 241-264.

______. "New Divinity Theology and the Idea of Moral Accountability." Ph.D. dissertation, Yale University, 1978.

Brown, Irene Quenzler. "Death, Friendship, and Female Identity During New England's Second Great Awakening." *Journal of Family History* 12 (4): 367-387.

Brown, Kathleen M. "Brave New Worlds: Women's and Gender History." *William and Mary Quarterly*, 3d series, L (April 1993) 2: 311-328.

Brumberg, Joan Jacobs. "The Ethnological Mirror: American Evangelical Women and Their Heathen Sisters, 1870-19 10. " In Barbara J. Harris and JoAnn K. McNamara, eds. *Women and the Structure of Society*. Durham, NC: Duke University Press, 1984, 108-128.

_______. *Mission for Life: The Judson Family and American Evangelical Culture*. New York: New York University Press, 1984.

. "Zenanas and Girlless Villages: The Ethnology of American Evangelical Women, 1870-1910." *Journal of American History* 69 (1982) 2: 347-371.

Burg, David F. *Chicago's White City of 1893*. Louisville KY: University Press of Kentucky, 1976.

Buss, Dietrich. "The Meeting of Heaven and Earth: A Survey and Analysis of the Literature on Millennialism in America, 1965-1985." *Fides et Historia* 20 (1988) 1: 5-28.

______. "The Millennial Vision as Motive for Religious Benevolence and Reform: Timothy Dwight and the New England Evangelicals Reconsidered." *Fides et Historia* 16 (1984) 1: 18-34.

Carwardine, Richard. *Transatlantic Revivalism: Popular Evangelicalism in Britain and America, 1790-1865*. Westport, Conn.: Greenwood Press, 1978.

Chambers-Schiller, Lee Virginia. *Liberty, A Better Husband: Single Women in America, The Generation of 1780-1840.* New Haven: Yale University Press, 1984.

Chatterjee, Sunil Kumar. *Hannah Marshman: The First Woman Missionary in India.* Calcutta: People's Little Press, 1987.

______. "Serampore Missionaries and Christian-Muslim Interaction in Bengal 1793-1834)." *Bulletin of the Christian Institute of Islamic Studies* III (Jan 1980) 1-4: 115-132.

Christensen, Torben and William R. Hutchison, eds. *Missionary Ideologies in the Imperialist Era, 1880-1820.* Copenhagen: Aros, 1982.

Clymer, Kenton J. *Protestant Missionaries in the Philippines, 1898-1916: An Enquiry into the American Colonial Mentality.* Urbana: University of Illinois Press, 1986.

Coakley, J. F. *The Church of the East and the Church of England: A History of the Archbishop of Canterbury's Assyrian Mission*. Oxford: Clarendon Press, 1992.

Cohen, Paul A. *China and Christianity: The Missionary Movement and the Growth of Chinese Anti-Foreignism, 1860-1870.* Cambridge, Mass.: Harvard University Press, 1963.

Collins, Aileen. "Calista Holman Vinton: Not Just a Missionary's Wife." *American Baptist Quarterly* 12 (September 1993): 210-222.

Conforti, Joseph. "David Brainerd and the Nineteenth Century Missionary Movement. " Journal *of the Early Republic* 5 (Fall 198 5): 3 09-3 29.

______. *Jonathan Edwards, Religious Tradition, and American Culture.* Chapel Hill: University of North Carolina Press, 1995.

______. "Jonathan Edwards's Most Popular Work: 'The Life of David Brainerd' and Nineteenth-Century Evangelical Culture." *Church History* 54 (1985) 2: 188-201.

______. "Mary Lyon, the Founding of Mount Holyoke College, and the Cultural Revival of Jonathan Edwards." *Religion and American Culture* 3 (1993) 1: 69-89.

______. "Samuel Hopkins and the New Divinity: Theology, Ethics and Social Reform in Eighteenth Century New England." *William and Mary Quarterly* XXXIV (October 1977) 4: 572-589.

______. *Samuel Hopkins and the New Divinity Movement: Calvinism, the Congregational Ministry, and Reform in New England Between the Great Awakenings.* Grand Rapids,MI: Christian University Press, 1981.

Conkin, Paul K. *Cane Ridge: America's Pentecost.* Madison, WI: University of Wisconsin Press, 1990.

______. *The Uneasy Center: Reformed Christianity in Antebellum America.* Chapel Hill: University of North Carolina Press, 1995.

Constable, Pamela, for the *Washington Post.* "Backlash shutters schools in Afghanistan: Taliban feared in attacks on girls' education." *The Tennessean* (Nashville), Monday, September 15, 2003, 4B.

Cott, Nancy F. *The Bonds of Womanhood. 'Woman's Sphere' in New England, 1780-1835.* New Haven: Yale University Press, 1977.

______. "Young Women in the Second Great Awakening in New England. *Feminist Studies* 3 (1975) 1/2: 15-29.

Cross,Whitney R. *The Burned-Over District: The Social and Intellectual History of Enthusiastic Religion in Western New York, 1800-1850.* Ithaca: Cornell University Press, 1950.

Curry, Dayna and Heather Mercer. *Prisoners of Hope: The Story of Our Captivity and Freedom in Afghanistan*. New York: Doubleday, 2002.

Das, Veena. "The Imaging of Indian Women: Missionaries and Journalists. " In Sulochana. Raghavan Glazer and Nathan Glazer, eds., *Conflicting Images: India* and *the United States.* Glenn Dale, MD: Riverdale Co., 1990, 203 -220.

Datta, V. N. *Sati: A Historical, Social and Philosophical Enquiry into the Hindu Rite of Widow Burning.* London: Sangam Books, 1988.

Donaldson, Margaret. "'The Cultivation of the Heart and the Moulding of the Will': the Missionary Contribution of the Society for Promoting Female Education in China, India, and the East." In W. J. Sheils and Diana Wood, eds., *Women in the Church: Papers Read at the 1989 Summer Meeting and the 1990 Winter Meeting of the Ecclesiastical History Society.* Oxford: Basil Blackwell, 1990.

______.. "The Invisible Factor: 19th Century Feminist Evangelical Concern for Human Rights." *Journal for theStudy of Religion* 2 (September 1989) 2: 3-15.

Donegan, Jane B. *Women* and *Men Midwives: Medicine, Morality, and Misogyny in Early America.* *W*estport,Conn.: Greenwood Press, 1978.

Dougherty, Mary Agnes. "The Methodist Deaconess: A Case of Religious Feminism." *Methodist History* 21 (1983) 2: 90-98.

Douglas, Ann. *The Feminization of American Culture.* New York: Knopf, 1977.

Downs, Frederick S. "Social Influences on Nineteenth Century Baptist Missionaries in India." *American Baptist* Quarterly 8(1989) 4: 247-56.

Drucker, Alison R. "The Influence of Western Women on the Anti-Footbinding Movement, 1840-1911. " In Richard W. Guisso and

Stanley Johannesen, eds., *Women in China: Current Directions in Historical Scholarship.* Youngstown, NY: Philo Press, 1981, 179-199.

Elbert, Sarah. "'Anywhere with Jesus, Everywhere with Jesus': American Women's Foreign Mission." *American Quarterly* 37 (Winter 1985): 755-761.

Elsbree, Oliver Wendell. *The Rise of the Missionary Spirit in America, 1790-1815.* Philadelphia, PA: Porcupine Press, 1980 (reprint), c 1928.

______. "Samuel Hopkins and His Doctrine of Benevolence." *New England Quarterly* 8 (Dec. 1935): 534-550.

Entrikin, Isabelle Webb. *Sarah Josepha Hale and Godey's Lady's Book.* Philadelphia: University of Pennsylvania Press, 1946.

Estep, William R. *Whole Gospel, Whole World: The Foreign Mission Board of the Southern Baptist Convention, 1845-1995.* Nashville, TN: Broadman & Holman Publishers, 1994.

Fairbank, John King, ed.. *The Missionary Enterprise in China and America.* Cambridge, Mass.: Harvard University Press, 1974.

Falls, Helen Emery. "Baptist Women in Missions Support in the Nineteenth Century. *Baptist History and Heritage XII* (January 1977) 1:26–36.

Findlay, Alice. "A Worthy Woman Who Can Find?: Anna Kay Scott, M. D." *American Baptist Quarterly* 12 (September 1993): 223-234.

Findlay, James F. "Nineteenth-Century Protestantism." *Pennsylvania Magazine of History and Biography* 107 (1983) 1: 137-142.

Finley, Ruth E. *The Lady of Godey's: Sarah Josepha Hale.* Philadelphia: J. B. Lippincott Company, 1931. Reprint, New York: Arno Press, 1974.

Forman, Charles W. "'Sing to the Lord a New Song': Women in the Churches of Oceania." InDenise O'Brien and Sharon W. Tiffany, eds., *Rethinking Women's Roles: Perspectives from the Pacific.* Berkeley, CA: University of California Press, 1984, 153-172.

Forrester, Duncan B. *Caste and Christianity: Attitudes and Policies on Caste of Anglo-Saxon Missions in India.* London: Curzon Press, 1980.

Foster, Charles I. *An Errand of Mercy: The Evangelical United Front, 1790-1837.* Chapel Hill, NC: University of North Carolina Press, 1960.

Freedman, Estelle. "Separatism as Strategy: Female Institution Building and American Feminism, 1870-1930." *Feminist Studies* 5 (Fall 1979) 3: 512-529.

Gall, Carlotta, for the *New York Times News Service.* "Advocates, victims gather to draft Afghan women's rights bill." *The Tennessean (Nashville),* Sunday, September 28, 2003, 4A.

George, Timothy. *Faithful Witness: 1he Life and Mission of William Carey.* Birmingham, Ala.: New Hope Press, 1991.

Ghosh, Jayati and C. P. Chandrasekhar. "Women in India: A Status Report." *The Hindu Business Line Online Edition*, September 3, 2002. [http://www.thehindubusinessline.com/bline/2002/09/03/stories/2002090300080900.htm], accessed 9/28/03.

Gifford, Carolyn DeSwarte, ed. *The American Deaconess Movement in the Early Twentieth Century*. New York: Garland Pub., 1987.

Gillespie, Joanna Bowen. "'The Clear Leadings of Providence': Pious Memoirs and the Problems of Self-Realization for Women in the Early Nineteenth Century." *Journal of the Early Republic* 5 (Summer 1985): 197-221.

Gimelli,Louis B. "'Borne Upon the Wings of Faith': The Chinese Odyssey of Henrietta Hall Shuck." *Journal of the Early Republic* 14 (Summer 1994): 221-245.

Ginzberg, Lori. *Women and the Work of Benevolence: Morality, Politics, and Class in the Nineteenth-Century United States*. New Haven: Yale University Press, 1990.

Gleeson, Kristin L. "The Stethoscope and the Gospel: Presbyterian Foreign Medical Missions, 1840-1900. *American Presbyterians* 71 (Spring 1993) 1: 127-138.

Grabill, Joseph L. *Protestant Diplomacy and the Near East: Missionary Influence on Foreign Policy, 1810-1927*. Minneapolis: University of Minnesota Press, 1971.

Graham, Gael. *Gender, Culture, and Christianity: American Protestant Mission Schools in China, 1880-1930*. New York: Peter Lang, 1995.

Green, Elizabeth Alden. *Mary Lyon and Mount Holyoke: Opening the Gates*. Hanover, New Hampshire: University Press of New England, *1979*.

Gribben, William. *The Churches Militant: The War of 1812 and American Religion*. New Haven: Yale University Press, 1973.

Grimshaw, Patricia. *Paths of Duty: American Missionary Wives in Nineteenth - Century Hawaii*. Honolulu: University of Hawaii Press, 1989.

Grundman, Christoffer. "Proclaiming the Gospel by Healing the Sick? Historical and Theological Annotations on Medical Mission." *International Bulletin of Missionary Research* 14 (July 1990): 120-126.

Gulick, Edward V. *Peter Parker and the Opening of China*. Cambridge, Mass.: Harvard University Press, 1973.

Haber, Samuel. *The Quest for Authority and Honor in the American Professions, 1750-1900*. Chicago: University of Chicago Press, 1991.

Hamilton, J. Taylor and Kenneth G. Hamilton, *History of the Moravian Church: The Renewed Unitas Fratrem, 1722-1957*. Bethlehem PA: Interprovincial Board of Christian Education, Moravian Church in America, 1967.

Hardesty, Nancy A. "The Scientific Study of Missions: Textbooks of the Central Committee on the United Study of Foreign Missions." In Daniel H. Bays and Grant Wacker, editors, *The Foreign Missionary Enterprise at Home: Explorations in North American Cultural History*. Tuscaloosa AL: University of Alabama Press, 2003.

Hardman, Keith. *Charles Grandison Finney, 1792-1875: Revivalist and Reformer*. Syracuse, N.Y.: Syracuse University Press, 1987.

Hatch, Nathan O. *The Sacred Cause of Liberty*. New Haven, Conn.: Yale University Press, 1977.

Hedrick, Joan D. *Harriet Beecher Stowe: A Life*. New York: Oxford University Press, 1994.

Hill, Patricia R. *The World Their Household: The American Woman's Foreign Mission Movement and Cultural Transformation, 18 70-1920*. Ann Arbor, MI: University of Michigan Press, 1985.

Hinnells, John R., ed. *New Dictionary of Religion*. Oxford: Blackwell Ltd., 1995.

Hoyt, Frederick B. "'When a Field was Found too Difficult for a Man, a Woman Should be Sent Adele M. Fielde in Asia, 1865-1890. " *The Historian* 44 (1982) 3: 314-334.

Hunter, Jane. *The Gospel of Gentility: American Women Missionaries in Turn of the Century China*. New Haven: Yale University Press, 1984.

Hutchison, William R. *Errand to the World. American Protestant Thought and Foreign Missions*. Chicago: University of Chicago Press, 1987.

Ingham, Kenneth. *Reformers in India, 1793-1833: An Account of the Work of Missions in Behalf of Social Reform*. New York: Octagon, 1973.

Jackson, Carl T. *The Oriental Religions and American Thought: Nineteenth-Century Explorations*. Westport, Conn.: Greenwood Press, 1981.

Jong, James A de. *As the Waters Cover the Sea: Millennial Expectations in the Rise of Anglo-American Missions, 1640-1810*. J. H. Kok N. V. Kampen, 1970.

Joseph, John. *The Nestorians and Their Muslim Neighbors*. Princeton NJ: Princeton University Press, 1961.

Juster, Susan. "'In a Different Voice': Male and Female Narratives of Religious Conversion in Post-Revolutionary America." *American Quarterly* 41 (March 1989): 34-62.

Katz, Nikki. "Women Under the Taliban." http://womenissues.about.com/library/weekly/aa102601a.htm], accessed 9/29/03.

Keller, Charles R. *The Second Great Awakening in Connecticut*. New Haven: Yale University Press, 1942.

Keller, Rosemary S. "Lay Women in the Protestant Tradition." In Keller and Rosemary Radford Ruether, eds., *Women and Religion in America: Volume I, The Nineteenth Century, A Documentary History*. San Francisco: Harper and Row, 1981.

______. "Women and the Nature of Ministry in the United Methodist Tradition." *Methodist History* 22 (1984) 2: 99-114.

Kerber, Linda K. *Women of the Republic: Intellect and Ideology in Revolutionary America*. Chapel Hill: University of North Carolina Press, 1980.

King, William McGuire. "Denominational Modernization and Religious Identity: The Case of the Methodist Episcopal Church." *Methodist History* 20 (1982) 2: 75-89.

Kling, David W. *A Field of Divine Wonders: The New Divinity and Village Revivals in Northwestern Connecticut, 1792-1822.* University Park, Penn.: Pennsylvania State University Press, 1993.

Kuhn, Anne Louise. *7he Mother's Role in Childhood Education: New England Concepts, 1830-1860.* New Haven: Yale University Press, 1947.

Lee, Bernice J. "Female Infanticide in China." Richard W. Guisso and Stanley Johannesen, eds., *Women in China:Current Directions in Historical Scholarship.* Youngstown, NY: Philo Press, 1981, 163-177.

Leonard, Elizabeth D. *Yankee Women: Gender Battles in the Civil War.* New York: W. W. Norton & Co., 1994.

Limerick, Patricia Nelson. "The Multicultural Islands." *American Historical Review* (February 1992): 121-135.

Marshall, P. J. and Glyndwr Williams. *The Great Map of Mankind: Perceptions of New Worlds in the Age of Enlightenment.* Cambridge: Harvard University Press, 1982.

Massey, Mary Elizabeth. *Bonnet Brigades.* New York: Alfred A. Knopf, 1966.

Mathews, Donald G. "The Second Great Awakening as an Organizing Process, 1780-1830." In John M. Mulder and John F. Wilson, *Religion in American History: Interpretive Essays.* Englewood Cliffs, N.J.: Prentice Hall, 1978.

McLoughlin, William C. *Revivals, Awakenings, and Reform: An Essay on Religion and Social Change in America, 1607-1977.* Chicago: University of Chicago Press, 1978.

Meckel, Richard A. "Educating a Ministry of Mothers: Evangelical Maternal Associations, 1815 -1860." *Journal of the Early Republic* 2 (Winter 1982): 403-423.

Mellor, Anne K. "'A Revolution in Female Manners."' In Duncan Wu, ed., *Romanticism: A Critical Reader.* Oxford: Blackwell, 1996.

Melman, Billie. *Women's Orients: English Women and the Middle East, 1718-1918.* Ann Arbor, Mich.: University of Michigan Press, 1992.

Merquerian, Barbara J. "Mt. Holyoke Seminary in Bitlis: Providing an American Education for Armenian Women." *Armenian Review* 43 (Spring 1990) 1/169: 31-65.

Mild, Mary L. "Whom Shall I Send?': An Overview of the American Baptist Woman's Foreign Mission Society for 1873 -1913. " *American Baptist Quarterly X11* (September 1993) 3: 194-209.

Moorhead, James. "Between Progress and Apocalypse: A Reassessment of Millennialism in American Religious Thought, 1800-1880." *Journal of American History* 71 (December 1984) 3: 524-542.

_______. "The Millennium and the Media." In Leonard 1. Sweet, ed., *Communication and Change in American Religious History.* Grand Rapids: Eerdmans, 1993, 216-238.

Morantz- Sanchez, Regina. "The Female Student Has Arrived: The Rise of the Women's Medical Movement. " In Ruth J. Abram, ed., *"Send Us a Lady Physician": Women Doctors in America, 1835-1920.* New York: W. W. Norton, 1985.

______. *Sympathy and Science: Women Physicians in American Medicine.* New York: Oxford University Press, 1985.

Myers, Mitze. "Reform or Ruin: 'A Revolution in Female Manners'." *Studies in Eighteenth Century Culture 11* (1982): 199-216.

Nair, Janaki. "Uncovering the Zenana: Visions of Indian Womanhood in Englishwomens Writings, 1813-1940." *Journal of Women's History* 2 (Spring) 1: 8-29.

Narasimhan, Sakuntala. *Sati: Widow Burning in India.* New York: Doubleday, 1990.

Neill, Stephen. *History of Christianity in India, 170 7-1858.* Cambridge: Cambridge University Press, 1985.

Norton, Mary Beth. *Liberty's Daughters: The Revolutionary Experience of American Women, 1750-1800.* Boston: Little, Brown, and Co., 1980.

Patterson, James A. "Motives in the Development of Foreign Missions Among American Baptists, 1810-1826. *Foundations XIX* (Oct. -Dec. 1976): 298319.

Paul, John J. "Religion and Medicine in South India: The Scudder Medical Missionaries and the Christian Medical College and Hospital, Vellore. " *Fides et Historia* 22 (Fall 1990): 16-29.

Payne, Ernest A. *The Great Succession: Leaders of the Baptist Missionary Society During the Nineteenth Century.* London: Carey Press, 1938.

Phillips, Clifton Jackson. *Protestant America and the Pagan World: The First Half Century of the American Board of Commissioners for Foreign Missions, 1810-1860.* Cambridge, Mass.: East Asian Research Center, Harvard University, 1969.

Porterfield, Amanda. *Mary Lyon and the Mount Holyoke Missionaries.* New York: Oxford University Press, 1997.

Potts, E. Daniel. *British Baptist Missionaries in India, 1793-1837: The History of Serampore and Its Missions.* Cambridge: Cambridge University Press, 1967.

Pruitt, Lisa J. "Possessed of a Missionary Spirit?: British Baptist Women and Bengali Missions in the Nineteenth Century." *American Baptist Quarterly* XVII (December 1998): 285-304.

Reynolds, David S. "The Feminization Controversy: Sexual Stereotypes and the Paradoxes of Piety in Nineteenth-Century America." *New England Quarterly* 53 (March 1980): 96-106.

Robert, Dana. *American Women in Mission: A Social History of Their Thought and Practice.* Macon, GA: Mercer University Press, 1996.

______. "Evangelist or Homemaker? Mission Strategies of Early Nineteenth Century Missionary Wives in Burma and Hawaii." *International Bulletin of Missionary Research* January 1993: 4-12.

Roberts, Phil. "Andrew Fuller." In Timothy George and David Dockery, eds. *Baptist Theologians.* Nashville: Broadman Press, 1990, 121-139.

Rubinstein, Murray A. *The Origins of the Anglo-American Missionary Enterprise in China, 1807-1840.* Lanham, Md.: Scarecrow, 1996.

Ryan, Mary P. *Cradle of the Middle Class: The Family in Oneida County, New* York, 1790-1865. New York: Cambridge University Press, 1981.

______. "A Women's Awakening: Evangelical Religion and the Families of Utica, New York, 1800-1840." *American Quarterly* 31 (1978) 5: 602-623.

Said, Edward. *Orientalism.* New York: Vintage Books, 1979.

Schuyler, David. "Inventing a Feminine Past." *The New England Quarterly* 51 (September 1978): 291-308.

Scudder, Dorothy J. *A Thousand Years in Thy Sight: The Story of the Scudder Missionaries of India.* New York: Vantage Press, 1984.

Seabrook, Ginny. "Pagoda Shadows: The Life of Adele Marion Fielde, Missionary to China, 1865-1889." *American Baptist Quarterly* 12 (September 1993) 235-241.

Shenk, Wilbert R. *Henry Venn: Missionary Statesman.* Maryknoll, N. Y.: Orbis Books, 1983.

Shiels, Richard D. "The Feminization of American Congregationalism, 1730-1835." *American Quarterly* 33 (Spring 1981): 46-62.

Sklar, Kathryn Kish. *Catharine Beecher: A Study in American Domesticity.* New York: W. W. Norton, 1976.

Smalley, William A. *Translation as Mission: Bible Translation in the Modern Missionary Movement.* Macon, GA: Mercer University Press, 199 1.

Smith, Geoffrey E. "Patterns of Missionary Education: The Baptist India Mission, 1794-1824." *Baptist Quarterly* 20 (July 1964): 293 -312.

Smith, George. *Twelve Pioneer Missionaries.* London: Thomas Nelson & Sons, 1900.

Smith, Karen E. "The Role of Women in Early Baptist Missions. " *Review and Expositor* 89 (1992): Smith, Timothy L. *Revivalism and Social Reform: American Protestantism on the Eve of the Civil War.* Nashville: Abingdon Press, 1957.

Stanley, Brian. *The Bible and the Flag: Protestant Missions and British Imperialism in the Nineteenth and Twentieth Centuries.* Leicester: Apollos, 1990.

Starr, Cindy. "More Chinese Girls find 'forever homes' in US." *Washington Times* June 22, 1999, E4 [http://www.theadoptionguide.com/complaints/chinalove.html],accessed 9/28/03.

Stone, Frank A. "Mt. Holyoke's Impact on the Land of Mt. Ararat." *Muslim World* LXVI (January 1976) 1: 44-57.

Summers, Anne. "Ministering Angels." *History* Today 3 9 (February 1989): 31-37.

Sweet, Leonard I. *The Minister's Wife: Her Role in Nineteenth-Century American Evangelicalism.* Philadelphia: Temple University Press, 1983.

Tiffany, Sharon W. "Introduction: Feminist Perceptions in Anthropology." In *Rethinking Women's Roles: Perspectives from the Pacific.* Berkeley, CA: University of California Press, 1984, 1-11.

Thomson, James C., Jr., Peter W. Stanley, and John Curtis Perry. *Sentimental Imperialists: The American Experience in East Asia.* New York: Harper and Row, 1981.

Tucker, Ruth A. *Guardians of the Great Commission: The Story of Women in Modem Missions.* Grand Rapid, MI: Acadernie Books, 1988.

Tucker, Sara W. "Opportunities for Women: The Development of Professional Women's Medicine at Canton, China, 1879-190 1." *Women's Studies International Forum* 13 (1990) 4: 357-368.

Tuveson, Ernest. *Redeemer Nation: The Idea of America's Millennial Role.* Chicago: University of Chicago Press, 1968.

Ulrich, Laurel Thatcher. "'Daughters of Liberty': Religious Women in Revolutionary New England." In Ronald Hoffinan and Peter J. Albert, eds., *Women in the Age of the American Revolution.* Charlottesville, VA: Published for the United States Capitol Historical Society by the University Press of Virginia, 1989, 211-243.

USAID India: Women's Status." [http://www.usaid.gov/in/programareas/women.htm], accessed 9/28/03.

Vail, Albert L. *Mary Webb and the Mother Society.* Philadelphia: American Baptist Publication Society, 1914.

Welter, Barbara. "She Hath Done What She Could: Protestant Women's Missionary Careers in Nineteenth-Century America." *American Quarterly* 30 (1978) 5: 624-638.

______. "The Cult of True Womanhood, 1820-60." In Barbara Welter, *Dimity Convictions: The American Woman in the Nineteenth Century.* Athens: Ohio University Press, 1976, 21-41.

______. *Dimity Convictions: The American Woman in the Nineteenth Century.* Athens: Ohio University Press, 1976.

______. "The Feminization of American Religion, 1800-1860. " In Barbara Welter, *Dimity Convictions: The American Woman in the Nineteenth Century.* Athens: Ohio University Press, 1976, 83-102.

Wenger, J. C. *The Mennonite Church in America.* Scottdale PA: Herald Press, 1966).

White, Ann. "Counting the Cost of Faith: America's Early Female Missionaries." *Church History* 57 (1): 19-30.

Wiebe, Robert. *The Search for Order, 1877-1920.* New York: Hill and Wang, 1967.

Wosh, Peter J. *Spreading the Word: The Bible Business in Nineteenth-Century America.* Ithaca: Cornell University Press, 1994.

Zwiep, Mary. *Pilgrim Path: The First Company of Women Missionaries to Hawaii.* Madison, WI: University of Wisconsin Press, 1991.

Index